OCR

Economics

Colin Bamford | Susan Grant

The Learning Centre
Abingdon Campus
Wootton Road

OCR RECOGNISING ACHIEVEMENT   Heinemann

Official Publisher Partnership

Heinemann is an imprint of Pearson Education Limited, a company incorporated in England and Wales, having its registered office at Edinburgh Gate, Harlow, Essex, CM20 2JE. Registered company number: 872828

www.heinemann.co.uk

Heinemann is a registered trademark of Pearson Education Limited

General introduction and Part 1 © Colin Bamford 2008
Part 2 © Susan Grant 2008
Glossary © Colin Bamford and Susan Grant 2008

First published 2008

12 11 10 09 08
10 9 8 7 6 5 4 3 2

British Library Cataloguing in Publication Data is available from the British Library on request.

ISBN 978 0 435692 20 9

Edited by Bill MacKeith
Designed by Tek-Art
Typeset by Tek-Art
Original illustrations © Pearson Education Ltd 2008
Illustrated by Tek-Art
Picture research by Sally Claxton
Cover photo/illustration © Corbis / Lawrence Manning
Printed in the UK by Scotprint

Websites
There are links to relevant websites in this book. In order to ensure that the links are up-to-date, that the links work, and that the sites are not inadvertently linked to sites that could be considered offensive, we have made the links available on the Heinemann website at www.heinemann.co.uk/hotlinks. When you access the site, the express code is 2209P.

Contents

About the authors

Susan Grant is a Principal Examiner for a major examining body and has years of experience in setting examination papers and assessing candidates' performance. Susan is currently teaching economics at Abingdon and Witney College and Wood Green School in Witney, Oxfordshire. She is the author of more than 15 economics books and is a regular contributor to the *British Economy Survey*.

Professor Colin Bamford is OCR's Chief Examiner in GCE Economics. He has over 30 years' experience of teaching economics and assessing and setting A Level examination papers. He is well known among students for the range of textbooks and articles he has produced on various aspects of the subject. He is Associate Dean and Head of the Department of Logistics and Hospitality Management at the University of Huddersfield, West Yorkshire, and the current President of the Economics and Business Education Association.

Acknowledgements

The authors should like to thank their OCR colleague Mark Jackson for his helpful comments on the first draft of the manuscript. Thanks also go to Diane Bramley for word-processing, to the students at the University of Huddersfield, Witney College and Wood Green School, and to the staff at Heinemann for their advice and support.

The author and publisher would like to thank the following individuals and organisations for permission to reproduce photographs:

Alamy / Mediablitzimages (UK) Ltd / Martin Lee p 24; Alamy / Alex Segre p 49; Bananastock p 152; Corbis / EPA / Andy Raine p 144; Corbis / Jack Fields p 8; Corbis / Andrew Holbrooke p 72; Corbis / Richard Klune p 116; Corbis / Charles O'Rear p 35; Corbis / Eye Ubiquitous / John Hulme p 118; Corbis / Reuters / Vito Lee p 59; Corbis / Sion Touhig p 10; Corbis / Zefa / Jose Fuste Raga p 26; Digital Stock p 100, Getty Images / AFP / Prakash Singh p vii; Istockphoto / Nicola Stratford p 100; Jupiter Images / Photos.com p 94; PA Photos / AP p 129; PA Photos / AP / Nabil Al-Jurani p 142; PA Photos / AP / Oded Balilty p 133; PA Photos / AP / Stefen Chow p 37; PA Photos / AP / Petr David Josek p 18; PA Photos / AP / Daniel Ochoa De Olza p 154; Photos / AP / Kirsty Wigglesworth p 83, PA Photos / Andy Butterton p ix; PA Photos / Owen Humphreys p 60; PA Photos / Andrew Parsons p 142; PA Photos / Stefan Rousseau p 159; Pearson Education Ltd / Arnos Design p 14; Pearson Education Ltd / Naki Photography p 110; Pearson Education Ltd / Tudor Photography p 43; Rex Features / Dmitris Legakis p 65; Still Pictures / Joerg Boethling p 20

Every effort has been made to contact copyright holders of material reproduced in this book. Any omissions will be rectified in subsequent printings if notice is given to the publishers.

General introduction

This book introduces you to the study of economics, a fascinating and important subject. We all play a role in the economy and all our lives are influenced by economic events.

Our aims in writing this book are to stimulate your interest in the subject, to develop your skills as an economist and to help you prepare for the AS examinations.

This book explicitly follows the OCR AS specification. It is divided into two parts, with three chapters in each. The first part focuses on the basic principles and concepts of microeconomics. As its name implies, microeconomics is concerned with economics on a small scale. It examines the behaviour of buyers and sellers in particular markets. Part 2, in contrast, concentrates on macroeconomics. This is the study of the whole economy and includes topics such as unemployment and inflation.

Each chapter starts with a list of learning objectives. Keep these in mind as you work through the chapter. When you have finished the chapter, go back to them and make sure that you have achieved all of them.

Each of the chapters also includes a range of activities and a number of learning tips. The activities are designed to test your understanding of the topics covered and to build up your skills. Try to work through all of these. You may do some in class and some for homework. The learning tips include advice on avoiding common mistakes, how to label diagrams and what you can do to increase your understanding.

At the end of both parts there is an Exam Café. This is designed to help your examination preparation. It includes tips from students, a revision checklist, a quick-fire quiz, some students' answers to a question, some tips from us and an exam practice question.

We hope that you will find this book interesting, informative and useful. We also hope that you will enjoy your course and do well in the examinations. Good luck!

The economist's 'tool kit'

The economist's tool kit is used in the same way as a motor mechanic uses a tool kit when servicing a car. The principles and concepts of economics, in other words the body of subject knowledge that constitutes economics, can be viewed as the car. To understand the subject effectively, though, economists use a variety of skills and techniques of investigation, in the same way as the mechanic uses various tools and techniques when servicing a vehicle. While the emphasis of this book is on the subject matter of AS Economics, it is also important to be able to use and apply the fundamental skills that are necessary to understand economics in an effective way. These skills are what is sometimes referred to as the 'tool kit'.

For AS Level, two elements of the tool kit are relevant. These are:

● the ability to interpret economic information and use it to enhance your understanding of economics

● the ability to write in a clear and effective way, in particular to develop the writing skills that will enable you to demonstrate that you really understand what you have been studying.

Each of these will now be considered. Don't worry if you do not fully comprehend what is said here – this will become much clearer as you progress in your AS studies. So, do keep looking back at this section from time to time. You will also find it very useful if you progress to A2 Economics.

DATA HANDLING SKILLS

In economics, the term 'data' is used in a broad sense. It means economic information that is available on a particular topic including numerical data, data represented by graphs and diagrams and also text. The following are the skills that you need at AS level to be confident in handling the first two types of data:

- the ability to pick out the main features in a data set

- a knowledge of trends and how to understand what is meant by the rate of change in a set of data

- a basic understanding of index numbers and how these are used

- what is meant by an average value in a data set

- how to interpret data that is presented in a variety of visual forms.

Each of these skills will now be looked at. It is important for you to feel confident in handling data, as this will help you understand the subject content, particularly when you study the National and International Economy unit. You will also find these data-handling skills useful when you tackle many of the self-assessment tasks.

Consider the data in Table 1 below. This shows the average percentage unemployment in the various member states of the Caribbean Community (CARICOM) in 2005.

Table 1 Average unemployment, 2005 (% of working population)

Country	%	Country	%
Antigua & Barbuda	11.0	Jamaica	13.0
Bahamas	7.8	St Kitts/Nevis	4.5
Barbados	10.4	St Lucia	18.1
Belize	12.8	St Vincent & the Grenadines	15.0
Dominica	23.1	Suriname	10.6
Grenada	17.0	Trinidad & Tobago	14.2
Guyana	9.1	Average CARICOM	11.9

Source: Caribbean Community Secretariat, 2006

So, what can we tell from Table 1? The first point to note is that the data shown are for one year only, 2005 – a kind of snapshot taken at a given point in time. Another basic point to bear in mind is the title and source of the data. The title should give

Unemployed Jamaicans hoping for casual employment

you a clear steer as to what the data is about; the source should give you some indication as to the likely accuracy of the data. (In this case, it is from an official source and therefore ought to be reasonably accurate, assuming that it is possible to measure Caribbean unemployment in an accurate way in the first instance.)

The first skill you need to develop is what is known as *eyeballing*. All this means is looking at a data set and picking out the main features. This is a useful skill, as it will give you an introductory insight into the economic issue that is represented.

ACTIVITY ⋯⋮

Study the data in Table 1. Write a few sentences about what it shows and why it may not necessarily be as precise as indicated in the table.

Let us now look at what Table 1 shows. You should be able to see that:

● there is a wide variation in average unemployment rates in 2005

● Dominica has the highest at around 23 per cent, while average unemployment is lowest in St Kitts/Nevis at 4.5 per cent

● the CARICOM average therefore is not very representative, as only three or four of the 13 members have an unemployment average close to that for the organisation as a whole

● the data gives no indication of the absolute or actual numbers unemployed or the size of the populations in each member state.

The average of 11.9 per cent is a widely used measure to summarise a set of data. It is also known as the **arithmetic mean** and, in the case of Table 1, can be best described as a **weighted average**. This is because it is calculated by taking into account the respective working populations in each of the 13 countries.

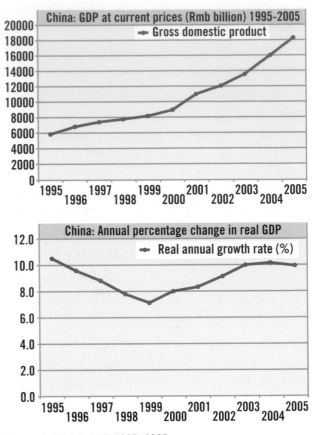

Figure 1 China's GDP, 1995–2005

DEFINITIONS

Arithmetic mean: the sum of the items divided by the number of items.

Weighted average: an average that takes into account the relative importance of the different items.

DEFINITION

Time series: information shown at successive points or intervals of time.

The main problem with any average value is that it tends to be affected by extreme values in a data set. The data in Table 1 is a case in point, given the wide range of average unemployment rates. To some extent this is compensated for by using a weighted average, although a large country with a high unemployment rate will inevitably affect such a central indicator.

Consider Figure 1, which shows two economic indicators that are used by economists when analysing an economy, in this case the economy of China. This information is the form of two **time series**, the term used to denote that the data is recorded over a period of time.

ACTIVITY ····⁝

Study the data in Figure 1.

a) Identify what time periods are involved.

b) Consider each of the graphs and make some brief notes on what each shows.

Let us now look at what Figure 1 shows. You should be able to see that:

● each chart has the same horizontal scale (showing time period) but a different vertical scale (showing the annual changes for each variable)

● GDP at current prices increased annually over the ten-year period

- in 2005 GDP at current prices was almost three times greater than in 1995
- the real annual growth rate fluctuated over the period shown
- the average annual growth rate was around 9 per cent from 1995 to 2005.

What each of the two variables means will be introduced later, in Unit 2. At this stage it is important to clarify what is meant by 'annual percentage change' or 'year-on year' change, as it is sometimes called, as many students struggle to get to grips with this particular measure.

Let us look more closely at the lower chart in Figure 1. The data shown are for the mid-point in each year, as this is the best way to represent annual change. In 1995 the annual percentage change in China's GDP was 10.5 per cent; for the following year, it fell to 9.6 per cent and continued to fall until 1999. What this means is that there was a minor falling off of annual GDP growth from 1995 to 1999. What this does *not* mean is that GDP fell over this period or indeed for any period covered by this chart. (This is confirmed by the top, time-serried graph in Figure 1.) A common error that many students make when looking at data such as this is to deduce that GDP has fallen. This is not so. All that has happened between 1995 and 1999 is that the annual rate of increase of GDP has slowed.

With time series, especially, the raw data is often shown in terms of an **index number** with a base year of 100. Table 2 shows a typical example.

Rail fares rose by nearly 50 per cent between 1993 and 2005

> **DEFINITION**
>
> **Index number:** a number showing the variation in, for example, wages or prices, as compared with a chosen base period or date.

> **learning tip**
> When dealing with data that shows year on year changes, think carefully about what any one change really means.

Table 2 Transport costs and retail prices, 1993–2003 (1993 = 100)

Year	Rail fares	Private car costs	Retail prices
1993	100.0	100.0	100.0
1995	109.1	105.3	106.0
1997	115.8	114.3	112.0
1999	125.0	120.7	117.6
2001	132.0	124.6	123.2
2003	137.3	125.3	128.9
2005	144.2	128.1	132.9

Source: Office for National Statistics, 2006.
Crown Copyright material reproduced by permission of the Controller of HMSO and the Queen's Printer for Scotland

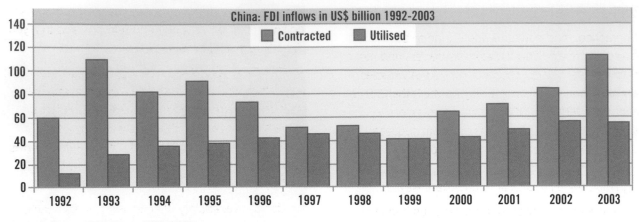

Figure 2 China: FDI inflows, 1992–2003

When data is shown in this way, some of the difficulties mentioned earlier when considering the rate of change are avoided. Table 2 shows clearly that:

● rail fares have increased consistently above the rate of inflation over the period 1993–2005

● the increase in the cost of running a car has been slightly less than inflation over the whole period; between 1997 and 1999 the opposite was true.

To construct a set of index numbers:

● assign an index of 100 to a base year. Ideally the quantity in the chosen year of the item measured should be typical and not influenced by one-off external influences

● for subsequent years, divide the base year value by 100 and then divide every value by this figure to calculate the index number.

Finally, let us look more closely at data that are represented in a more visual form. The data on foreign direct investment (FDI) in Figure 2 is in the form of a **bar chart**. The principle behind this is that the height of each bar represents the value of the data as shown on the vertical scale; in this case, FDI inflows measured in US$. At a glance it is possible to make deductions about the annual level (in value terms), changes in the annual level and the trend (over the whole period).

Newspapers and magazines increasingly represent economic information in highly attractive ways, using pictures and a variety of charts. These are invariably more eye-catching than a simple table or chart. *The Economist* and the business section of *The Times* are particularly good examples of publications that use this form of presentation.

learning tip
When you see the term 'trend' used, this means you need to look at the general direction of the data over a period of time.

ACTIVITY ⋯⋗

a) Study the information in Figure 2.

   i) Describe the trends in contracted and utilised FDI.

   ii) Describe the changing relationship between contracted and utilised FDI from 1992 to 2003.

   (Note: contracted FDI is where provisional plans to commit FDI have been agreed; utilised FDI is what has actually been spent in a given year.)

b) Search through recent copies of *The Times* and *The Economist* to obtain a selection of recent pictures and charts showing economic information. For each example, summarise what it shows.

Writing skills

In practice, most economic ideas tend to be expressed in a written form in newspapers and other publications, and on websites. For your AS studies, a written examination is the way in which the Oxford and Cambridge RSA (OCR) examiners assess whether you have understood what is needed to succeed. The key to success, for both professional economists and yourself as a budding economist, is to be able to express yourself in a clear and relevant way.

Writing is an activity at which most of us become more proficient over time. Many people find writing in a technical way – for example, when expressing economic ideas and concepts – difficult. This need not be so. As you progress with your AS studies, you should be able gradually to improve in the way you express yourself and feel confident that you can tackle your examinations in a positive way.

There are four main guidelines you need to bear in mind when communicating your knowledge of economics in an examination. These are:

● Present clear, accurate and relevant information. In other words, keep to the point of the question. You may need to explain some things and elaborate others, but keep focused on the question. This particularly applies to the last 18 mark question in the exam, where you are required to write a short essay. There may also be an opportunity to include a diagram in your answer, but do make sure that, if you do so, it is 'clear, accurate and relevant' and that you directly refer to it in your answer.

● Put down your ideas in an organised and coherent way. When writing a paragraph or short essay, link your information and ideas in an ordered way. For some answers, especially those with only a few marks, you might find it a good idea to write in terms of bullet points or phrases that may not be a full sentence.

● Use the vocabulary of economics. In this book, key terms are shown in bold where they are first used, and then defined. Use them where you can. If you need to explain or apply a particular term, think back to the definition that has been given.

● Make sure that what you write is legible and that your spelling, punctuation and grammar are correct.

OCR examiners will be impressed when your examination answers match these criteria. More information and advice on how to succeed in the AS examinations are provided in the two Exam Café sections of the book.

As you systematically work through the two parts of the book, and tackle the various activities, you will become increasingly familiar with the subject matter of OCR's AS Economics and what is needed in order to succeed.

PART 1

Markets in action

INTRODUCTION

This part of the book concentrates on microeconomics, the study of economics on a small scale. It concentrates on the choices people make, how and why the price and output of particular products change and why the decisions that some of us make can have a beneficial or harmful effect on others.

In Chapter 1, you will be introduced to the problem facing all economies. This is that we want more products than our firms are capable of producing. You will examine the nature of the resources that are used to make these products. You will also learn about opportunity cost and production possibility curves. A production possibility curve is one of a number of diagrams you will come across in economics. You will get used to drawing and interpreting diagrams. They are a useful way of illustrating what is happening in a market or in the economy as a whole, and also of analysing the effects of any changes.

Chapter 2 also contains diagrams. This time they are demand and supply diagrams. This chapter focuses on how buyers and sellers of particular products interact and how prices are determined. Most people realise that if the price of a product rises, people tend to buy less of it and as people become richer they tend to buy more. Economists, however, explore these relationships in more depth. Working through this chapter will enable you to measure and interpret the key influences on the demand for and supply of products.

Chapter 2 concentrates on markets working efficiently; Chapter 3 explores what can go wrong and what governments can do to improve the situation.

When you have completed this part you should be able to:

- describe why and how people make choices
- draw and interpret production possibility curves
- analyse how the price and output of products is determined
- measure the extent to which demand and supply changes when key influences alter
- explain how markets may not work efficiently
- assess government measures to reduce market failure.

1 The reasons for individuals, organisations and societies having to make choices

On completion of this chapter, you should be able to:

● describe what economists mean by 'the economic problem'

● understand the different factors of production as economic resources

● explain how specialisation can be used to address the problem of scarcity

● understand the role of markets in allocating scarce resources

● explain what is meant by opportunity cost

● explain how production possibility curves can be used to show scarcity, choice and opportunity cost.

What is economics?

Economics as a subject covers a wide range of issues, most of which tend to be topical and receive daily coverage in newspapers and on television and the Internet. Over time, economists have developed their own language of terms and concepts in order to explain and, in many cases, evaluate these issues.

In this book you will systematically and progressively come across this terminology. Some of the words will seem familiar, for example 'demand', 'market', 'unemployment', 'inflation'. Other terms, though, will be new to you. All in all, by the end of your AS Level studies, you should be able to use these words and terms in a useful way to be more aware of the world in which you live. Hopefully, you will have started to think like an economist!

For a start, let us take a few newspaper headlines from around the world to get a brief indication of the sort of issues and questions that interest professional economists.

'*Price* of oil to rise after *supply* crisis'

'Record high in wheat *costs* sends *price* of bread soaring'

'Rail bosses' salaries outstrip *inflation* for second year running'

'Is China's *growth* increasing global warming?'

'Panic in world *markets* as dollar hits all time low'

The words in *italics* are all ones that you should have come across as they are in general everyday use. They do, however, have very specific meanings when used in economics, as you will see as you study this book.

ACTIVITY ...⋗

a) Look through (say) today's newspapers and look on the BBC News website and write down some of the key economic terms you can find. For the BBC News website, go to www.heinemann.co.uk/hotlinks, insert the express code 2209P and click on 'BBC News'.

b) Select one article from a newspaper and one from the BBC News website. Summarise the main points and say why these items may be of interest to economists.

learning tip Do try to read a good newspaper on a regular basis. You might be surprised at how much economics it usually contains!

A DEFINITION OF ECONOMICS

At times, as you will learn, economists do not always agree. This is hardly surprising, given the range of issues they study. Having said this, most economists would not disagree with the definition of the subject as the study of how to allocate scarce resources in the most effective way.

DEFINITION

Economics: the study of how to allocate scarce resources in the most effective way.

So what does this mean? Let us take yourself first of all. Most teenagers find that they want to lead a full and exciting life but, unfortunately, most do not always have the money that is necessary to buy everything and do everything that they would like to do. Does this sound familiar? So, choices have to be made among the many alternatives that are available. This is the so-called **economic problem** of scarcity and choice that is central to economics as a subject.

DEFINITION

Economic problem: how to allocate scarce resources among alternative uses.

It is not only teenagers and other people who are faced with this problem. Firms, for instance, have to decide what they should produce and how they can do this in the most efficient way. Governments, too, face having to make choices. For example, how much should the UK government spend on state education or the National Health Service? And if more is spent on these, given the government's limited income from taxation, should less be spent on defence or law and order? The government's problem is really no different to that facing all of us, but on a different scale, involving a complex range of processes of decision-making.

ACTIVITY ...⋗

Make a list in your own words of some of the economic choices that

● you are facing

● your family has to take

● the country has to take.

As should now be clear, economics and, more specifically, the economic problem, can be studied at different levels. It is possible to study decisions made by individuals, **households** and firms. Or we can study the operation of an economy or groups of economies such as those that make up the European Union (EU). We can also study the economic problem of emerging economies such as China and the 'Asian Tigers', or of the world's poorest countries in sub Saharan Africa. In so doing, we are considering the

DEFINITION

Household: group of people whose spending decisions are connected.

two traditional fields of economics, **microeconomics** and **macroeconomics**.

ACTIVITY ···⋗

a) Go back to the material you produced for the first activity. Divide the issues you found into microeconomic and macroeconomic topics.

b) Have you found it easy to classify economic problems in this way?

It will be surprising if your answer to part (b) in the activity is 'Yes'. This is because many economic problems cannot be satisfactorily classified as being micro or macro – they encompass both of the two branches of the subject. Complex inter-relationships can come into play, and it is these that make economics a fascinating subject to study. Despite this, though, the two branches of economics are distinct. They invariably consider different questions and issues, involving different methods of economic analysis and approach.

As you work though this AS Level book, you will be introduced to concepts, theories and simple **models** which are used by economists to explain a range of problems and issues that come within the scope of economics. Virtually all models have their origin in some sort of empirical investigation, that is, a study of real-world economic behaviour. Some concepts and models go back 200 years; others, particularly those in Chapter 3, on market failure, are much more recent or have been revised and refined in the light

DEFINITION

Model: a simplified view of reality that is used by economists as a means of explaining economic relationships.

of the growing complexity of the present-day global economy. This serves to enhance the interesting nature of economics.

The basic economic problem

This is the fact that resources are scarce in relation to wants that are unlimited, leading to choices having to be made. (See Figure 1.1.)

The resources available in an economy are known by economists as **factors of production**. As this suggests, they are the means by which an economy produces a whole range of **goods** and **services** to meet the needs of its population. There are four main types of factors of production:

● **Land**. This is a natural resource. It includes a wide range of things such as mineral deposits like oil and

DEFINITIONS

Factor of production: the resource inputs that are available in an economy for the production of goods and services.

Goods: tangible products, i.e. products that can be seen and touched, such as cars, food and washing machines.

Services: intangible products, i.e. products that cannot be seen or touched, such as banking, beauty therapy and insurance.

Land: natural resources in an economy.

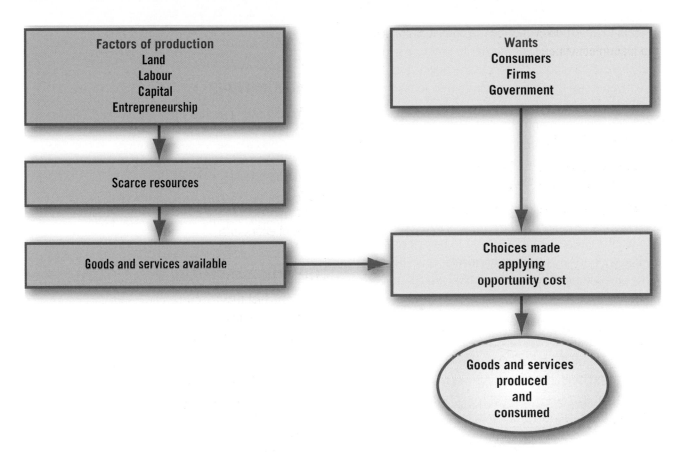

Figure 1.1 The basic economic problem

coal, the earth's rivers and lakes, and the land itself, in terms of the quality of soil for agriculture and availability of trees and vegetation. This factor of production can also be used to describe the natural resources such as sea, sand and sun that have been so important for the development of tourism and leisure activities.

● **Labour**. This is the human resource that is available in any economy. Quantity and quality are key considerations here. Some economies, particularly the world's poorest countries, often have large populations but suffer from a lack of a well-trained and well-educated workforce. Other countries, for example Germany and Italy, have declining populations and have to rely on immigrant workers to do both skilled and unskilled jobs. The quality of labour is essential for economic progress, as clearly evidenced by the growing importance of India in the global economy.

● **Capital**. This is a form of physical resource covering anything that can be regarded as a man-made aid for **production**. The function of capital is that it is combined with land and labour to produce goods and services that are required by the population. It covers a wide range of items such as factories, office blocks, machinery, information technology, transport vehicles and infrastructure in the form of roads, railways, pipelines, electricity supplies and so on.

● **Entrepreneurship**. This is a very particular form of human capital. It has two main functions. First,

DEFINITIONS

Labour: the quantity and quality of human resources.

Capital: man-made aids to production.

Entrepreneurship: the willingness of an entrepreneur to take risks and organise production.

Entrepreneur: someone who bears the risks of the business and who organises production.

it refers to enterprise whereby the other factors of production are organised in order to produce goods and services. Second, it refers to the ability and inventiveness of those who are prepared to take *risks*. Well-known **entrepreneurs** are Jack Cohen, who set up Tesco, Philip Green (Arcadia), Richard Branson (Virgin Group) and of course, Bill Gates (Microsoft Corporation). More typical, though, are the millions of people who own a small business and organise the factors of production in order to make a profit.

The world's poorest countries tend to have few and/or poor quality **factor endowments**, while the most prosperous economies, such as the US, have invariably exploited their factors of production for substantial economic development.

Why some countries are rich and others remain poor is a complex topic and one that economists have debated and deliberated over for many years. Factor endowment alone is not the only explanation for the huge inequalities in well-being between the world's economies.

DEFINITIONS

Factor endowment: the stock of factors of production.

Production: the output of goods and services.

Returning to the basic economic problem, it should now be clear that resources as explained by the factors of production are invariably scarce. In contrast, our individual and collective **wants** tend to be unlimited. In other words, most people would like to consume more but are unable to do so usually because they do not have the income or possibly the time to do so. This situation involves three fundamental economic concepts, namely **scarcity**, **choice** and **opportunity cost**. Many of the problems that economists study and write about are underpinned in this way.

Let us return to what economists call *wants*. All of us are in a position where we would like more, whether this be more spending money, the latest electronic

DEFINITIONS

Want: anything you would like, irrespective of whether you have the resources to purchase it.

Scarcity: a situation where there are insufficient resources to meet all wants.

Choice: the selection of appropriate alternatives.

Opportunity cost: the cost of the (next) best alternative, which is foregone when a choice is made.

device or more designer clothing. For most, these items are above the basic needs of food, clothing and housing that for poorer families, particularly in developing countries, can be regarded as wants. So, what may be essential for some is not necessarily essential for others. Equally, what may be a luxury item for someone may well be an essential item for someone else. This also raises the issue of choice. As individuals, due to personal, social, cultural and economic reasons, we have a list or scale of preferences. Our wants tend to be consciously put in rank order in terms of their perceived value to us. No two individuals will have the same scale of preferences.

To some extent none of us can ever be satisfied (even if you are Bill Gates, Li Ka-shing or even Roman Abramovich!). There will always be some things that we want – say a new product comes onto the market, due to a fashion change, or a new business opportunity arises. Much as we would like the latest mobile phone, MP4 player or HD television, our income (resources) will constrain what we are able to buy. As a consequence of such scarcity, we have to make choices.

The idea of the economic problem can also be applied in business or to the economy as a whole. Entrepreneurs, like those mentioned above, are in the same way constrained in what they might be able to acquire. Within a firm, managers have to decide what to produce and in what quantities, as they are unable to produce everything due to the limited factor endowment at their disposal.

At a macroeconomic level, as will be shown in Part 2, the UK's chancellor of the exchequer is faced with the economic problem when drawing up the annual spending round or budget. Government ministers will always be seeking more funding for their departments (an example of unlimited wants). Revenue from taxation, though, is limited, so the chancellor has to decide how much should be spent on defence, social services, education, transport and the National Health Service (NHS). In turn, in each of these areas of government spending, crucial decisions have to be made about how best to spend the money that has been allocated. This is particularly critical in the NHS at present due to an expanding yet ageing population in the UK. So, decisions have to be made by health authorities on whether to build new hospitals to replace those that are run-down or whether resources are better spent on new, expensive drugs or community care.

In all these cases, therefore, because of unlimited wants, choices have to be made due to the limited resources that are available. In making choices, economists usually consider possible alternatives. The next best alternative forgone is called the *opportunity cost*. For a given amount of resources or income, this is a statement of the true cost of what has been sacrificed. A few examples will explain this important concept.

Suppose you have won a £100 prize from the Premium Bonds you were given for your birthday a few years ago. How might you spend it? Or should you re-invest the prize in more Premium Bonds? If you do the latter, then the opportunity cost is not spending the £100 on the various things you could have bought. Alternatively, you might decide to spend the money on either (say) a new personal DVD player which costs £100 or you might buy a new pair of jeans and other pieces of clothing to the value of £100. You cannot have both, so the opportunity cost of the DVD player is the clothing you might otherwise have bought. This is the best alternative that you have had to sacrifice in making this choice.

ACTIVITY ⋯⟶

There is currently increasing unease about the so-called 'postal lottery' in the treatment of patients by the NHS. The problem arises because local health authorities have a major say on how their budgets are spent. The drug Herceptin, which can help control certain forms of cancer, is available to patients in some parts of the country but not in others. Explain how this example can illustrate scarcity, choice and opportunity cost.

learning tip
Make sure you understand the terms used in this section. All economic problems can be expressed in this form.

Specialisation and exchange

The problem of scarcity can to some extent be addressed through what is known as **specialisation**. This is a situation where individual workers, firms, regions or economies concentrate on a particular task or upon producing some goods and services and not others. It is distinct from a situation where everyone does everything for themselves and so produces everything that they need.

Specialisation lies at the heart of the modern global economy. Trade, which involves the **exchange** of goods and services normally using money, enables specialisation to take place. Even in the most primitive of economies, it is necessary to exchange goods or to provide services in exchange for other goods, although no money changes hands. This form of exchange is known as barter.

DEFINITIONS

Specialisation: the concentration by a worker or workers, firm, region or whole economy on a narrow range of goods and services.

Exchange: the process by which goods and services are traded.

In developed economies, trade can be either internal (domestic) or external (international). The latter refers to transactions between countries and is recorded in the *balance of payments* (see Part 2). Irrespective of which type of trade we are dealing with, specialisation produces a range of benefits to both countries involved in the exchange process. These benefits include:

● an increase in the output of goods and services when compared to circumstances where each country provides itself with everything it needs. Globally, this has had an important bearing on raising living standards, since there is more output from a particular volume of resources.

● a widening of the range of goods that are available in an economy. A typical example is bananas and other types of fruit that cannot be grown in the UK for climatic reasons. Caribbean countries specialise in growing bananas; these are traded with the UK and, in return, the money from their sale can be used to purchase, say, financial services or pharmaceuticals from the UK.

● exchange between developed and developing economies. Trade has been important in facilitating export-led growth for economies such as China, Thailand, Malaysia and the new members of the European Union.

So trade permits countries to specialise in products which they are able to make or grow relatively efficiently. Why this occurs is mainly due to the availability of factors of production (see above). Economies which have naturally occurring resources such as oil, copper or bauxite can exploit these and trade them on the world market. Alternatively, the climate or soils of a country may make it able to produce agricultural crops and commodities or be a good destination for international tourists. Other economies may have a highly skilled workforce, so giving them an advantage in the production of high-technology precision-manufactured goods. Significantly, emerging economies such as China and Poland have labour costs that are below those of most other economies, enabling them to produce clothing, electrical goods and vehicles at relatively low costs. These examples indicate how a country's factors of production influence what it produces.

A small Tongan banana producer with products for the Australian and South-East Asian markets

Specialisation is not without risks. For example:

● If a country has finite resources such as oil or copper, when these run out, the economy is likely to suffer unless the revenues earned from exports have been wisely invested for the future.

● De-industrialisation – the loss of manufacturing capacity and jobs – has posed serious problems for parts of the UK economy. Many thousands of jobs have been lost in textiles, clothing, engineering, vehicle manufacturing and other sectors. The benefits of cheap imported goods may not be seen as such by workers who have been displaced and who are unable to find a new job.

● Bad weather, as experienced in parts of the Caribbean, may wipe out a whole year's crops, reducing incomes and creating widespread economic chaos.

● The taste or needs of consumers may change, leaving a country's exports in a vulnerable position. As certain goods may no longer be needed, hardship among those producing them is almost inevitable.

● Political rather than economic factors may result in risks due to specialisation. The world's economies now rely heavily on each other, so that any unplanned shocks to the system (for example 9/11 or the Asian tsunami of 2004) are likely to be more acutely felt in the more specialised economies.

DEFINITION

Subsidy: a payment by a governing body to encourage the production or consumption of a product.

ACTIVITY ⋯⋙

An increasing volume of consumer goods sold in the UK are manufactured in China, Malaysia, Thailand, Czech Republic, Hungary and Poland.

Look through the clothes and other things you possess and make a list of where they are produced. Is there a pattern emerging? If so, why might specialisation have taken place in these economies?

DIVISION OF LABOUR

We have already looked at specialisation as far as the economy is concerned. In order to be competitive, labour costs need to be kept as low as possible. By specialising in a particular task, the production process can be broken down into a series of separate processes. This form of specialisation of labour is known as the **division of labour**.

Writing at the end of the 18th century, Adam Smith showed in a simple way how the production of pins was more efficient when the production process was split up into a series of individual tasks. In this way, each employee undertook just one part of the operation. Consequently, output per employee, or **productivity,** was many times greater than when each

ACTIVITY ⋯⋙

Sugar cane is a valuable export crop for some of the world's poorest economies in the Caribbean area. The UK company, Tate & Lyle, has long supported such producers. In addition, beet sugar is produced and refined in the UK by the British Sugar Corporation; **subsidies** from the EU help offset the higher costs of production.

a) Why is it possible for producers in both the Caribbean and the UK to specialise in sugar production?

b) Identify two benefits and two risks that affect producers of sugar in the Caribbean and in the UK.

DEFINITIONS

Division of labour: the specialisation of labour where the production process is broken down into separate tasks.

Productivity: output, or production of a good or service, per worker.

worker was tasked with producing the whole finished product.

A particularly good example today of the division of labour is in the manufacture of motor vehicles. This is a highly competitive industry, with price as well as quality important reasons why some manufacturers survive and prosper while others do not. The assembly of vehicles is a highly specialised and sophisticated process whereby parts such as engines, body panels, electrical components and seating are put together in a continuous production process. Much of this process is automated, but supervised by assembly workers. The result is usually high productivity in terms of vehicles produced per worker per day.

A controversial example of the division of labour is in the clothing, toy and electronics factories of China, India and Thailand. Millions of workers are employed in thousands of factories to produce goods for the European and American markets. A combination of low labour costs and the division of labour makes these products very price competitive. As a consequence, much domestic manufacture of these products has been forced to close.

This form of division of labour is not without problems. Many workers are low paid and have to work long hours to earn a decent wage. The monotonous nature of the work can lead to intense boredom and a poor-quality product from a generally unhappy, dissatisfied labour force. Cheap goods may be fine for UK and US consumers … but are they good for those who produce them?

Production possibility curves

Let us now return to the basic economic problem that applies to all economies, namely that of scarcity,

Production line in a Chinese electronics factory

choice and opportunity cost. We can use a simple economic model, a **production possibility curve** to show how resources are allocated.

> ### DEFINITION
>
> **Production possibility curve:** this shows the maximum quantities of different combinations of output of two products, given current resources and the state of technology.

In any economy, what is produced is determined by the quantity and quality of resources that are available. In **developed economies**, for example, many thousands of goods and services are produced as a result of the extensive availability of factors of production. For **developing economies**, the quantity and quality of resources will be much lower and consequently less will be produced and there will be less variety of production. These factors of production therefore determine an economy's so-called production possibilities.

> ### DEFINITIONS
>
> **Developed economy:** an economy with a high level of income per head.
>
> **Developing economy:** an economy with a relatively low level of income per head.

To show how this simple model works, we need to imagine that the economy produces just two goods, say cars and television sets. It is further assumed that these two industries use all of the economy's current resources in their respective production and that the production technology available is also being fully utilised. The production possibility curve shows the

maximum level of output of the two goods that can be produced. It is sometimes called the production possibility frontier, since it draws a type of boundary between what can be produced and what cannot be produced.

> ## ACTIVITY ·····⋮
>
> The data below shows the various production possibilities for an economy that produces two goods, cars and television sets.
>
> | Cars | Televisions |
> |---|---|
> | 1,000 | 0 |
> | 800 | 400 |
> | 600 | 800 |
> | 400 | 1,200 |
> | 200 | 1,600 |
> | 0 | 2,000 |
>
> **a)** Draw the above combinations of products on a graph. Put cars on the vertical axis and televisions on the horizontal axis.
> **b)** How many televisions can be produced when car production is 700? How does this change when 550 cars are produced?
> **c)** How does your diagram illustrate:
>   **i)** choice
>   **ii)** scarcity?

Figure 1.2 (see over) is another example of a production possibility curve, only here, the relationship between the two products is in the form of a curve (and not a straight line as in the above Activity). The maximum output of both types of product remains the same.

If all resources were being used in the production of cars, then 1,000 would be produced and no televisions. Alternatively, if all resources were allocated to making televisions, then 2,000 would be produced and no cars. These end points represent the extreme possibilities of what can be produced. Between these extremes there are many points on the production possibility curve where other

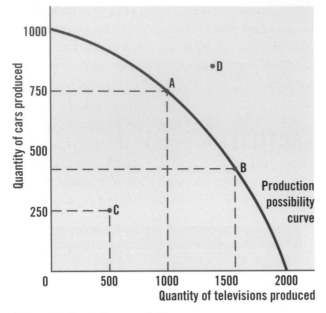

Figure 1.2 Production possibility curve

combinations of the two products can be made while maximising total output. At point *A*, 750 cars and 1,000 television sets are produced; at point *B*, the number of cars produced falls to 400 and the televisions produced increases to 1,650. The points, like any on the production possibility curve, are important since they are indicative of an efficient allocation of resources. In other words, the economy is getting all it can from the resources available and the present state of technology. It is clearly sensible and beneficial for the economy to be producing on its production possibility curve.

Now consider point *C*. This is within the production possibility curve and at this point, only 250 cars and 500 televisions are being produced. This is inefficient, since the economy is producing less than it could from the resources available. This also applies to any other points that are located within the production possibility curve. In contrast, point *D* which is outside the production possibility curve is not a possible outcome, since here the economy does not have the resources that are required to sustain this level of output of both types of good. Hence point *D* represents a position of scarcity.

The production possibility curve in Figure 1.2 can also be used to show the opportunity cost of one good measured in terms of the other good. When the economy reallocates its factors of production from point

A to point *B*, resources are being moved from the car industry to the production of televisions. When this occurs, 350 cars are being given up in order to get 650 more television sets. In other words, if the economy is operating at point *A*, the opportunity cost of producing 650 more televisions is 350 cars. The production foregone of these cars is the opportunity cost.

The shape of the production possibility curve is also significant. If you look at Figure 1.2, you will see that it is bowed or curves outwards. When the economy is devoting most of its resources to producing televisions, the production possibility curve is relatively steep. This means that in order to produce more televisions, an increasing amount of productive capacity for making cars has to be sacrificed. In contrast, when the economy is using most of its resources to produce cars, the production possibility curve is slightly flatter. This means that each television that is sacrificed gives a much smaller increase in the number of cars produced.

Figure 1.2 can be further used to show what is known as the **trade-off** involved in the production of these two products. As the name suggests, this is the process of deciding whether to give up some of one good in order to obtain more of another. So, if it is decided that more televisions are to be produced, the trade-off is that, as current resources are being fully used, less cars can be produced. The extent of any trade-off can be shown from the production possibility curve.

> **DEFINITION**
>
> **Trade-off:** the calculation involved in deciding on whether to give up one good for another.

Let us now relax the assumption that the resources available are fixed. Over time, there is technological advance in most forms of production. This is particularly the case in the electronics industry, which includes television production. The norm now is for televisions to be slim with high-density widescreens, which can be assembled more quickly than bulky conventional sets. For the economy, productivity (output per worker) increases, resulting in more

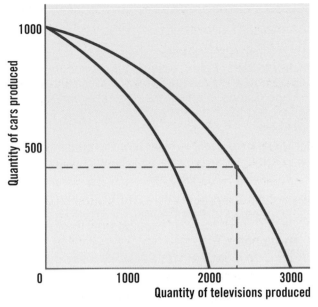

Figure 1.3 Increase in ability to produce televisions

are produced, the relative efficiency gain increases. So, where previously the economy could produce 400 cars and 1,650 televisions, it can now produce 2,300 televisions and the same amount of cars.

There are also circumstances where the production possibility curve shifts in its entirety, either to the right or to the left of its current position. What this means is that the productive capacity of the economy has changed. A shift to the right indicates an increase in productive capacity, whereas a shift to the left indicates that productive capacity has decreased. These new situations are shown in Figure 1.4.

television sets being produced for a given number of cars. This new state of affairs results in a change in the shape of the production possibility curve as in Figure 1.3.

This shows that the production possibility curve pivots outwards from its previous position on the vertical axis. It changes shape in this way because there has been no change in the conditions affecting car production. It is now possible to produce 3,000 televisions with current resources, an increase in efficiency of television production of 50 per cent. So, for any quantity of cars produced, it is now possible to produce more televisions. As more television sets

ACTIVITY ⋯⋮

The car production industry in an economy is facing increasing competition from producers elsewhere. In order to offset this, car manufacturers have developed more advanced robots to carry out production.

a) Re-draw Figure 1.2, assuming that 1,200 cars can now be produced.

b) Approximately how many more cars can be produced when the number of television sets made is 1,000?

c) How does the number of cars that can be produced change as television production falls below 1,000?

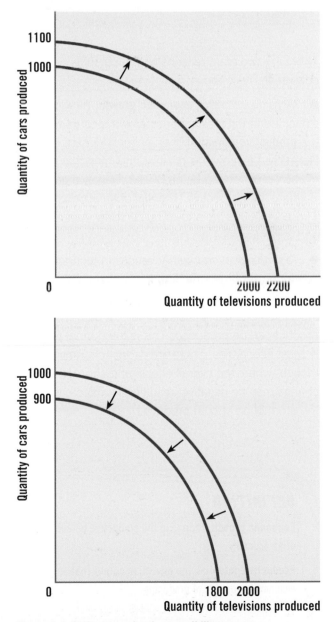

Figure 1.4 Shifts in production possibility curves

ACTIVITY ····⟩

It has been estimated that, since 2004, more than a million migrant workers have come to the UK from new EU member states in Central and Eastern Europe. Many of these workers are highly skilled and have had little difficulty getting a good job.

a) Using a diagram, explain how the production possibility curve might have been changed as a result of this migration.

b) Using a diagram, explain how the production possibility curve in the new EU member states might have changed as a result of this migration.

There are two main reasons why such shifts have occurred. These are:

● *More resources* or **economic growth**. As will be explained in Part 2, economic growth occurs where the **productive potential** of an economy changes. Normally this growth is positive, meaning that more of each product can be produced. Negative growth is where the productive potential of an economy falls. These situations are shown respectively in parts (a) and (b) of Figure 1.4.

● *Technological change*. Advances in technology continue over time, affecting the position of the production possibility curve of an economy. Where the overall change is positive, more of both types of product can be produced. This is the normal position in most economies. There are certain circumstances, though, where the overall effects of technological change may be negative, resulting in a decrease in the production of both products.

DEFINITION

Economic growth: change in the productive potential of an economy.

Productive potential: the maximum output that an economy is capable of producing.

Other applications

Production possibility curves can also be used to show the difficult choices that have to be made by many developing economies. As you will learn in Part 2, such economies invariably have low standards of living, expanding populations and little or no economic potential. Consequently, scarce resources have to be allocated to meeting present needs at the expense of investing in capital goods that would increase economic potential in the longer term.

The production possibility curve in Figure 1.5 shows the problem that many such economies have to face.

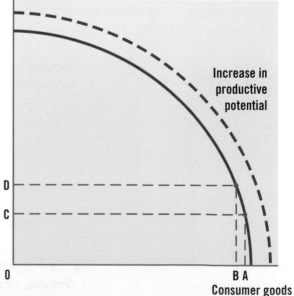

Figure 1.5 **Choice between consumer and capital goods for a developing economy**

The production of consumer goods is approaching its maximum, leaving only a small amount of resource for capital goods. With such a small allocation, new investment in capital goods is often only to replace existing resources. What is needed to raise economic potential is that a greater proportion of resources should be devoted to capital goods in order to shift the production possibility curve outwards. A small reduction in the amount of consumer goods produced from A to B can produce a greater relative increase in the amount of capital goods from C to D. The effect of this is to increase the economy's potential for economic growth as shown by an outward shift of the production possibility curve.

A contrasting application is to the command economy (see page 17). Here the choice faced by its regime is again one of choosing between capital goods and consumer goods; this time, though, the production of consumer goods is held down, with more resources being allocated to capital goods, which are seen as being essential for future economic growth and well-being. Current consumption therefore is being sacrificed for future prosperity … in theory at least.

Figure 1.6 shows this situation. Ideally, to meet consumer needs, the economy should be producing B quantity of consumer goods. This means that the quantity of capital goods produced is at D. In order to realise future growth, and so shift the production possibility curve outwards, the amount of capital goods produced is C with consumer good production restricted to A. The loss of current consumption is the difference between point B and point A. The usual criticism made of this type of economy is that the volume of consumer goods available is deliberately held down so that resources can be allocated to increasing economic potential and the benefits that this will bring in the future.

Finally, it must be made clear that the above analysis of the production possibility curve is highly simplified in order to establish, as well as clarify, some fundamental economic ideas, namely scarcity, choice and opportunity cost. These ideas are central to the study of economics and will re-appear in various forms throughout both parts of this book. At this early sage of studying economics, the use of production possibility curves should have made you aware of what these ideas are and why you should always keep them in your mind.

Economic systems and the role of the market

To conclude this first chapter, let us return yet again to the fundamental problem of scarcity, which in turn requires choices to be made. This problem is common to all economies, rich and poor. The choices that are made and how they are made is determined by the **economic system** of a particular country. This is the term that is used to describe the means by which a country's people, organisations and government make decisions with respect to:

● what goods and services are to be produced

● how these goods and services are produced and

● who should receive these goods and services.

Traditionally, economists have recognised three main types of economic system. These are the **market**

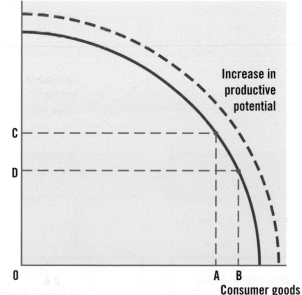

Capital goods

Increase in productive potential

Consumer goods

Figure 1.6 Choice between consumer and capital goods for a command economy

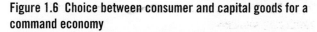

DEFINITION

Economic system: the way in which production is organised in a country or group of countries.

economy, the **command** or **centrally planned economy** and the **mixed economy**. Over the past 20–30 years, the planned economy has been replaced by the mixed economy in countries such as Poland, Estonia and the former Soviet Union. The market now has an increasing role to play, albeit to a varying degree, as such economies seek to cope with the problems and prospects that are being presented to them.

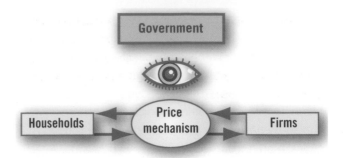

Figure 1.7 The market economy

> ## DEFINITION
>
> **Market economy:** an economic system whereby resources are allocated through the market forces of demand and supply.

THE MARKET ECONOMY

In the market economy, resources are allocated by the forces of **demand** and **supply** though the price mechanism. Decisions on how resources are to be allocated are invariably taken by millions of people and thousands of firms. The government has little or no direct involvement in this process. (See Figure 1.7). Households and firms interact as buyers and sellers. Price and the free operation of the **price system** (see page 22) are central to the way in which resources are allocated.

> ## DEFINITION
>
> **Price system:** a method of allocating resources by the free movement of prices.

Figure 1.8 shows a typical sequence of events to show how the market operates with no government interference. The starting point is that there is excess supply in the market – too much is being produced compared to demand, resulting in goods being stockpiled in shops and warehouses. To clear such stocks, the obvious response is to reduce price. This may well clear the excess supply, but it is also likely to mean that some firms that previously produced the good will now no longer be willing to do so. With less supply in the market, the price rises. In time, assuming no change in demand, firms may choose to

> ## DEFINITIONS
>
> **Supply:** the quantity of a product that producers are willing and able to provide at different market prices over a period of time.
>
> **Demand:** the quantity of a product that consumers are able and willing to purchase at various prices over a period of time.

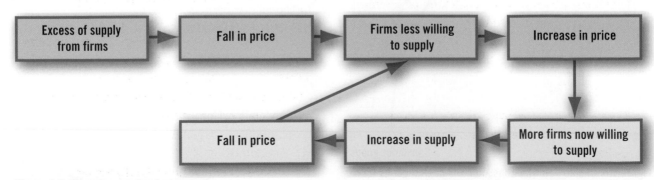

Figure 1.8 The price mechanism at work

re-enter the market. The increase in supply will lead to a fall in price and this whole process will continue. Prices and the self-interest of people and businesses therefore act as a barometer or guide to the decisions that have to be made.

ACTIVITY ⋯⋗

Using a similar diagram to Figure 1.8, map out the way in which the market responds to a situation where a firm is faced with a sudden yet substantial increase in demand for one of its products.

In principle, the government should have no direct role in the workings of the market economy and the natural operation of the price mechanism. Providing these are working efficiently, the government's role is to 'keep an eye' on what is happening and only interfere where these processes do not provide the best allocation of resources. As we shall see in Chapter 3, this is where the market 'fails'. Examples of such circumstances are where the government has to provide goods such as health care and national defence and where it seeks to regulate situations where the prices that are charged are not an accurate reflection of the true cost.

It must, though, be made clear that the true market economy is in certain respects an ideal. Even in the US, federal and state governments still have important roles to play in providing certain but limited public services.

THE COMMAND OR CENTRALLY PLANNED ECONOMY

Like the market economy, the command or centrally planned economy in its true form only exists in

DEFINITION

Command economy: an economic system in which most resources are state owned and also allocated centrally.

theory. In this economic system, the government has a central role in all decisions that are made. The decisions in terms of what to produce, how to produce and for whom to produce are all centralised. Decision-making is by planning boards and organisations and, in principle, production is controlled by the state. What is available to consumers and manufacturing organisations are again determined through centralisation.

The key features of a command economy are that central government and its organisations are responsible for the allocation of resources. Production targets are set for the main sectors of the economy, such as agriculture and manufacturing. These invariably are linked to planning for long-term growth through an increase in productive potential (see Figure 1.6). Prices of most essential items and the determination of wages are also controlled. Finally, the ownership of most productive resources and property is in the hands of the state. In short, the market does not have a substantive role in the allocation of resources.

In practice, there is always some government intervention in any economy. Even in a market economy, governments intervene. They find it necessary, for largely political reasons, to control the workings of the market mechanism. A typical example is where basic foodstuffs such as bread and meat are heavily subsidised to keep prices at a low, fixed level. The fluctuation of prices, so important in the market economy, does not take place. A consequence of artificially low prices is often one of excess demand relative to supply – queuing becomes a way of life. Private ownership of productive resources is restricted to small shops, restaurants and personal services such as hairdressing.

Governments of command economies tend to set goals which are different from those of governments in market economies, as explained earlier. Invariably, the objective is to achieve a high rate of growth in order to catch up on the progress made by the advanced market economies.

THE MIXED ECONOMY

The mixed economy is undoubtedly the typical economic system. As its name indicates, both

DEFINITION

Mixed economy: an economic system in which resources are allocated through a mixture of the market and direct public sector involvement.

private and public sectors have a part to play in the allocation of resources. Decisions involve an interaction between firms, labour and the government, mainly through the market mechanism. There is private ownership of most productive resources, although public ownership does exist to varying degrees.

Over the past 20 years or so, the trend has been one of privatisation, the transfer of resources from public ownership to the private sector. This has been the case in many economies including the UK and, equally significant, the economies of central and eastern Europe. Many of the latter economies have had to move along this path prior to becoming full members of the EU. The introduction of an increased emphasis on market forces has not been without its problems. The UK, especially, has suffered a tremendous loss of jobs in manufacturing as plants have closed and production has moved to lower-cost locations mainly in China, South-east Asia and central and eastern Europe.

ECONOMICS IN CONTEXT

THE CZECH REPUBLIC – TRANSITION FROM A COMMAND TO A MIXED ECONOMY

A communist regime was established in Czechoslovakia – the territory that today is the Czech Republic and Slovakia – in 1948. Thereafter, virtually all of industry, agriculture and trade were nationalised. Central planning was introduced and this resulted in an economic strategy that saw the country as a supplier of heavy equipment to the Soviet Union and other members of COMECON (Council for Mutual Economic Aid). Little trade was allowed with countries outside of this organisation.

This state of affairs persisted until the so-called 'velvet revolution' of 1989, when the Soviet Union announced that it would not intervene in countries which challenged the former communist regime and command economy. The split with Slovakia came later in 1993.

Since 1993, the Czech Republic's transition to a market economy has been extremely successful, although not without problems. Real GDP growth in recent years has been 5–7 per cent. This increase in productive capacity has resulted in the Czech Republic concentrating its productive resources on machinery and transport equipment, which now account for nearly 60 per cent of total exports. Total exports of all products have increased by 150 per cent since 2002.

Structurally, through privatisation and the benefits of economic growth, private consumption in 2006

was about 50 per cent of GDP. Public consumption was just over 20 per cent, compared to over four times this percentage when the command economy was at its strongest.

Much of the Czech Republic's productive capacity is in the motor manufacturing industry. VW-Audi has been a leading player in this market for many years; more recently, Kia and Peugeot/Toyota have invested heavily in new vehicle assembly plants. In contrast, agricultural production in 2006 was around half the level of the mid-1990s.

Elsewhere there have been similar trends. One of the most dramatic has been in the former Soviet Union, where the economy has been restructured (*perestroika*). This has also been the case in its former satellites such as Poland, the Czech Republic, Slovakia, Hungary, Lithuania and Estonia. Opening up the economy in this way has resulted in huge inward flows of foreign investment, particularly in the manufacturing and retail sectors. Opportunities have also occurred for private sector businesses to be developed – cafés, small shops and garages, and local ownership of productive resources is now the norm. In some cases, such as where former state-owned companies have been sold off, the new private owners have made vast sums of money in a very short time through adapting these businesses to make the most of the opportunities of the market mechanism. Even in Albania, once seen as one of the few remaining command economies, the government has recently decided to allow limited privatisation and a greater emphasis on the market mechanism.

The experience of the Asian 'Tiger' economies is also interesting. Some, such as Singapore and Hong Kong, have consistently had a strong focus on the market to allocate resources. Through this their governments have created an economy where free enterprise is encouraged The rewards can be high. Others, such as Malaysia, the Philippines and Indonesia, have placed more emphasis on central

ACTIVITY ···

a) Use the information available in the *Economics in context* to draw the production possibility curves that show the choices made in the Czech Republic with respect to the production of vehicles and agricultural goods

   i) in 2006

   ii) in the mid-1990s.

b) Use a diagram to show how the country's high rate of economic growth has affected its possible production possibility frontiers over the past few years.

c) Use production possibility curves to explain the changes in the opportunity cost of more resources being allocated to the production of vehicles.

d) What evidence is there that the Czech Republic is now a mixed economy?

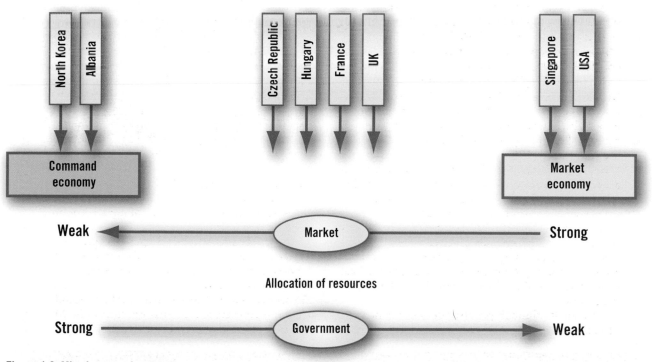

Figure 1.9 Mixed economic systems

planning. China's phenomenal sustained growth over the past 15 years or so has been based on the controlled management of the economy, but with very clear opportunities for foreign investors as well as domestic companies to influence the allocation of resources.

Figure 1.9 (see page 19) provides a broad explanation of where selected economies fall in terms of the relative strengths of the market and planned systems of resource allocation. To varying degrees, all countries would seem to fit within the definition of a mixed economy.

ECONOMICS IN CONTEXT

MALI'S FARMERS DISCOVER THE POWER OF JATROPHA

Mali is one of the world's poorest countries. It lacks the quantity and quality of factors of production that are needed to increase its productive potential. But all of this could be changing due to poisonous black seeds from a seemingly worthless weed, jatropha.

Jatropha originates in South America and is believed to have been spread around the world by Portuguese explorers. In Mali it has been used for decades as a living fence to keep animals off the fields – its smell and taste repel animals. It has also been planted to protect the precious soil from erosion.

All of this is now changing. It has been discovered that jatropha seeds can be used as a source of bio-fuel. This is very good news for Mali's farmers and those in India, China, Malaysia and the Philippines who have switched production from low-value arable crops to jatropha. An estimated 1 million acres is now under cultivation in these countries; farmers are being spurred on by big companies such as BP and D1 Oils to alter what they grow in favour of jatropha.

A number of small-scale projects have started in Mali to modify generators so they can use jatropha seeds to produce much-needed electricity in poor rural areas. There is less of an opportunity cost than in, for example, India, since jatropha tends to be grown on waste land or in between food crops. In this it

differs from other bio-fuels, such as palm oil and sugar cane, which require cultivable land and other resources in order to thrive.

Cultivating jatropha is not without risk, however. If it is a success, farmers, as other countries are finding out, will see it as being more valuable than the food crops they grow. In turn this could end up crippling food supplies and plunging many of Mali's people into even deeper poverty. This would not appear to be one of the benefits of specialisation.

2 Competitive markets and how they work

On completion of this chapter, you should be able to:

- understand what is meant by a 'competitive market' and explain the role of a market in allocating scarce resources
- understand what is meant by demand and consumer surplus
- explain how demand is influenced by price and other factors such as income, the prices of other goods, and changes in tastes and fashion
- analyse the difference between a shift in demand and a movement along a demand curve
- explain what is meant by supply and producer surplus
- understand the factors that will influence the supply of a particular product, including the impact of changing costs of production on supply
- analyse the difference between a shift in supply and a movement along a supply curve.

You should also be able to

- explain what is meant by the concepts of price, income and cross-elasticity of demand
- make simple calculations of price, income and cross-elasticity of demand
- explain the concept of elasticity of supply and make simple calculations
- discuss the business relevance of different elasticity estimates
- explain how equilibrium price and quantity are determined
- analyse how and why the equilibrium position changes
- explain what allocative efficiency is and the conditions under which it is achieved
- discuss whether competitive markets always lead to allocative efficiency.

What is a 'competitive market'?

At the end of Chapter 1, the market economy was described as one of the three main types of economic system. In it, the best way to try to resolve the economic problem is considered to be by the forces of demand and supply through the price mechanism. The purpose of this chapter is to examine markets and how they work. It will show how markets allocate scarce resources in relation to our infinite wants. This is fundamental to the study of economics.

Let us start by looking at the term **market**. We need to be clear from the start what we are studying. In some respects, a market may seem obvious – most of our towns have buildings for their markets or parts of streets which are used on certain days for markets. A growing trend is towards farmers' markets, for instance. Looking at the term more broadly, we can identify other examples such as the:

● foreign exchange market

● stock market

● holiday market

● housing market

● retail market, to include a full range of goods and services

● commodity market, to include agricultural and mineral products

● labour market

● eBay.

There are many more examples of markets, but each has the same basic characteristics. These are:

● a physical place where, or some mechanism whereby, buyers and sellers can meet or contact each other. The Internet has been a great enabler through various forms of home shopping and, of course, eBay.

● a willingness to trade or exchange goods and services. This is usually done using money. In many developing countries, exchange may take place through a simple system of bartering physical quantities of goods or providing services in exchange for goods.

Markets, though, are also competitive. This is because they provide for the resolution of the basic economic problem by providing a means through which scarce resources are allocated. This is the **price system**. In every market where money is used,

the products that are bought and sold command a price. This price reflects what suppliers wish to sell their product for; it also indicates the price that buyers are willing to pay to consume a product. The interaction of sellers and buyers, therefore, determines the price in any type of market situation.

The fact that markets are competitive invariably means that prices fluctuate. So, if producers put more of their products on the market, the most likely result is that prices will fall. This will also be the result if buyers hold back from purchasing a product. In contrast, if producers decide to restrict what they are willing to sell, then prices are expected to increase. A sudden surge of demand from consumers will also cause prices to increase.

ACTIVITY ⋯⋮

The graph below shows the annual percentage change in house prices in the UK from 1977 to 2007.

a) Briefly describe the trend in annual house prices over this period.

b) How might demand and supply be used to explain the fluctuations in annual house prices?

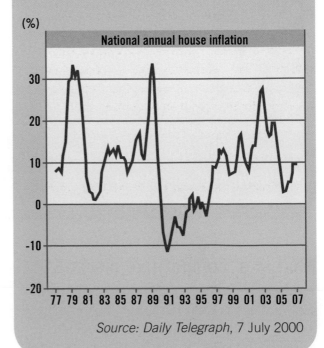

Source: Daily Telegraph, 7 July 2000

ACTIVITY ···▶

In August 2007, Tesco, the UK's largest and most powerful retailer, started to sell the UK's cheapest digital Freeview box for just £10. On the shelf it sat next to Tesco's new £9 DVD player. This was great news for consumers – but it did beg the question 'How did they get to be so cheap?'

a) How might demand and supply be used to explain the rock-bottom prices that Tesco was seemingly charging?

b) Who might benefit and who might lose out to Tesco's low prices for electronics goods such as digital Freeview boxes and DVD players?

When studying markets, it is also important to recognise that, in practice, a market may be a relatively complex concept to describe. Take the case of the retail market referred to above. This is particularly wide-ranging, covering a huge range of products that are bought by consumers. A more accurate explanation is to refer to the various distinguishable parts or **sub-markets** within the retail market. They could include, for instance, food and non-food sub-markets, or segments as they are sometimes known. In turn, each of these can be split down. The food market includes fresh food, frozen food and ambient food (food that can be stored for a long period at room temperature); it can also be considered in terms of its many products, such as fish, meat, fruit, vegetables, bread, household goods, pet food and so on. In all cases, the same general principles for the operation of markets apply.

DEFINITION

Sub-market: a recognised or distinguishable part of a market. Also known as a market segment.

ACTIVITY ···▶

Consider the holiday market. On what basis might this market be divided up into a series of sub-markets?

---

learning tip

A market in economics has the same functions as any street market that takes place where you live.

Demand

The term **demand** has been used a few times already in Chapter 1 and in this chapter. In simple terms, demand is what consumers want. What consumers want, however, and what they actually demand are not the same thing for two reasons.

● As shown in Chapter 1, wants are unlimited. We would all like more of the things we currently consume as well as to be able to consume things we currently aspire to such as (say) an expensive sports car, an exotic holiday or a Rolex watch.

● The point about demand is that to consume a product, consumers must have the ability to pay. In other words, they must be able to afford what they demand either in terms of their own income or in terms of what they may be able to borrow in order to fund a purchase.

DEFINITION

Demand: the quantity of a product that consumers are able and willing to purchase at various prices over a period of time.

This distinction between wants and demand can be made clear in terms of what are referred to as **notional demand** and **effective demand**. The former is the same as wants. It refers to the sort of things

DEFINITIONS

Notional demand: the desire for a product.

Effective demand: the willingness and ability to buy a product.

any consumer might desire, given personal tastes and preferences. Effective demand is different; it is demand supported by the ability and willingness to pay the market price. When we use the term 'demand' in this book, and indeed when professional economists use it, it is referring to effective demand.

Demand, therefore, can be defined as 'the quantity of a product that consumers are able and willing to purchase at various prices over a period of time'.

Two other points need to be made.

● The above definition assumes that all other things that affect the demand for a product do not change. In other words, any changes in the quantity demanded are due to changes in the price of the product alone. This important assumption is referred to by economists as **ceteris paribus** – which literally means 'other things remaining equal'.

● As the definition indicates, the quantity demanded must be time-related in the sense that it needs to be specified whether it is over the period of a day, a week, a month, a year and so on. If, say, sales of holidays were for a given week, then the quantities demanded will be clearly less than if the information is for annual sales.

DEFINITION

Ceteris paribus (Latin: other things being equal): assuming other variables remain unchanged.

Relationship between price and quantity demanded

The relationship between price and the quantity demanded of a product is in certain respects obvious. From our own experience, we know that in general if there is a sale and the price of something we want falls, then we are more likely to purchase it. Similarly, in the supermarket, a price reduction on a product we normally buy or one we might buy occasionally, will result in an increase in the quantity demanded (bought). Our big retailers know this

behaviour well. Conversely, if there is an increase in price of a particular product, the usual reaction from consumers is to buy less of it.

This relationship is a key consideration in microeconomics. More explicitly, it means that:

● there is an inverse relationship between the price of a product and the quantity demanded

● the lower the price, the more that will be demanded

● the higher the price, the less that will be demanded.

One further assumption needs to be made: that consumers are rational. By this we mean that they will behave in the manner stated above. They will also opt for the cheaper product when two otherwise identical ones are available in the market.

ACTIVITY ···⋗

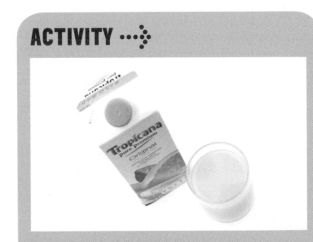

In September 2007, Sainsbury's, a major supermarket, reduced the price of its own-label 'Taste the Difference' orange juice by one third to £1.49 a litre. The price of Tropicana orange juice, a competing product, remained at £1.62 per litre.

a) How would you expect the quantity demanded of each product to be affected?

b) Why might the expected change in the quantity demanded for Tropicana orange juice not be the same as the actual change in the quantity demanded?

The demand curve

The **demand curve** is a simple representation of the relationship between the price of a product and the quantity that is demanded. It is usually represented in the form of a simple graph; price is plotted on the vertical (*y*) axis, the quantity on the horizontal (*x*) axis.

The data from which a demand curve is derived is taken from what is known as a **demand schedule**. Essentially, this is a data set which shows how much of a product will be demanded over a range of prices. Obtaining such information in practice can be quite difficult, particularly for a wide range of prices at a given point in time. One way in which such data can be compiled is from past records. A supermarket or other firm, for example, will have a record of how much of a product they have sold at particular prices, albeit over time. Another way of collecting data for the demand schedule is by means of a questionnaire. Package holiday companies do this and often ask their customers at the end of their holiday whether they would be willing to pay more (or less) for the holiday they have taken. And if so, how much more or how much less?

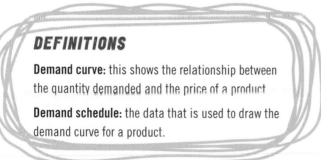

DEFINITIONS

Demand curve: this shows the relationship between the quantity demanded and the price of a product

Demand schedule: the data that is used to draw the demand curve for a product.

Let us take a simple example. The data in Table 2.1 has been collected by a market research company on behalf of a large tour operator. It is for a one-week self-catering holiday in Ibiza during June. We can now plot the market demand schedule on a graph to indicate how the quantity demanded changes when there is a change in the price of holidays. This is shown in Figure 2.1.

Points to note from this figure are:

● There is the normal inverse relationship between price and quantity demanded. As the price of a holiday falls, then so the quantity demanded increases.

Table 2.1 Demand schedule for a one-week self-catering holiday in Ibiza in June

Price per person (£)	Quantity demanded
500	300
450	500
400	650
350	800
300	1,000
250	1,150
200	1,300
150	1,500

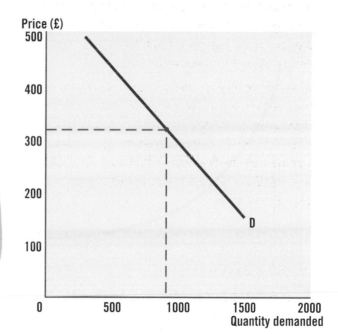

Figure 2.1 Market demand curve for June holidays to Ibiza

● The relationship is linear – the market demand curve is a straight line.

● The relationship only applies for holidays that are taken in June.

● It is possible to use the market demand curve to extrapolate the expected quantity demanded at any particular price. For example, at a price of £325, 900 holidays will be demanded.

Information on the demand of an individual can also be represented by a demand curve. The basic principles remain the same. In many cases, this information may not be linear. A very usual shape for the demand curve is for it to be curvilinear. An example of this is shown in Figure 2.2. Here the demand curve shows how an individual's demand for trips to the cinema (per month) changes as the price of cinema admission changes. The curve slopes downwards from left to right. This indicates that less will be demanded at a higher price than at a lower price. So, when the price is £4 per visit, this person will make just one cinema trip per month. Where price falls to £3, then two trips will be made. The curve slopes down rather steeply – at £1.50, a massive five trips per month will take place!

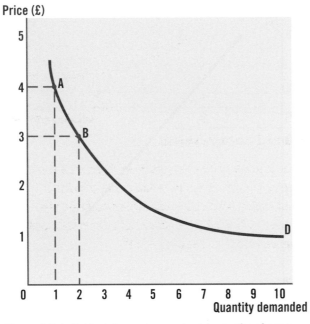

Figure 2.2 Individual demand curve for trips to the cinema

As stated above, Figure 2.2 shows that, as the price of trips to the cinema falls from £4 to £3 (from *A* to *B*), the quantity demanded increases. Alternatively, if price increases from £3 to £4 (*B* to *A*), the quantity demanded falls. These changes are often referred to as **movements along the demand curve**. They are only caused by a change in the price of the product. Where the movement is upwards along the demand curve, then it is known as an extension in demand; where the movement is downwards, then it is referred to as a contraction of demand.

ACTIVITY ····⟫

Market research for a large inclusive tour operator has shown that the typical peak period demand for a hotel holiday to Benidorm is as follows:

Price per person (£)	Quantity demanded
500	50
450	90
400	110
350	150
300	200
250	300
200	400
150	600
100	1,000

a) Use this data to plot the market demand curve.

b) How many holidays might the tour operator expect to sell if the price is £225 per person?

DEFINITION

Movement along the demand curve: this is in response to a change in the price of a product.

> **learning tip** An *extension in demand* is where a fall in price results in a greater quantity demanded; a *contraction in demand* is where a higher price results in a lesser quantity demanded.

Consumer surplus

In almost every market situation, holidays and trips to the cinema being typical, there will always be some individuals who will be willing to pay above what they actually have to pay in order to satisfy their demand. Take the case of a holiday to Benidorm. There are some people who are so fond of Benidorm that they go there year after year for their holidays. These people will be prepared to pay above the typical price of £200 per person on the grounds that they really must go to Benidorm and nowhere else. For the cinema, the release of a new Bond movie will mean that Bond fanatics will want to see the film when it is first released almost irrespective of the ticket price. If they were prepared to wait, then they would find they could see the film more cheaply.

These examples illustrate the concept of **consumer surplus**. This is the extra amount that consumers are prepared to pay for a product above the price that they actually pay. If we go back to Figure 2.2, this person would have been prepared to pay £4 for the first cinema trip, £3 for the second trip, £2.25 for the third trip and so on. If the actual price of admission is only £1.50, this person will go to the cinema five times per month. The consumer surplus therefore is £2.50 (the difference between £4 and £1.50 actually paid) for the first trip, £1.50 (£3 minus £1.50) for the second and so on. When demand is five trips per month, this individual has received a consumer surplus of £5.05p.

> ***DEFINITION***
>
> **Consumer surplus:** the extra amount that a consumer is willing to pay for a product above the price that is actually paid.

Figure 2.3 shows how consumer surplus can be represented by the area under the demand curve. This area indicates the additional money that this consumer is willing to pay to consume the product when the price is *P* and when *Q* is the quantity demanded.

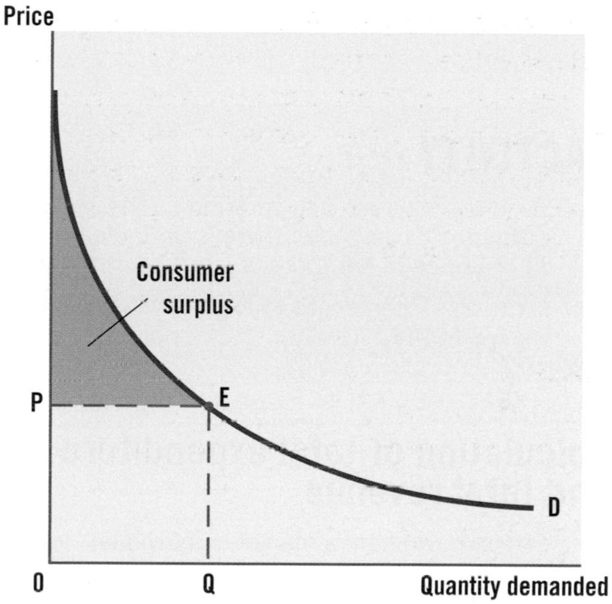

Figure 2.3 Consumer surplus

If the market price changes from P, the consumer surplus will also change. A fall in the price to P_1 results in an increase in consumer surplus (see Figure 2.4 below). The additional consumer surplus is represented by the area $PEFP_1$.

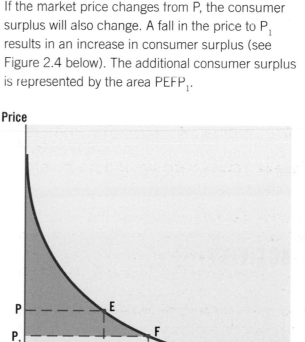

Figure 2.4 An increase in consumer surplus

An interesting example of consumer surplus is in the case of low-cost airlines such as easyJet and Jet2. Where passengers book early, the fare can be very low, even when taxes are added. In most cases, the fare is well below what prospective customers would be prepared to pay. This therefore generates considerable consumer surplus.

ACTIVITY ⋯⋮

a) Re-draw Figure 2.3 to show how consumer surplus changes when there is an increase in the price of the product.

b) Write a few sentences to explain what this means to the consumer.

Calculation of total expenditure and total revenue

Data that is drawn from a market or individual demand curve can be used to calculate the total expenditure made by the consumer. In turn, this is the total revenue or sales of the producer.

total expenditure = price x quantity demanded

If we go back to Figure 2.1, this market demand curve indicated that at a price of £300, 1,000 holidays to Ibiza would be demanded. So, total expenditure by these consumers is £300 x 1,000 = £300,000. This is the total revenue of the tour operator. If the price rises to £325, then 900 holidays are demanded, giving total expenditure of £292,500. As we shall see later, this is good news for consumers but not such good news for the tour operator.

ACTIVITY ⋯⋮

In Figure 2.4, assume that

P = £6   P₁ = £5
Q = 30   Q₁ = 40

a) Calculate the change in total expenditure when the price falls from £6 to £5.

b) What area represents the increase in consumer surplus when the price falls from £6 to £5?

Other factors affecting demand

It is clear from what has been described above that price has a major effect on the quantity of a product that is demanded. Whenever there is a sale involving price reductions or special offers in the supermarket, the purpose is quite clear – to sell more and to get consumers to buy more. Equally, for many types of product, a steep rise in price will mean that the quantity demanded falls. Price, however, is not the *only* reason or factor that affects the demand for a product.

Three non-price factors are recognised by economists as influencing the demand for most types of product. These are:

● consumer income

● the prices of other products

● tastes and fashion.

Let us consider each in turn.

CONSUMER INCOME

It is almost stating the obvious to say that income, our ability to purchase a product, has an important influence on whether we actually buy a good. (The basic economic problem again!) If we return to the example of holidays, then certain types of holiday may be outside the price that we are prepared to pay as we cannot afford to spend so much on a holiday. The same is true for clothes, electronic goods and so on. Income therefore has a major bearing on whether a good is demanded.

To be more specific, income is best seen in terms of what is left in our pockets once direct tax has been deducted and any state benefits have been added and the effects of inflation have been taken into account. This is referred to in economics as **real disposable income**. For most young people **disposable income** is the allowance that is given or what is earned from a part-time job after deductions are made. The 'real' element is rather more difficult to explain. If the money you receive increases by 5 per cent over a period of time but prices rise by 3 per cent, then real income has increased by the smaller amount of just 2 per cent. If the rise in prices is greater then the rise in money income, then real income has actually fallen, assuming no change in deductions such as income tax. This is not good, since the ability to pay for goods and services has fallen.

With this in mind, it is most usual for the demand for a product to increase if consumers' income increases. With more income, consumers have more spending power available, and so buy more of most goods and services. This is certainly true for most consumers of holidays, cars, televisions, computer equipment, visits to the cinema or clubs, take-away meals, clothes and so on. Such products, where demand increases with an increase in income, are known as **normal goods**.

In some cases, the relationship between income and demand is inverse, that is, as income rises, demand for the product actually falls. These goods and services are known as **inferior goods**. This term can be rather misleading – the products may not necessarily be of poor quality. They are products that are consumed only because more desirable alternatives cannot be purchased with available income. So, as income increases, a better alternative can be purchased. A typical example could be trainers. A top brand such as Nike, Reebok or Adidas could cost as much as £70 or even £80 a pair. Lesser brands or ones bought from a market stall will cost less. They may still be decent trainers, but they are perceived as being less prestigious. So, as income increases, less of the non-branded trainers will be purchased.

It is really quite difficult to generalise about inferior goods. What is an inferior good for one person may well be a normal good for someone else. Why this is so depends upon the consumer's income. For example, a pair of new lesser brand trainers is likely to be a normal good for someone who is used to buying second-hand cast-offs from a charity shop. For holidays, some consumers may regard a holiday to Benidorm as inferior – other people, who have not been able to afford a holiday, will view such a trip as a normal good. Despite this qualification, products such as supermarket own-label goods (relative to recognised brands), bus travel (relative to car travel) or a basic mobile phone (relative to one that takes photographs and downloads) can be regarded as inferior goods. The final outcome is determined by what happens to the total demand for a product following a change in income, not one individual's demand.

> **learning tip**
> The demand for many products we buy is mainly determined by our real disposable income.

THE PRICES OF OTHER PRODUCTS

The demand for a particular product can also be affected by a change in the price of another, different product. Two possible cases are recognised. These are where there are **substitutes** and **complements** to the product in question.

Most products have substitutes. They occur where a good or service faces competition from another product. In such a situation, there is competitive demand. A few examples will make this clear:

● Own-label baked beans compete with various brands such as Heinz and HP.

● BMW and Audi cars are top of the range substitutes.

● Car and train travel are substitutes for certain types of trip.

● A take-away pizza and a Chinese meal might be alternatives for some consumers.

● A holiday in Ibiza may be a substitute for a holiday in Majorca.

The list is almost endless. To the economist, there is a relationship between the price of one product and demand for the substitute. If the price of, say, holidays to Ibiza goes up, then there is likely to be an increase in the demand for holidays to Majorca since both destinations are close substitutes. Alternatively, if the price of holidays to Ibiza falls, there will be more of these holidays demanded. In turn, this may result in a fall in demand for holidays to Majorca as these are no longer as price competitive.

Complements, on the other hand, tend to be jointly demanded. Examples here are maybe not quite as obvious as in the case of substitutes. They could include:

● car prices and petrol prices

● car prices and car insurance premiums

● the price of air travel and air-inclusive holiday prices.

In this case, if the price of air travel increases, then it will lead to a rise in the price of air-inclusive holidays and a subsequent fall in their demand. Although unlikely, a fall in the price of air travel will be passed on to consumers by way of reduced prices for holidays and hence there will be an increase in their demand. There is, therefore, an inverse relationship between the price of the complement and the demand for the product that is jointly demanded.

In order to be able to make rational decisions with respect to demand in general, and with respect to substitutes and complements in particular, it is very important that consumers are fully aware of market prices. The Internet, and the widespread use of eBay and various search engines, have provided consumers with accurate, up-to-date information on a whole range of prices. It is now possible to compare grocery prices of the main supermarkets, international flight prices, car insurance premiums, the prices of electrical goods and many other items from the comfort of your own home. This, in turn, has put increased pressures on all retailers to be price competitive.

TASTES AND FASHION

Over time, consumer tastes change. In the fast-moving world in which we live, the life cycle of many products may be quite limited. Take the case of mobile phones again. To many teenagers, these are now a fashion accessory as well as a means of communication. It is seen to be 'cool' to have the latest model with all the latest features as well as the facility to make telephone calls. It is the same with clothing: fashions come and go, often in a very short time. With holidays, some destinations are more fashionable than others – bad publicity can often harm the reputation of a resort relative to somewhere else. With cars, the BMW Mini or a Smart car are fashionable to some; to others they are not.

Taste, to some extent, is rather more personal. Some people may like a particular product, while others may not want to consume it, irrespective of its price: a vegetarian, for instance, would never buy beef or chicken.

Various forms of advertising can have a very substantial influence on tastes and fashion. Informative advertising, where the positive features of a product are promoted, can have a powerful effect on demand. On the other hand, negative publicity such as has occurred with respect to child obesity and junk food can have an adverse effect on the demand for a product or group of products. In general, producers will only advertise if they believe it can have a positive effect on the demand for their product.

A change in demand due to a change in non-price factors

It is clear from the above explanation that changes in consumer income, the prices of other products and tastes and fashion can cause a **change in demand** for a product. When this occurs, it results in a shift of the demand curve or demand schedule. What this means is that a different amount of the good or service is now demanded at the same price. This must not be confused with a movement along the demand curve, which is due to a change in the price of the product and results in a change in the quantity demanded.

DEFINITION

Change in demand: this is where a change in a non-price factor leads to an increase or decrease in demand for a product.

A change in demand can produce two results:

● an increase in demand, where the demand curve shifts to the right. This means that more of the product is being demanded at the same price.

● a decrease in demand, where the demand curve shifts to the left. This means that less of the product is now demanded at the same price.

Table 2.2 summarises how each of these possibilities can occur.

Table 2.2 Summary of effects of a change in non-price factors on the demand curve.

Change in demand due to	Effect on the demand curve
An increase in consumer income	
A rise in the price of substitutes	
A fall in the price of complements	A shift to the RIGHT
A positive change in tastes and fashion	
A fall in consumer income	
A fall in the price of substitutes	
A rise in the price of complements	A shift to the LEFT
A negative change in tastes and fashion	

Figure 2.5 shows these changes in the form of a diagram. The original demand curve is *D*. An increase in demand, due to the factors referred to

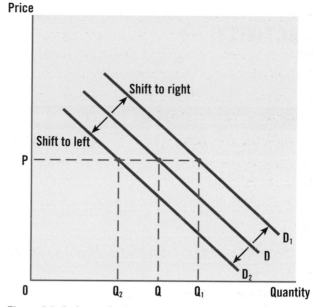

Figure 2.5 A change in demand due to a change in non-price factors

in Table 2.1, results in the demand curve shifting outwards to the right. At any price, for example *P*, more is demanded. This is represented by the demand curve D_1. A decrease in demand causes the demand curve to shift outwards to the left. Less is now demanded at price *P*. D_2 is the new demand curve resulting from this change.

> **learning tip**
>
> A change in any of the non-price factors affecting demand will lead to a shift in the position of the demand curve. Do not confuse this with a movement along the demand curve, which is due to a change in price alone.

ACTIVITY ⋯⟶

Explain how you would expect the demand for self-catering holidays to Ibiza to change if:

a) There is a substantial fall in the price of holidays to Florida.

b) There is an increase in the price of holidays to Majorca.

c) There is a serious outbreak of food poisoning in Ibiza and this has generated adverse stories in the media.

In each case, use a market demand curve to support your explanation.

ACTIVITY ⋯⋯⋗

The data below shows the estimated average quarterly sales of diving holidays to Cuba for a small, specialist UK company.

Price per person (£)	Quantity demanded
1,000	60
900	80
800	110
700	150
600	200
500	300
400	400
300	600

a) Using the above data, plot the demand curve.

b) For environmental reasons the company has been forced to limit the number of diving holidays to 230 per quarter. What price should it charge?

c) The above data was collected three years ago. Since then the UK economy has experienced a period of growth, with real disposable incomes rising by 10 per cent. The demand for diving holidays has also risen by 10 per cent. On the same diagram, draw the new market demand curve. What changes do you observe? What price should the company now charge in order to limit the number of holidays to 230 per quarter?

Supply

The term **supply** has been used a few times so far, In short, it is what producers of any type of product provide from the scarce resources that are available to them. Through supply, they are seeking to meet the unlimited wants of consumers.

Supply in the market is in the hands of producers. This is so whether we are dealing with tangible goods, such as mobile telephones, processed food and clothing, or with services, such as banking, hairdressing and transport. Supply seeks to satisfy the wants of consumers, but we need to remember that the motives of suppliers in most cases have little to do with goodwill and everything to do with making profits. Crudely, **profit** is the difference between the total revenue (sales revenue) of a producer and total cost. Economics assumes that the behaviour of suppliers is governed by the consistent need to maximise profits.

The producer's function is to combine the factors of production in an efficient and profitable way. To do this, a producer needs to decide how to use the various factors of production to find the least costly, and hence most profitable, combination for the output they produce. If we take the example of a mobile phone, when the producer combines the various factors of production, this involves:

- the assembly of components and parts

- employing skilled labour

- producing at a suitable location

- having the business skills and contacts to survive.

To some extent, in producing mobile phones, the producer has to decide the right combination of labour and capital to achieve the profit maximisation objective. The world's largest manufacturer of mobile phones is Nokia, a Finnish company that continues to produce in its own country. Labour costs elsewhere, especially in developing economies, are relatively cheaper than Finland. So when producing

DEFINITIONS

Supply: the quantity of a product that producers are willing and able to provide at different market prices over a period of time.

Profit: the difference between the total revenue (sales revenue) of a producer and total cost.

outside Finland, more labour is used relative to capital; in Finland, the production process is more capital intensive, with state of the art machines replacing labour.

Supply, therefore, can be defined as the quantity of a product that producers are willing and able to provide at different market prices over a period of time. It can be increased by producing more or by releasing stocks of goods held in a warehouse.

RELATIONSHIP BETWEEN PRICE AND QUANTITY SUPPLIED

Given the producer's motivation to supply, it should be clear that there is a greater willingness to increase the quantity supplied when there is a rise in prices. This is because firms are likely to be making greater profit. So, when price increases, the quantity supplied also increases. Conversely, if the market price of a product falls, then there is a decrease in the quantity that producers will wish to supply because they are likely to make less profit.

THE SUPPLY CURVE

The **supply curve** is a simple representation of the relationship between the price of a product and the quantity that is supplied. It is usually represented in the form of a simple graph; price is plotted on the vertical (*y*) axis, the quantity on the horizontal (*x*) axis.

The data from which a supply curve is derived is taken from what is known as the **supply schedule**. This is a data set which shows how much of a product is likely to be supplied over a range of prices. In some respects, in practice, obtaining this data is rather easier than in the case of a demand schedule

(see above, page 33). This is because suppliers can control how much they are willing and able to supply at a particular price. Past records may be of some help, yet, at the end of the day, if the price is not right, they will withhold their supply.

Let us take a simple example. The data in Table 2.3 shows how many holidays a large tour operator is willing and able to supply at various prices. We can now plot the supply schedule on a graph to indicate how the quantity supplied changes with the price of holidays. This is shown in Figure 2.6.

Table 2.3 Supply schedule for a one-week self-catering holiday in Ibiza in June.

Price per person (£)	Quantity supplied
500	1,200
450	1,150
400	1,100
350	1,050
300	1,000
250	950
200	900
150	850

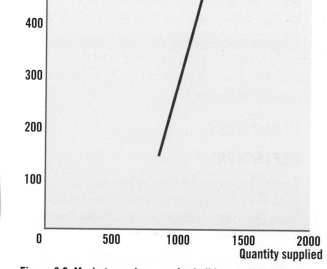

Figure 2.6 Market supply curve for holidays to Ibiza in June

> ### DEFINITIONS
>
> **Supply curve:** this shows the relationship between the quantity supplied and the price of a product.
>
> **Supply schedule:** the data used to draw up the supply curve of a product.

33

Points to note from this figure are:

● There is a normal positive relationship between price and quantity supplied. As the price of a holiday increases, the quantity supplied increases.

● The relationship is linear – the market supply curve is a straight line. It is, though, rather steep, the significance of which will be explained later.

● The relationship only applies for holidays taken in June.

● It is possible to use the market supply curve to extrapolate the likely supply at any price. For example, at a price of £325, 1,025 holidays will be supplied.

We have assumed here that there is just one supplier of self-catering holidays to Ibiza in June. In other words, the supply curve in Figure 2.6 is also the market supply curve. If there is more than one supplier, the market supply curve is the sum of the individual supply curves of all producers.

> **learning tip**
> A movement along the supply curve is due to a change in the price of the product that is being supplied.

Producer surplus

In certain respects, **producer surplus** is a similar concept to that of consumer surplus, explained earlier. As the term indicates, though, here we are looking at the situation from the producer's perspective. As the objective of all producers is normally one of maximising profits, it follows that they will be very keen to supply consumers who are willing to pay a price above that which they, the producers, are prepared to accept.

> **DEFINITION**
>
> **Producer surplus:** the difference between the price a producer is willing to accept and what it is actually paid.

Let us go back to Table 2.3. Suppose the producer has a base-line price of £350 per holiday. This is

what on average the firm might see as a fair price that it is prepared to accept for a one week self-catering holiday to Ibiza in June. There are likely to be consumers who are willing to pay above this price. These could be ones who really like going to Ibiza or maybe those who have no choice but to go in June. So, such consumers will be providing additional revenue to the producer, above what is the normal expectation. This is what is meant by producer surplus.

Figure 2.7 shows the extent of producer surplus. Suppose the typical selling price is *P* and at this price *Q* is the quantity supplied. The producer surplus is the shaded area above the supply curve but below the price line at *P*. Anything the firm sells for below price *P* is because it is willing to sell to consumers at this price. There is, however, a point P_1 on Figure 2.7, below which the firm is completely unwilling to supply. A change in price affects producer surplus – a fall in price reduces producer surplus, while a rise in price increases producer surplus.

> **learning tip**
> Be careful not to confuse producer surplus with consumer surplus.

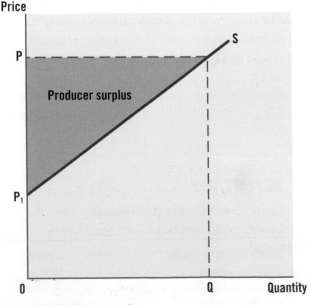

Figure 2.7 Producer surplus

ACTIVITY ⋯⋮➤

The table below shows the weekly supply schedule for a product.

Price (£)	Quantity supplied (per week)
4.00	320
3.75	280
3.50	240
3.25	220
3.00	180
2.75	140
2.50	100

a) Plot the supply curve.

b) Use this curve to calculate the producer surplus if the firm is willing to accept a price of £3.25.

c) Re-draw Figure 2.7 to show how
  ● a rise in price
  ● a fall in price
  affects producer surplus.

Other factors affecting supply

A change in price is not the only factor that affects a producer's willingness to supply. There are other factors including:

● costs of production
● size and nature of the industry
● government policy, and
● other factors.

COSTS OF PRODUCTION

There are many things that can affect the costs of production; any change in any input can have an effect on the firm's profits and willingness to supply the market.

The most obvious is a change in the cost of factors of production. For example, world prices of oil and of many types of minerals, metals and food have

been rising in real terms in recent years. This clearly impacts upon a firm's production costs. How much it does will depend upon how important these particular factors are within a firm's total costs. In the case of oil, the rapid increase in price has affected all types of business, small as well as large. For some products, like cars and engineering machinery, the effect of rising metal prices on costs is likely to be much greater than in some other forms of production that have less reliance on such inputs. A rise in oil prices leads to a rise in the cost of fuel and this affects the distribution costs of all businesses.

In some types of activity, labour costs are a high proportion of total costs. This is particularly true in service sector activities, such as most forms of retailing, transport and personal services. It is also true for some types of manufacturing where the price of the products is quite low. So, an increase in labour costs has to be passed on to the consumers in the form of higher prices.

In practice, it is quite difficult to generalise. Labour in plentiful supply will usually not increase in price to the same extent as labour which is specialist and in short supply. The extent of any change in the supply price will also depend upon the extent to which efficiency gains can be made by the producer, for example by replacing labour with capital.

Robots have replaced some types of labour in vehicle manufacturing

Technological change has a bearing on the costs of production. Many tasks, both in manufacturing and in services, can now be done by technologically advanced machines instead of by human labour. The assembly of vehicles, which is done mainly by robots under human control, is a typical example. Banks and retailers have cut costs by making many parts of their operations 'self-service'. Computer-aided production is the norm in most mass-market clothing businesses, even in countries such as China and India that have low labour costs. The application of computerisation in many types of firm has had a substantial impact on production costs. This has invariably been downwards.

SIZE AND NATURE OF THE INDUSTRY

Some industries are more competitive than others. Where this is the case, for example, in grocery retailing or food production, very minor increases in costs can have a big impact on supply. In other markets, for example, where there is a strong brand or just a few producers, price competition is likely to be less important. Any cost increases can usually be passed on to consumers, with very little or no effect on profits.

GOVERNMENT POLICY

Governments can affect the supply of a product in many different ways. Most products that firms supply are subject to some form of indirect taxation such as Value Added Tax (VAT). Any increase in this taxation will have to be passed on to the consumer through increased prices. In turn, the increased prices will affect the willingness of producers to supply.

Legislation and regulations can also affect a firm's costs. UK businesses frequently complain about compliance and the impact of bureaucracy on their costs. Health and safety regulations, for example, invariably lead to higher production costs, compared to costs in countries that have less demanding standards. Such regulations tend to affect all firms. So any effect on the costs of production tends to affect all firms in a fair way.

In a few instances, the government is prepared to give an annual subsidy to firms. This is in the form

of a payment to reduce costs, and hence prices to consumers. European Union (EU) payments to farmers and subsidies to rail passenger transport companies are typical examples. As a result, the supply of products is increased.

OTHER FACTORS

The supply of many products is subject to a whole range of other outside factors over which suppliers often have little or no influence. A good example is in agriculture, where producers are subject to the vagaries of the weather. In 2005, for example, Hurricane Katrina devastated the banana crops of some Caribbean producers. Closer to home, the floods of summer 2007 destroyed many vegetable stocks, reducing total supply from within the UK.

The supply of food products can also be affected by unexpected health scares. In summer 2007, there was a reported new case of foot and mouth disease. This temporarily reduced the supply of beef and pork coming onto the market in the UK. In contrast, around the same time, nutritionists concluded that pomegranate juice was very beneficial in reducing cholesterol and blood pressure. To meet the increased demand, producers of pomegranates have frantically tried to increase production.

A change in supply due to a change in non-price factors

Changes in the costs of production, the size and nature of an industry and government policies can therefore result in a **change in supply** of a product. This means that a different quantity is now being supplied at the same price. When this occurs, the supply curve shifts either to the right or to the left depending on the direction of the change. There are two possibilities:

DEFINITION

Change in supply: occurs when a change in a non-price influence leads to an increase or decrease in the willingness of a producer to supply a product.

● an increase in supply, meaning that more will be supplied at the same price. A technological advance or breakthrough or a reduction in the rate of indirect taxation will result in the supply curve shifting to the right.

● a decrease in supply, where less of a product is being supplied at the same price. Here, the supply curve shifts to the left. Typical causes are an increase in the rate of indirect taxation or a rise in price of an essential factor of production.

A change in supply must not be confused with a change in the quantity supplied, which is due to a change in the price of the product alone, all other factors remaining constant.

Table 2.4 provides a summary of how shifts in the supply curve can occur.

Table 2.4 Summary of effects of a change in non-price factors on the supply curve.

Change in supply due to	Effect on the supply curve
A fall in raw material costs	
An improvement in labour efficiency	
A reduction in the rate of indirect taxation	A shift to the RIGHT
A positive technological advance	
Any other positive factor	
An increase in cost of raw materials	
An increase in labour costs	
An increase in the rate of indirect taxation	A shift to the LEFT
A failed technological advance	
Any other negative factor	

Figure 2.8 shows these changes in the form of a diagram. The original supply curve is S. An increase in supply, for the reasons given in Table 2.4, will result in the supply curve shifting outwards to the right. At any one price, for example P, more will be supplied. The new supply curve is S_1. A decrease in supply causes the supply curve to shift upwards and

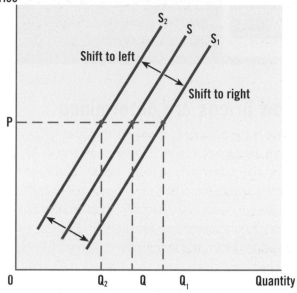

Figure 2.8 A change in supply due to a change in non-price factors

to the left. Less is now supplied at price P. S_2 is the new supply curve resulting from this change.

ACTIVITY ⋯⋮

a) Go back to the supply curve you have plotted in the previous activity. Suppose the government imposes a new indirect tax of 10 per cent of the selling price on this product. Draw the new supply curve.

b) Briefly describe any changes you observe.

ACTIVITY ⋯⋮

In October 2007 the new Airbus A380 went into service with Singapore Airlines, following various production delays, which have resulted in an escalation of production costs.

a) How in theory might this rise in costs affect the supply curve for A380s?

b) Why in practice might the increase in production costs have no particular effect on the final price of A380s?

learning tip

Be careful not to confuse a change in supply with a change in the quantity supplied.

How prices are determined

Price is the amount of money that is paid for a given amount of a particular good or service. As consumers, for many of the things we purchase, price is a very important consideration. For high-value purchases, we invariably 'shop around' or look at price comparisons on the Internet. Even for lower-value products, like sandwiches or a can of Coke, we are tempted to buy from shops where their price is cheapest. Price is also important for suppliers. Their decision on whether to supply the market is usually heavily dependent on the price they can obtain. Within the market system, therefore, price is central to the way in which resources are allocated.

This leads us to what is the most fundamental principle in economics, namely that

The price of any product is determined by demand and supply.

The **equilibrium price** is where demand and supply are equal. It is sometimes referred to as the **clearing price**, since this is where the amount consumers wish to buy and the amount producers wish to put up for sale are equal. In other words, both parties in the market are satisfied – demand is being met and there are no unsold products, so neither side in the market has any particular reason to want change. This situation is shown in Table 2.5 and Figure 2.9.

Table 2.5 Market demand and supply schedules for one-week self-catering holidays in Ibiza in June.

Price per person (£)	Quantity demanded	Quantity supplied
500	300	1,200
450	500	1,150
400	650	1,100
350	800	1,050
300	1,000	1,000
250	1,150	950
200	1,300	900
150	1,500	850

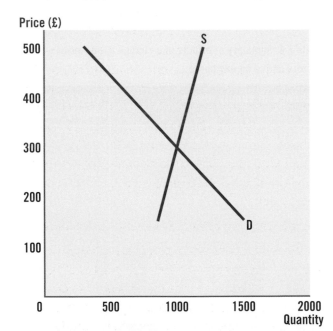

Figure 2.9 Price determination

learning tip

Think of the equilibrium price as being the price where the market 'clears'.

The equilibrium price is £300 per holiday. On Figure 2.9 this is where the demand and supply curves intersect or cross. At this point, the **equilibrium quantity** is 1,000 holidays. The total expenditure by consumers, and hence revenue for producers, is £300 x 1,000 = £300,000.

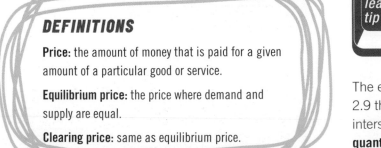

DEFINITIONS

Price: the amount of money that is paid for a given amount of a particular good or service.

Equilibrium price: the price where demand and supply are equal.

Clearing price: same as equilibrium price.

In practice, markets are often unstable and not always in equilibrium. When this happens, the market is said to be in **disequilibrium**; in other words, demand and supply are not equal. Where this happens, the natural forces in the market result in the market price and output moving to the equilibrium position. Two cases are:

● Where the price set by producers is too high. Referring back to Table 2.5, the tour operator may be of the opinion that tourists would be prepared to pay £400 for the holiday in Ibiza. At this price, the firm would be willing to supply 1,100 holidays; consumers, though, would only be willing to buy 650 holidays at this price. Consequently, the tour operator would be left with unsold holidays or a **surplus**. For many reasons, this situation cannot persist. So, what happens is that the tour operator is forced to reduce the price of these holidays to clear the surplus supply. This is another fundamental principle of economics namely that

When supply is greater than demand, price will fall.

● Where the price set by producers is too low. Table 2.5 indicates that if the price is set at £200 per holiday, consumers will see this as a good bargain and will be willing to buy 1,300 holidays. At this price, the tour operator is only willing to provide 900 holidays. In such a market situation there is a **shortage**. Holidays have sold very quickly, leaving

consumers who would otherwise be willing to purchase this holiday unsatisfied.

So, in this situation, companies seeking to maximise their profits will see this as an opportunity to raise their prices and provide more holidays for the market. (This assumes they can actually increase supply, which in practice can sometimes be difficult.) Prices will rise to the equilibrium price. In this process, some consumers may decide the price is too high for them and will drop out of this market. So, a further fundamental principle of economics is

When demand is greater than supply, price will rise.

In general terms, these two situations are shown on Figure 2.10.

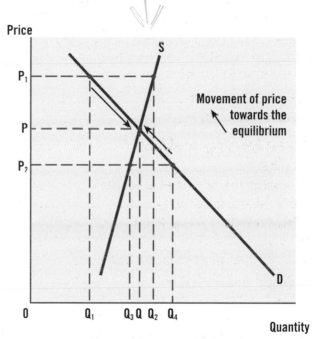

Figure 2.10 Disequilibrium in the market

ACTIVITY ···

a) In Figure 2.10, the equilibrium price is P and the equilibrium quantity is Q.

Use your own words, and the relevant symbols, to explain what happens in the market when price is set at

i) P_1

ii) P_2

b) i) In October 2007, on the day of the World Cup final, it was reported that English rugby union fans were willing to pay as much as £1,000 for a ticket to watch the match. The actual price of the ticket was £60. Use demand and supply concepts to explain this situation.

ii) Earlier in 2007, it was reported that on the day of the match, local cricket fans in Barbados were being offered tickets to watch a World Cup tie for as little as $10. The actual price of the ticket was $80. Use demand and supply concepts to explain this situation.

Effects of a change in demand or supply on the equilibrium position

Within any market, the equilibrium position is subject to change. This can come about for three reasons:

● a change in demand, whereby the demand curve shifts to the right or to the left

● a change in supply, whereby the supply curve shifts to the right or to the left

● a more or less simultaneous change in demand and supply.

In looking at the effects of any of these changes, it is necessary to be mindful of the time scale. Markets, particularly on the supply side, cannot adjust quickly unless the product has been stored. On the demand side, especially if tastes and fashion change, the effect on the market can be quick. A food scare, such as a foot and mouth epidemic, can have an extremely rapid effect on the equilibrium price and quantity. The usual assumption made is that all other factors affecting the market remain unchanged.

Figure 2.11 shows how the equilibrium position changes with an increase or decrease in demand. A change in demand can occur for the reasons discussed earlier. Take the case of holidays to Ibiza. Demand could fall if there were adverse reports in the media about drunkenness in Ibiza; it could increase if a television programme gave a glowing report of Ibiza as a holiday destination. In both cases, there would be a quick response in the market. A fall in demand would see the demand curve shift downwards and

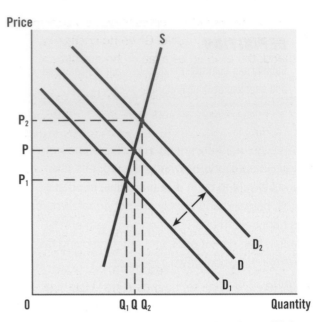

Figure 2.11 Effects of a change in demand on the equilibrium position

to the left. This would result in a fall in both the equilibrium price and quantity.

An increase in demand would see a shift to the right and upwards of the demand curve resulting in an increase in both the equilibrium price and quantity.

Figure 2.12 shows how the equilibrium position changes with an increase or decrease in supply. In the case of holidays, for example, there could be a reduction in supply if a tour operator went out of

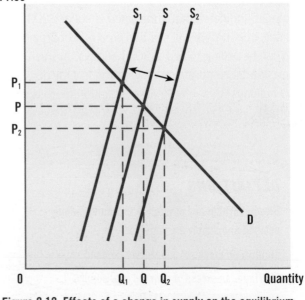

Figure 2.12 Effects of a change in supply on the equilibrium position

business. This would be represented by a shift to the left of the supply curve. Given no change in demand, there would be a fall in the equilibrium quantity but a rise in the equilibrium price. An increase in the supply of holidays to Ibiza could come about if tour operators were able to increase their arrangements for accommodation, flights and so on. This would take time but would lead to an increase in the equilibrium quantity and a fall in the equilibrium price.

A third way in which the equilibrium position might change is when there is a simultaneous change in demand and supply. This can involve various possibilities. It could also result in an unchanged equilibrium price if the two respective shifts cancel out each other. This situation is shown in Figure 2.13. Here, there has been a fall in demand combined with

Price

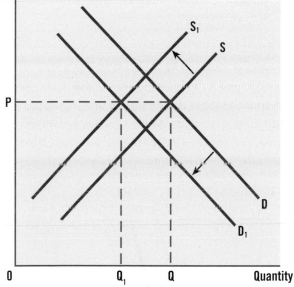

Figure 2.13 **Effects of a simultaneous fall in demand and supply in the equilibrium position**

THE ESCALATING PRICE OF FOOD – A CASE OF DEMAND AND SUPPLY

1 May, Labour Day, is a public holiday in Hong Kong and China. In 2008 it also marked the arrival of the Olympic torch at Hong Kong International Airport, en route to its final destination, Beijing. Not all of Hong Kong's residents were as bothered about this unique event as they were about the escalating price of food and the availability of cooking oil, an essential ingredient in Chinese stir-fry and deep-fry cooking. Since January the price of cooking oil has increased by 40 per cent; panic buying is prevalent, with supermarket shelves being cleared almost as soon as new stocks are received. This is the latest in a string of food price increases, which have seen chicken, duck and pork prices rise in Hong Kong and China by up to 30 per cent in the last year.

Why is this? The simple reason is demand and supply. More specifically, the demand and supply of maize, the common factor in all the cases mentioned. Over the last two years the demand for maize has increased owing to:

- an increase in demand for maize to be processed into bio-fuel. Higher prices have tempted farmers into selling their crops for this type of processing rather than for processing into cooking oil and animal feed.
- an increase in demand for meat from China's booming middle classes.

These factors account for a doubling in maize prices over the last year.

A second example is rice. Between January and May 2008 the world price of rice rose 150 per cent. In this case the price rise owes more to a fall in supply than an increase in demand. The harvest in Thailand and elsewhere in southern Asia was poor in 2007. There was also a dwindling stockpile in the USA, which meant that additional supplies could not be released to keep down prices. Wal-Mart, the mega US retailer, took the unprecedented step of restricting its customers to four packets of rice each, and at about the same time the Indian government banned the export of all rice except for premium-quality basmati.

ACTIVITY ····

In June 2007, it was announced that Tata Motors, the vehicle arm of the powerful Indian conglomerate, was planning to produce 250,000 cars a year from a new factory in 2008. The reasons given for this massive venture were that, for the past decade, India had a burgeoning middle class with money to spend, there was a rising population and a need to provide an alternative to the country's ailing public transport system.

a) Use a diagram to show how the price of cars in India might have changed between 1997 and 2007.

b) Modify this diagram to explain how production by Tata motors might affect the equilibrium from 2008.

a simultaneous fall in supply, the combined effect of which is to reduce the equilibrium quantity from Q to Q_1 yet maintain the equilibrium price. In practice, this outcome is rather difficult to achieve; it may happen say if a supermarket stockpiles products when there is a sudden decrease in demand.

Elasticity

We have shown so far in this chapter that there are many factors that can affect the demand and supply of products. What we have not yet done is to say by how much demand and supply changes when any of these factors, including the price of the product, changes. This is where **elasticity** comes into our analysis of competitive markets. It is the term that is used in general to *measure* the extent to which buyers and sellers respond to any particular *change* in market conditions. The two words in *italics* are crucial to understanding what elasticity is about, that:

● it is a numerical estimate

● it measures the response to a change in price or to a change in any other factors that determine the demand or supply of a product.

> **DEFINITION**
>
> **Elasticity:** the extent to which buyers and sellers respond to a change in market conditions.

Elasticity is an important concept in understanding how markets work. From a business standpoint, it goes a long way towards explaining why:

● the price of a return rail ticket between Leeds and London for arrival before 10.30 was £185 in October 2007 (assuming no prior booking)

● the price of a summer holiday in May or June is around two-thirds of the price it is in August

● the demand for some products increases more than others when real disposable income rises

● it is often difficult for suppliers to respond quickly when there is a surge in demand for their products.

PRICE ELASTICITY OF DEMAND

Price elasticity of demand (PED) measures how responsive the quantity demanded of a product is to a change in its price. For measurement purposes, we assume that all other factors that affect demand remain unchanged. PED is measured by the following formula:

$$\text{Price elasticity of demand} = \frac{\text{\% change in quantity demanded}}{\text{\% change in price}}$$

Mathematically (if you can remember GCSE!), it is no more than the gradient of the demand curve, either for the market or for an individual demand curve.

> **DEFINITION**
>
> **Price elasticity of demand:** the responsiveness of the quantity demanded to a change in the price of the product.

Let us take a simple example. Suppose a tour operator sells 5,000 holidays per month to Majorca for a price of £400. When the price is increased to £440, demand falls to 4,000 holidays per month. So,

$$\text{Price elasticity of demand} = \frac{-1,000/5,000}{40/400} \times 100 \text{ per cent}$$

$$= \frac{-20}{10}$$

$$= -2$$

> **learning tip**
>
> When calculating a percentage change, remember to divide the change by the original figure.

The estimate of –2 indicates that the demand for holidays to Majorca is responsive to a change in the price of these holidays. This is known as a **price elastic** or **price sensitive** situation. The negative sign is indicative of the fact that the quantity demanded has fallen as a result of the increase in price. (It is common practice to leave out the minus sign.)

The demand for water tends to be price inelastic

Not all products we buy are very responsive to a change in their price. Take the case of water. If the price of household water were to rise by 10 per cent, it is quite likely that demand would fall by a very small percentage, say 1 per cent. This would produce an estimate of price elasticity of demand of −0.1. This is **price inelastic** or **price insensitive**, indicating that the quantity demanded is not particularly responsive to a change in price.

DEFINITIONS

Price elastic: where the percentage change in the quantity demanded is sensitive to a change in price.

Price inelastic: where the percentage change in the quantity demanded is insensitive to a change in price.

Table 2.6 shows some empirical estimates of price elasticity of demand.

Table 2.6 Estimates for price elasticity of demand in the UK.

Dairy produce	−0.05
Bread and cereals	−0.22
Alcohol	−0.83
Alcoholic spirits	−1.27
Entertainment	−1.40
Foreign leisure travel	−1.63

As the table indicates, there are substantial differences between the various products. For example:

● the demand for food items is not particularly price sensitive

● the demand for alcoholic drink in general is relatively price inelastic although the demand for spirits is price elastic

● the demand for both entertainment and leisure travel seems to be price sensitive.

learning tip

Remember: PED>1: elastic; PED<1: inelastic; PED=1: unit PED. (PED=1: here a change in price causes an exactly proportional change in demand.)

Variations such as these lead us to ask the obvious question, 'What determines the price elasticity of demand for a product or group of products?' There are three main determinants. These are:

● *The availability and closeness of substitutes*

A **substitute** is an alternative to a particular product. In general, the greater the number of substitutes and the greater their closeness to a given product, then the likelihood is that such a product will be price elastic. A very specific example would be baked beans where there are many brands – a rise in the price of one brand would result in more consumers buying an alternative brand.

Referring back to Table 2.6, entertainment and foreign leisure travel are broadly defined products. There are clearly substitutes for both, as the price elasticity estimates might suggest. If we define the product more narrowly, such as a type of entertainment or foreign travel to a specific place, the estimate of price elasticity of demand becomes even more price elastic. This means the demand for these products is very price responsive.

In the case of dairy products, the very low estimate of price elasticity is indicative of a genuine lack of substitutes in the eyes of most consumers. The same is largely true for bread and cereals.

● *The relative expense of the product with respect to income*

If a product takes up a very small proportion of a person's income (for example, a banana), then a doubling in price will not result in much change in the quantity demanded. In such situations demand is likely to be price inelastic. Items such as bus fares, newspapers and cheap food items are other typical examples.

Where a product takes up a larger proportion of income, for example a holiday or eating out, it is more likely that demand will be more sensitive to changes in price and so be more price elastic. A possible exception is the case of habit-forming items, such as cigarettes and certain types of alcohol. A rise in these prices, even for those on low incomes, is unlikely to lead to much of a fall in the quantity demanded.

● *Time*

In the short term, most consumers find it difficult to alter their spending habits. This means they are quite likely to continue to purchase a product despite a price increase. Over time, as consumers find out more about possible substitutes, demand for a product is likely to become more price elastic. Still concerning time, where consumption of a product can be delayed, demand for that product is likely to be price elastic. Such products tend not to be necessities and are likely to take up a large proportion of income, for example, a replacement car or a home improvement such as a new bathroom.

ACTIVITY ⋯⋮⋗

In 2003, Sony sold 22.5 million Play Station 2 games consoles for a typical selling price of £129.99. As a result of falling sales, in 2005 the price was reduced to £99.99 and there were sales of 14 million. What might you deduce about the price elasticity of demand?

INCOME ELASTICITY OF DEMAND

Income elasticity of demand (YED) measures how responsive demand is following a change in income. It is assumed that all other factors affecting demand are unchanged. It is measured by the following formula:

$$\frac{\text{income elasticity}}{\text{of demand}} = \frac{\%\ \text{change in quantity demanded}}{\%\ \text{change in income}}$$

The sign, positive or negative, is an essential element of this elasticity measure as it indicates whether there is an increase or decrease in the quantity demanded following change in income.

> **DEFINITION**
>
> **Income elasticity of demand:** the responsiveness of demand to a change in income.

Most products have a positive income elasticity of demand and are known as **normal goods**. This means that, as real disposable income increases, demand for these products will also increase. Typical examples are hotel breaks, most types of holiday,

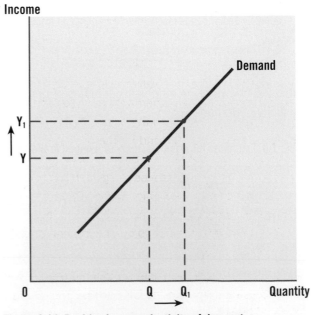

Figure 2.14 Positive income elasticity of demand

wine, new clothes, eating out, organic food, electronic goods and home improvements. The relationship between a change in income and a change in quantity demanded for such goods is shown in Figure 2.14. Here, as income increases from Y to Y_1, the quantity demanded also increases from Q to Q_1.

The extent of the response of demand to the change in income can vary. Two particular cases are:

● where the estimate of income elasticity of demand is less than 1. For such a product, demand is said to be **income inelastic.**

● where the estimate of income elasticity of demand is greater than 1. For such a product, demand is said to be **income elastic**.

DEFINITIONS

Normal goods: goods with a positive income elasticity of demand.

Income inelastic: goods for which a change in income produces a less than proportionate change in demand.

Income elastic: goods for which a change in income produces a greater proportionate change in demand.

Some goods that have a relatively large income elasticity of demand are referred to as superior goods. They are 'normal' in the sense of our earlier definition, but demand for them increases considerably more in relation to the change in income. It is really quite difficult to give examples of such goods as far as individual consumers are concerned – what may be a normal good for one person could be a superior good for someone on a lower relative income.

Table 2.7 gives some estimates of income elasticity of demand using data from the UK Family Expenditure Survey (2006).

Table 2.7 Estimates of income elasticity of demand

Dairy produce	0.53
Foreign travel	1.14
Recreational goods	1.99
Wines and spirits	2.60

It should be stressed that the data in Table 2.7 is estimated and is for a typical family unit. Having said this, the table shows the following.

● All of the products are normal goods.

● The income elasticity of demand for dairy products is inelastic; for all other products it is elastic.

● The quantity demanded of wines and spirits increases most significantly as income increases.

● If income were to fall, then the quantity demanded for all these products would fall but to varying extents.

ACTIVITY ⋯⋮

Prior to an increase in income, a person bought 200 units of a product per year with an income of £15,000. After an increase in income of £1,500, this person bought 240 units of the product. Calculate the income elasticity of demand and say what it means.

A small number of products have a negative income elasticity of demand. These are known as **inferior goods**. The relationship between their demand and a change in income is shown in Figure 2.15 (see over). This shows that as income increases from Y to Y_1, the quantity demanded falls from Q to Q_1. If income were to fall, then more of these goods would be demanded.

DEFINITION

Inferior goods: goods for which an increase in income leads to a fall in demand.

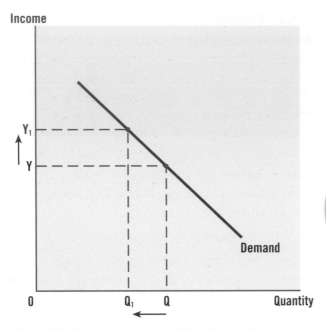

Figure 2.15 Negative income elasticity of demand

Typical examples of inferior goods are supermarket own-label 'value' products, most second-hand goods, cheap cuts of meat, and coach travel. The point about such products is that better-quality substitutes are available – but for families on a low income such alternatives are out of their reach.

> **learning tip**
> Normal goods have a positive YED; inferior goods have a negative YED.

ACTIVITY ···⋮·

Recent research for an inclusive tour operator produced the following estimates for the income elasticity of demand to selected holiday destinations:

Spain – Majorca	– 0.15
Croatia	1.10
USA – Florida	1.30
South Africa	2.05

Explain what each means.

CROSS ELASTICITY OF DEMAND

Cross elasticity of demand (XED) measures the responsiveness of demand for one product following a change in the price of another related product. It is assumed that all other factors that affect demand are unchanged.

> **DEFINITION**
>
> **Cross elasticity of demand (XED):** the responsiveness of demand for one product in relation to a change in the price of another product.

This elasticity measure is derived from what was stated earlier about the determinants of demand, namely that the prices of substitutes and complements can affect the demand for a particular product. It is measured by the following formula:

$$\text{Cross elasticity of demand} = \frac{\text{\% change in quantity demanded of product A}}{\text{\% change in price of product B}}$$

This measure is different from those for price and income elasticity of demand in so far as it measures the relationship between two *different* products. The sign and size of the cross elasticity of demand are relevant.

● A positive estimate indicates that the two products are substitutes; a negative estimate means that they are complements; a zero estimate means there is no particular relationship.

● The size of the cross elasticity of demand indicates the strength of the relationship between a change in the price of one product and the change in demand for another product. Where products are good or close substitutes, the value of the cross elasticity of demand will be higher than if they are only modest substitutes. Similarly, for complements, a high value of cross elasticity of demand is indicative of products with a high degree of complementarity.

Figure 2.16 shows the three possibilities with respect to the sign of the cross elasticity of demand estimate. Line *X* shows the position for substitutes where the cross elasticity of demand is positive in that a rise

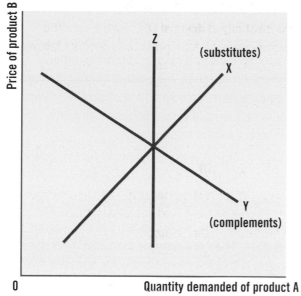

Figure 2.16 Positive, negative and zero cross elasticity of demand

in price of product *B* will result in an increase in the quantity demanded of product *A*. In the case of complements, line *Y* represents negative cross elasticity of demand. This shows that a rise in the price of product *B* will lead to a fall in the quantity demanded of product *A*. Finally, line *Z* indicates zero cross elasticity of demand – a rise in the price of product *B* has no bearing whatsoever on the demand for product *A*.

> **learning tip**
> Substitutes have a positive XED; complements have a negative XED.

PRICE ELASTICITY OF SUPPLY

We showed earlier that price elasticity of demand (see page 42) was a measure of the responsiveness of the quantity demanded to a change in the price of a particular product. It was represented by a movement along the demand curve. The **price elasticity of supply** (PES) of a product is the supply equivalent. It is measured by the following formula:

$$\text{Price elasticity of supply} = \frac{\% \text{ change in quantity supplied}}{\% \text{ change in price}}$$

> **DEFINITION**
>
> **Price elasticity of supply (PES):** the responsiveness of the quantity supplied to a change in the price of the product.

Price elasticity of supply indicates how much additional supply a producer is willing to provide for the market following a change in price of the product. Given the nature of the supplier's objective of profit maximisation, it follows that the value of the elasticity of supply will always be positive. (If the price falls, it will be highly unusual for the supplier to produce more goods for the market in a free market situation).

The size of the price elasticity of supply is therefore of crucial importance. It can take the following values:

ACTIVITY ····

Calculate the cross elasticity of demand in each of the cases below and say what the estimate means.

a)

	per kilo		kilos (000s)
Original price of lamb	£3.00	Quantity demanded of beef	200
New price of lamb	£3.75	Quantity demanded of beef	300

b)

	per litre		(000s)
Original price of petrol	£1.00	Quantity demanded of cars	200
New price of petrol	£1.05	Quantity demanded of cars	198

- between 0 and 1. This means that the elasticity of supply is inelastic. In other words, supply is not very responsive to a change in the price of the product.

- greater than 1. In this case supply is elastic, meaning that producers are able to respond with a relatively large change in supply if price rises.

- equal to 1. Here a change in price causes an exactly proportional change in the quantity supplied.

Figure 2.17 shows each of these possibilities. S_1 is where supply is inelastic to a price change. For a given change in price, the percentage change in the quantity supplied will be smaller. In contrast, S_2 represents a situation where suppliers are able to react strongly to a price change. The price elasticity of supply is elastic, meaning that for a given percentage change in price, there will be a larger percentage change in supply. S_3 is the case where the price elasticity of supply is equal to 1.

In practice, suppliers are not always able to respond to a change in price with the same speed as consumers. This is because, for most products, it takes time for producers to alter their production schedules in response to market need, unless they can draw upon stocks. For farmers, this time lag could be as much as a year, the time that it takes to alter the crop mix of their production.

Price

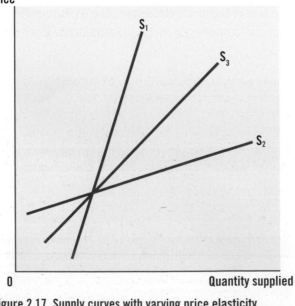

Figure 2.17 Supply curves with varying price elasticity of supply

Large parts of the service sector face a rather different supply issue. In the longer term, the supply of their products is more elastic than in the short term. In the case of a hotel or aircraft, supply is perishable in so far as the product cannot be stored. If a hotel room is not sold on a given night or aircraft seats remain unsold on a particular flight, this represents a loss to the business.

So, what determines the price elasticity of supply? There are three main factors. These are:

- *Availability of stocks of the product*

Stocks or inventory allow suppliers to store goods in a warehouse. Their relevance in considering elasticity of supply is that they can be quickly released if, say, an increase in demand results in a price rise in the market. Equally, if prices fall, the goods can be stored depending upon how perishable they are.

The large grocery retailers, such as Tesco, Sainsbury's and Asda, carry a certain amount of 'buffer stock', the term used in business for stock that can be released if market conditions change. Suppliers of vehicle parts, medicines and other consumer goods are also likely to have a reasonably elastic price elasticity of supply.

For service sector businesses, like hotels, restaurants, theatres and cinemas, supply is infinitely inelastic since the produce cannot be stored – it has to be consumed on a particular day or time period otherwise it is lost.

- *Availability of factors of production*

Labour is usually the most available factor of production. Provided there is spare capacity, additional workers can be used to produce more output, often in a relatively short period of time. Here, the elasticity of supply is relatively elastic. For some types of business, it is the availability of capital that determines whether a firm can increase output. Invariably, where new machinery has to be purchased and installed, the elasticity of supply will be inelastic. The risk for firms is that market conditions may well change before any increased production can reach the market.

- *Time period*

This has already been alluded to. Where it takes a lot of time for supply to be adjusted, then supply will be price inelastic. In the longer term, supply will normally be more price elastic. An example of this in the service sector is the provision of package holidays – companies invariably have to reserve flights and accommodation for potential clients up to one year ahead of consumption. This makes supply price inelastic. The problem companies then face is, if demand proves to be weak, they are left with unsold holidays on their hands. Inevitably, price will have to fall in order to clear excess supply.

ACTIVITY ⋯⋮

a) Consider the following product markets. State whether you think supply is elastic or inelastic following an increase in the price of the product:

- milk production
- bottling mineral water
- car manufacturing
- aircraft production such as the Airbus A380.

b) The following estimates have been made for the price elasticity of supply for two agricultural crops grown by US farmers:

green peppers 0.26   fresh spinach 4.70

Explain what the data mean and why there is a big difference in the elasticity of supply estimates for these crops.

BUSINESS RELEVANCE OF ELASTICITY ESTIMATES

The elasticity measures explained above have considerable practical business relevance. For example, a knowledge of price elasticity of demand is an essential input into the pricing strategy of firms, enabling them to maximise sales revenue. Before looking at how this and other measures can be used it will be useful to mention how the data might be collected and some of the general limitations of elasticity data.

All elasticity measures require information to be collected at two separate points in time – the formulas make this clear by indicating that it is 'change' that is being measured. This information can be collected by means of:

- sample surveys of consumers (for example, price and income elasticity of demand)

- past records from within a company (for example, price elasticity of supply)

- competitor analysis (for example, cross elasticity of demand)

Given the nature of how the data is collected, it is necessary to appreciate that:

- The data are estimates. In other words, they are not exact figures, since there may be some inaccuracies in how the data has been collected.

- Over time, it is often quite difficult to get data for, say, a full range of price changes. It is much easier to obtain data for price changes that are close to each other.

- Again, over time, there could be factors other than those in the elasticity calculations that affect the demand or supply of a particular product. An ongoing health scare, for instance, will affect the market for a product.

- Prices may fall for this reason, giving what is not necessarily a fair elasticity estimate.

Use of price elasticity of demand

Price elasticity of demand information is widely used by businesses when pricing their products in the market. It is particularly evident in the transport, leisure and communications markets where the market is segmented on a time basis. Most mainline rail and urban bus companies, tour operators and telephone service providers seek to maximise their revenue by charging peak and off-peak fares or rates.

Passenger train operators make extensive use of price elasticity of demand to maximise revenue

Table 2.8 'Walk on' rail fares between Leeds and London King's Cross in October 2007

Ticket type	Price	Notes
Open return	£185	Any train permitted
Business Saver return	£114	Arrive in London after 10.30
Saver return	£74.80	Restrictions on weekday use in both directions

Let us take an example. Table 2.8 shows three of the many rail fares that are available for travel between Leeds and London.

The variation in fares shown in this table is substantial and reflects the extent to which travel is essential. For peak period travel to London, for which an open return is required, demand is price inelastic. This is because those who purchase this ticket find it necessary to arrive in London before 10.30 a.m. In many cases, it is likely that firms and other employers will be paying the price of the ticket. At the other extreme, where travel plans are more flexible, demand is price elastic. The Business Saver ticket fits between these two extremes – it is likely to be price inelastic but not to the same extent as an open return ticket. In all cases, the actual journey experience is identical.

In applying a market knowledge of price elasticity of demand, the train operating company and others are pursuing an objective of maximising revenue.

They are very aware that, where demand is inelastic, an increase in price will lead to an increase in total revenue. This situation is shown in Figure 2.18. Here a price rise from £25 to £30 has reduced the quantity demanded from 800 to 720 units. The price elasticity of demand is –0.5. A fall in price, though, is more likely to lead to a fall in revenue, which is hardly an appropriate business strategy to implement.

Figure 2.19 shows a situation where the price elasticity of demand is elastic. Here a fall in price will increase total revenue. At the original price of £10, the quantity demanded is 100 units. When price falls to £8, the new quantity demanded is 140 units. This produces a price elasticity estimate of –2. Revenue increases by £120 as a result of the fall in price. In this situation, a rise in price will lead to a fall in revenue as consumers switch to other modes of transport.

The business situations shown in Figures 2.18 and 2.19 are clearly beneficial, as revenue increases;

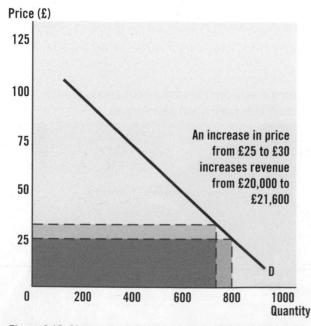

Figure 2.18 Change in total revenue where demand is inelastic

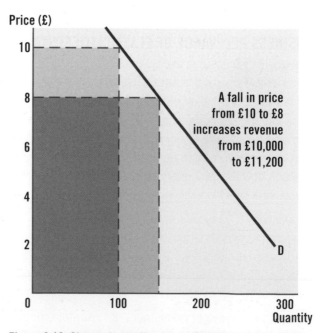

Figure 2.19 Change in total revenue where demand is elastic

what is not beneficial is for a firm to reduce prices where demand is inelastic or to increase prices where demand is elastic.

Use of income elasticity of demand

In most economies, real disposable incomes tend to rise over time. The business significance of this is that firms who produce goods and services

ACTIVITY ⋯⟩

a) Suppose the owner of a local restaurant has hired you, as a student of economics, to give some business advice. The problem faced is that the restaurant is running at a loss and there is an obvious need to increase revenue in order to continue in business. The restaurant is very busy on Friday and Saturday evenings, but there are very few customers at other times. The quality of food is not a problem, as the restaurant has won many awards. What would you suggest?

b) i) The National Health Service only pays a part of the cost of adult dental treatment; the remainder has to be paid by the patient. The Office of Health Economics has estimated that the price elasticity of demand for dental treatment is –0.6. Use this information to comment on the likely effects of raising dental charges by 10 per cent.

ii) The Office of Health Economics has also estimated that the price elasticity of demand for prescriptions is –0.32. Using your knowledge of elasticity, comment on whether raising prescription charges is an effective way of raising revenue for the National Health Service.

ECONOMICS IN CONTEXT

In June 2007 the English Beef and Lamb Executive (EBLEX) produced a report on the price elasticity of demand for beef. This report provided estimates of the price elasticity of demand for different cuts of beef. Data was also produced for beef from various countries of supply (see below). Using this data, the National Beef Association (NBA) then controversially argued that supermarkets and farm suppliers of beef in the UK could benefit from a rise in beef prices.

The UK is about 70 per cent self-sufficient in beef. Imports are required throughout the year, in particular between November and March, when domestic consumption most exceeds domestic supply.

The main argument in the report was that the price of most cuts of English beef (roasting joints excepted) could be increased to generate more revenue both from supermarkets and for farmers. The gain in revenue from a price increase would be less than the fall in sales due to customers switching to beef from elsewhere, to other types of meat or buying less English beef.

The NBA's view was that English beef is 'undervalued and undersold'. They claimed that retailers had not realised the significance of the price elasticity data and that they were holding down the prices of English beef because they saw cheap beef prices as a means of attracting some customers to their stores. The NBA claim that a 5.9 per cent rise in mince prices alone would produce additional retail income of £18.4m. As a result, English beef farmers could receive better prices and, in turn, this would make a contribution to the economic and environmental sustainability of the English livestock sector.

Source: English Beef and Lamb Executive

	Price elasticity of demand		Price elasticity of demand
English beef	–0.9	Beef mince	–0.17
Home-produced beef (incl. Scotland)	–1.2	Stewing steak	–0.32
Irish beef	–2.0	Sirloin steak	–0.38
Other imported beef	–2.1	Roasting joints	–1.61

with a positive, and in particular, high positive income elasticity of demand can expect to do well in the future. The converse is most likely for firms producing goods with a negative income elasticity of demand. An exception is when a business seeks to change the image of a product so that the income elasticity of demand becomes positive. 'Spam' and upmarket baked beans are typical examples of products that have been heavily marketed as superior products and yet, at one time, the basic product was regarded as inferior.

Within the UK, where living standards for most people have continued to increase, there has been substantial growth in the market for many types of service sector products such as overseas holidays, eating out, health spas and fitness centres, designer fashions, nail salons, dental implants and alternative medical therapies. So, these types of business, in the long term at least, would seem to have good business prospects. Estimates of income elasticity of demand, particularly if they are specific, can provide a basis for forecasting future market demand.

Similar tendencies can be seen in emerging economies. In China, for example, the income elasticity of demand for domestic air travel has been estimated at +3.0 and for new vehicle purchase, +1.8. Both would indicate good business prospects for firms in these markets.

ACTIVITY ····⋮⋗

Research at the University of Kent has produced the following estimates of the income elasticity of demand for imports into selected countries in Latin America:

Argentina	3.66
Chile	2.03
Dominican Republic	0.92
Peru	1.56

Account for possible variations in these estimates and comment on their likely significance for businesses that are located in these countries.

When economies face uncertain short term economic prospects or even recession, then demand for income elastic products will fall as consumers are forced to substitute their demand towards inferior goods and services. Products, however, with a low income elasticity of demand are least likely to be affected by either a rise or fall in living standards.

Use of cross elasticity of demand

Estimates of cross elasticity of demand are particularly important where firms are operating in markets that are very competitive. Where there are close substitutes, and hence a high positive cross elasticity of demand with other products, then firms are likely to be tempted to cut their own prices in order to steal market share from their rivals. There are many instances where this occurs in practice, for example between:

● low-cost airlines, train operating companies and bus companies that operate on identical routes

● well-known brands of virtually identical grocery or electronic products

● products such as wine or butter that are produced in different countries, yet are virtually the same.

In all cases, there are close substitutes. Increasing prices in such markets is a dangerous strategy – unless a rival producer follows with a similar price rise, market share can be quickly lost and is invariably difficult to regain without resorting to heavy price reductions.

The case of complements also has implications for firms, although it may not be as obvious or indeed as common as with substitutes. This is because the prices of the two complementary goods may not be particularly close. For example, a fall in the price of recordable DVD players may have only a slight effect on the quantity demanded of blank recordable DVDs. The effect of a fall in price of recordable DVD players on sales of High Density televisions may be much greater since they might be offered by the retailer as part of an all-in deal or to get more people to buy new televisions. The cross elasticity of demand can be expected to be low and negative for blank recordable DVD players and high and negative for High Density televisions respectively.

ACTIVITY ····⁝

An investigation conducted by Leeds University for the Competition Commission produced the following estimates of cross elasticity of demand for rail and coach travel between Norwich and London.

	Cross elasticity of demand
5% increase in rail fares	+3.10
10% increase in rail fares	+3.10
5% increase in coach fares	+0.30
10% increase in coach fares	+0.30

Explain what these estimates mean and their business significance for rail and coach operators.

Use of price elasticity of supply

As demonstrated earlier, the price elasticity of supply is always positive, a reflection of the positive relationship between price and the quantity supplied. In many types of business, supply is price inelastic in the short term as it is often difficult to switch resources into a market. The main exception to this is where it is practical and economic for firms to hold stocks in anticipation of a price rise. So, if a price rise is expected, firms are advised to have good stock availability. Over time, however, supply is likely to be more price elastic in the longer term as resources can be re-allocated to respond to the increase in market price.

Let us consider a few examples. In 2004, it was estimated that the price elasticity of supply of canned tuna in the US market was 0.2. In other words, producers found it difficult to respond to a change in price. This was a clear reflection of the fact that the supply of tuna was almost at its maximum, with fisheries being fully exploited. Despite the increased demand for tuna, for well publicised health reasons, supply was not forthcoming to the same extent. Consequently, the price of tuna increased in the US market.

The supply of housing is also price inelastic in many countries. In the UK, for example, an estimate of the elasticity of supply for new housing is 0.5. This is a fair indication of the time it takes to respond to increased prices. In contrast, in the USA and Germany, the price elasticity of supply for new housing has been estimated to be 1.4 and 2.1 respectively. Here, suppliers are more able to respond to increased prices for a wide range of reasons.

In general, firms will try to make their supply as elastic as possible, in the hope that they can cash in on a rise in prices by selling more of their product. If prices are falling, an elastic supply will enable them to move resources away from such products and into alternatives where the normal relationship between a change in price and a change in the quantity supplied holds true.

Allocative efficiency

It is appropriate to conclude this chapter with a brief explanation of **efficiency** and how this important economic term is used in competitive markets.

Efficiency occurs in a market when the best use is made of available resources; the market is operating in such a way as to most benefit consumers. For this to happen, the factors of production must be fully employed to meet consumers' needs, and the prices charged by producers should be at the lowest level.

Allocative efficiency is achieved in a market where consumer satisfaction is maximised. Scarce resources are used to produce those goods and services that consumers actually demand. To achieve this, the quantity supplied must be equal to the quantity that is demanded. In other words, the market must function at the equilibrium position.

DEFINITIONS

Efficiency: where the best use of resources is made for the benefit of consumers.

Allocative efficiency: where consumer satisfaction is maximised.

This is fine in theory, but does not always happen in practice. Figure 2.20 shows two positions of allocative inefficiency. At quantity Q_1, demand is not being met. Too few resources are being used in the supply of the product – suppliers are not matching the quantity that consumers are demanding. In contrast, if the quantity produced is Q_2, too many resources are being allocated to the production of this product in relation to demand. Consumers do not want all that is being produced. It is only when output is at Q that allocative efficiency is achieved. It is here that the competitive market is providing the best allocation of resources.

It is invariably the case that in practice markets do not work efficiently. Consumers are losing out, since it is not possible to produce what they want in the right quantities. This is how allocative efficiency is seen in a simple way from a microeconomic perspective.

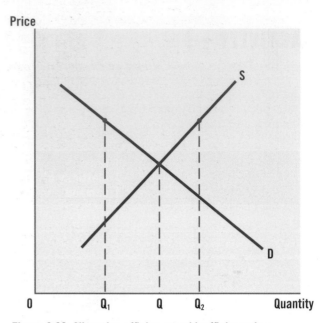

Figure 2.20 Allocative efficiency and inefficiency in a competitive market

3 Market failure and government intervention

On completion of this chapter, you should be able to:

- explain what is meant by 'market failure' in terms of an inefficient use of scarce resources
- explain what is meant by information failure and analyse its implications
- explain what is meant by negative externalities and how they arise as a result of the divergence between private and social costs
- explain how negative externalities lead to market failure
- explain what is meant by positive externalities and how they arise as a result of the divergence between private and social benefits
- explain how positive externalities lead to market failure
- explain what is meant by merit and demerit goods
- explain why the over-consumption of demerit goods and the under-consumption of merit goods leads to market failure
- explain the characteristics of public goods
- explain why the existence of public goods leads to market failure
- explain why governments intervene to correct externalities to influence the allocation of merit/demerit goods and to fund public goods
- evaluate the impact of indirect taxes, subsidies, regulation, tradable pollution permits and the provision of information as possible solutions to market failure
- discuss the effectiveness of these policies in correcting market failure.

What is meant by market failure?

As we saw in Chapter 2, where markets work efficiently, the market mechanism produces the best allocation of resources. This is an ideal situation. In reality, the problem is that markets do *not* always work in this way and when this happens, **market failure** occurs – resources are not being used in a way that produces the best allocation for consumers. It is therefore said that markets 'fail'.

Let us look at a few examples of relevant headlines:

'Overcrowded beaches make Brighton no picnic'

DEFINITION

Market failure: where the free market mechanism fails to achieve economic efficiency.

'Should we pay for plastic bags?'

'Gum bandits to be fined'

'Gridlock costs US workforce one week a year'

'Brown hails budget for schools'

'Public goods not just public services'

The common thread that links these examples is that the market is failing to produce the best use of scarce resources.

Take the case of the humble plastic carrier bag. In the course of a year, a typical family is given around 400 such bags by supermarkets, clothing retailers, take-away food shops and many other types of business. These bags cost money to produce and, in the production process, valuable resources (particularly oil-based ones) are being used up. Most plastic carrier bags are not bio-degradable and their disposal causes enormous problems. As most plastic carrier bags are provided free of charge, there is little incentive for consumers to recycle them. If a tax were to be introduced on new bags as in Ireland, customers might then have an incentive to re-use those they already possess. The purpose of the tax, therefore, is to make consumers aware of the true cost of the carrier bags that are being provided.

ACTIVITY ┄┄┄

Look through recent copies of your local newspaper to search for typical examples of market failures such as those outlined above. For each example, say why you think the market has failed to produce the best allocation of resources.

EFFICIENCY REVISITED AND THE CONCEPT OF INEFFICIENCY

Allocative efficiency was briefly described in the concluding section of Chapter 2. This is one of two types of efficiency that are recognised

in economics. The second type is **productive efficiency**. This is achieved when everything that is produced is produced using the least amount of scarce resources. We explained this in terms of the production possibility curve (PPC) shown in Figure 1.2 (see page 12).

To recapitulate, any combination of production that is located on the PPC is one in which all available resources are being used in an efficient way. In Figure 1.2, this applied to points A and B. Indeed, any other point anywhere along the PPC would similarly indicate that there is the fullest use of resources. In contrast, point C or any other point within the boundary of the PPC represents an inefficient use of resources. This is because more could be produced of one or both of the products with a more efficient use of the resources available.

It is, therefore, only when both allocative *and* productive efficiency are present that economists can conclude that scarce resources are being used in the most efficient way from a consumer's standpoint. This is known as **economic efficiency**.

Inefficiency, therefore, is a market situation in which resources are not being used in the best possible way – the products people want are not being produced in the quantities they desire and at the prices they are willing to pay.

Our definition of market failure can be elaborated to say that it exists in a market when the **free market mechanism** fails to achieve economic efficiency.

DEFINITIONS

Productive efficiency: where production takes place using the least amount of scarce resources.

Economic efficiency: where both allocative and productive efficiency are achieved.

Inefficiency: any situation where economic efficiency is not achieved.

DEFINITION

DEFINITION

Free market mechanism: the system by which the market forces of demand and supply determine prices and the decisions made by consumers and firms.

Economic efficiency is a very important concept in economics. Remember that it consists of allocative efficiency and productive efficiency.

ECONOMICS IN CONTEXT

TRAFFIC CONGESTION IN THE US

American drivers waste nearly an entire work week each year sitting in traffic on the way to and from their jobs, according to a national study carried out by the Texas Transportation Institute. Its report for 2005 contains some shocking figures:

- the worst US metropolitan areas for traffic congestion were Los Angeles, Atlanta, San Francisco, Washington and Dallas.

- US drivers languished in traffic delays for an estimated 4.2 billion hours, typically 38 hours per driver.

- 10.98 billion litres of fuel were used up while vehicles were sitting in stationary traffic.

- the cost of traffic congestion to the US economy was a staggering US$ 78.2 billion.

- around three-quarters of American commuters drive to work alone.

- higher petrol prices have reduced driving for other reasons but not commuting to work.

The study's co-author, Alan Pisarsky, commented 'Things are bad and they're getting worse. We've used up capacity and we have not replaced it. Too many people, too many trips over too short a time period on a system that is too small... There has to be a better way of allocating our resources!'

Source: Texas Transportation Institute

Information failure

The definition of economic efficiency, above, made clear that the free market is producing the best allocation of resources when consumers are maximising their welfare. This is fine in theory, but in practice the ability of consumers to benefit in these terms is entirely dependent upon them having accurate, up-to-date information on the quality and prices of the product they want to consume. It is lack of this information that underpins most instances of market failure.

Increasingly, particularly through the Internet and the ever-growing number of search engines, we are provided with a mass of information on the products we may wish to buy. In addition, better labelling on consumer products, such as food, drink and non-prescription medicines, helps in purchasing decisions. For some products, such as alcoholic drink, tobacco products and, again, medicines, the labelling may contain reasons to limit or stop the consumption of a product.

In principle, this boundless information should enable us to take the rational decisions that are needed to maximise our own welfare and that of society. If this is happening, then the market is working efficiently; if it is not, then there will be an inefficient allocation of resources and hence, market failure.

The problem of **information failure** is that the decisions taken by consumers (and also firms and even governments) are based on ignorance due to inaccurate or incomplete information. Typical examples are:

- where consumers are not aware of the benefits and, in some cases, the harmful effects of consuming a particular product

- where persuasive advertising results in consumption levels that are not in the best interest of consumers

---

DEFINITION

Information failure: a lack of information resulting in consumers and producers making decisions that do not maximise welfare.

● where product packaging makes claims that are inaccurate or misleading.

In some situations, the problem of information failure is known as **asymmetric information**. This occurs where information is not shared equally between two parties carrying out a transaction. Typical examples include:

● *Health care*. When you visit your doctor with an illness or problem (hopefully not too serious), you do not have the same medical knowledge as your doctor. You rely on the doctor's experience and competence to give you the diagnosis and treatment you need.

● *Environment*. As individuals we invariably know very little about the environmental consequences of driving cars, of flying in an aeroplane or tipping waste into landfill sites, drains and the sea. Environmental experts and the various authorities employing them are much more aware of the effects of our actions, as a result of their own research and studies that have been made.

● *Consumer purchases*. What might at first seem to be a good deal may not turn out to be so. A relevant example is the case of mobile phone contracts. These can be a nightmare to understand. The seller, who is likely to be on commission, has far more knowledge of the information than the purchaser, who may well make a bad choice as a result.

● *Insurance*. When applying for travel or car insurance, as a purchaser you know far more about your circumstances than the company that is selling you a policy. This contrasts with the previous example. Here, the seller relies upon your honesty and integrity in deciding whether to sell you a policy.

In these and in other similar circumstances, the lack of accurate information has distorted how the market allocates resources. In other words, the market has failed.

> **DEFINITION**
>
> **Asymmetric information:** information not equally shared between two parties.

ECONOMICS IN CONTEXT

CLAIMS 'MISLEADING'

An advert for a Clinique anti-wrinkle cream made misleading claims about its effect on the skin, the industry watchdog said today. The cosmetics giant's advert for Repairwear said that the cream enabled the skin to steer 'hearty cells' to the base of wrinkles. It then triggered the skin's own natural collagen production, the magazine advert claimed.

The Advertising Standards Authority (ASA) said Clinique could not support claims about their cream's physiological effect on users' skin. It found the advert in breach of the advertising code in relation to truthfulness, health and beauty products, cosmetics and substantiation.

The ASA told the cosmetics company not to repeat the claim and to consult an advice team for guidance on future adverts.

An expert working for the watchdog said a scientific study provided by Clinique was based on laboratory test results which had not been proven on consumers' skin.

Source: Huddersfield Examiner, 11 October 2006

Externalities

An **externality,** or spill-over effect as it is sometimes known, occurs when those not directly involved in a particular decision are affected by the actions of others. A few examples will make this clear:

● Residents living along the flight path to an airport will experience increased noise disturbance if the number of flights increases or an additional runway is opened.

● Residents and businesses in a rural village will experience a better quality of life and more local

> **DEFINITION**
>
> **Externality:** an effect whereby those not directly involved in taking a decision are affected by the actions of others.

Polluted rivers can kill off local fish stocks

trade when a new bypass is constructed to divert cars and lorries from the village.

● Anglers may not be able to fish in a river if a chemical factory nearby discharges waste into the river, killing fish stocks.

● A community will benefit when the local council agrees to let a major supermarket chain build a new indoor sports centre in return for obtaining planning permission for a new superstore.

Those people or groups not directly involved in decision making are known as **third parties**. So, in the above examples, the third parties are the residents living along the flight path; the anglers; residents and businesses in the rural village; and the community in the town where the new sports centre is to be built. None of these have had any real input into the decisions that affect their well-being.

DEFINITION

Third party: those not directly involved in making a decision.

learning tip

An externality is so-called because it is an action that has an effect on a third party.

Costs and benefits

Economists are interested in externalities because of the various costs and benefits that arise out of the actions of others. There are three types of costs and benefits.

● **Private costs** and **private benefits**. These are experienced by the people who are directly involved in the decision to take a particular action. Private costs therefore are the costs incurred by firms, individuals or others actually carrying out the particular action, either as producers or consumers. The private benefits are directly received by those who produce or consume the product of the action. An example will make this distinction clearer.

Take the case of the airport expansion referred to earlier. The private costs are the development costs that are paid by the owners of the airport. Private costs can also fall on users of the airport, such as airlines and passengers charged to use it. The private benefits in this case are the revenue received by the airport's owners and the pleasure that is gained by the additional passengers as a result of being able to travel by air from that extended airport.

● **External costs** and **external benefits**. These are a consequence of externalities that arise from a particular action. They are not paid by nor do they accrue to those responsible for the action. Instead they fall on third parties.

DEFINITIONS

Private costs: the costs incurred by those taking a particular action.

Private benefits: the benefits directly accruing to those taking a particular action.

External costs: the costs that are the consequence of externalities to third parties.

External benefits: the benefits that accrue as a consequence of externalities to third parties.

In the case of airport expansion, people who live on the flight path of the airport will experience additional noise pollution problems. They may be forced to soundproof their homes at their own expense through no fault or doing of their own. An external benefit could be if some flights transfer to the expanded airport from elsewhere, resulting in less noise pollution for those people who live on the flight path of that airport.

● **Social costs** and **social benefits.** These are the total costs and benefits incurred by or accruing to society as a result of a particular action. By definition, they consist of private costs and benefits and any external costs and benefits that arise.

The cost of fly-tipping has to be covered by society at large

In the case of the airport expansion, the social costs could include wider considerations, such as the costs of increased CO_2 emissions from aircraft, the increased congestion on roads near the airport and the cost of the loss of land to make way for airport expansion. The social benefits might include the additional jobs that are created at the airport and in related businesses or the additional convenience that all passengers might expect when using the airport.

For economists, a problem arises when the private costs or private benefits do not exactly equal the social cost or social benefit. The external costs or external benefits distort the efficient allocation of resources. It is for this reason that the market fails to produce the best allocation of resources.

Negative externalities

There are innumerable instances where **negative externalities** exist. Here, as stated above, the social cost of an activity is greater than the private costs. What this means is that there are costs imposed on a third party over and above the costs directly paid for by those who carry out the activity. Here are a few examples of such situations.

● *Illegal dumping of waste.* Fly-tipping is a growing problem that many local authorities have to deal with. Charges to dispose of refrigerators, washing machines, cars and used tyres mean that it can be cheaper and more convenient to dispose of such items on waste land, lay-bys and even at local beauty spots. The private cost to those dumping such things is minimal (unless they are found out!); the external cost has to be covered by those, such as local councils, responsible for maintaining the environment.

● *Chewing gum.* The disposal of chewing gum poses major problems in all our towns and cities. 'Pavement blight' is common. It is very unpleasant for pedestrians when used chewing gum sticks to their shoes. It has been estimated that it costs 10p

learning tip Remember that external costs are not the same as social costs.

to remove each piece of gum from a pavement. Westminster Council claims to spend over £100,000 annually removing gum from its streets. This is just a part of the cost of this rather disgusting negative externality.

● *Binge drinking.* This is a regular occurrence, particularly on Friday and Saturday nights, in our town and city centres. Late-night revellers drop litter, cause damage to property and invariably create noise disturbance. The private costs tend to be nil; the external costs have to be met by those responsible for policing and cleaning the streets, by the National Health Service and, in some cases, by business owners whose property has been damaged.

Each of these situations can be represented in principle by Figure 3.1. The market price is *P* and the quantity bought and sold is *Q*. At this price the supply curve only takes into account the private costs of a given action. If external costs are also taken into account, the supply curve would shift to the left, to S_1. The result would be an increase in price to P_1 and a fall in equilibrium quantity to Q_1. The problem, therefore, with negative externalities is that there is over-production of $Q–Q_1$ and that the price paid is lower than it should be. Too many scarce resources are being used. In other words, the market has failed because of allocative inefficiency.

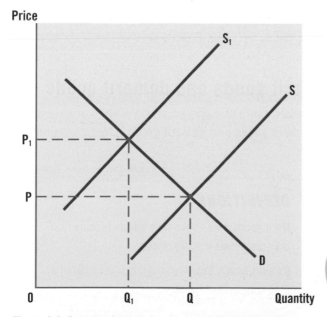

Figure 3.1 Over production due to a negative externality

ACTIVITY ⋯⋮

a) Pollution has killed dozens of trout along a stretch of a river used by members of an angling club. Environment Agency inspectors visited the river and concluded that the problem was due to a discharge of detergent into the river, causing the river to foam. The source of the discharge has not been traced. Local wildlife habitats have been badly affected and the pungent smell from the detergent foam has deterred walkers from using this part of the riverside path.

Explain the private, external and social costs that have occurred due to the discharge of detergent.

b) In August 2004, the BBC News reported the bizarre case of Jay Jay, a pet parrot, which had suffered from wheezing and laboured breathing. The bird's owners had to spend £600 on treatment before the cause of the problem was diagnosed by a vet as one of passive smoking suffered by the parrot!

Explain the private, external and social costs that have occurred in this situation.

Positive externalities

Examples of **positive externalities** are not as obvious or as common as instances of negative externality. A positive externality exists where the social benefit of an activity is greater than the private benefit. As a consequence, the benefits received by a third party are over and above those that are received by those responsible for carrying out a particular activity or action. A few examples are given below:

● *Inoculations.* It is now the norm in the UK for people over the age of 65 to be offered an annual flu inoculation. This should reduce the incidence of flu in this age group (private benefit) but also among others as the symptoms are less likely to be transmitted (external benefit).

DEFINITION

Positive externality: this exists where the social benefit of an activity exceeds the private benefit.

● *Crossrail.* Assuming it goes ahead, London's Crossrail project will provide millions of people with better rail transport connections through the west and east of London, including access to Heathrow airport. The external benefit will come through reduced road traffic congestion, as some passengers switch from cars and taxis to the new rail link. There will also be an external benefit to Underground passengers on the Central Line, due to a reduction in overcrowding.

● *Education and training.* All forms of education and training produce private benefits in the form of improved skills and, in most cases, better pay and job prospects. There are also external benefits that accrue to the community, such as better qualified employees for firms and enhanced longer-term competitiveness for the economy as a whole.

Each of these situations can be represented in principle by Figure 3.2. The market price is P and the quantity bought and sold is Q. At this price, the external benefits are not taken into account. If they are, the demand curve would shift to the right and, as a result, the market equilibrium would be at price P_1 and quantity Q_1. Where the market fails to operate in this way, there is under-production. This is shown by the difference between Q_1 and Q. Too few scarce resources are being used, hence the market failure.

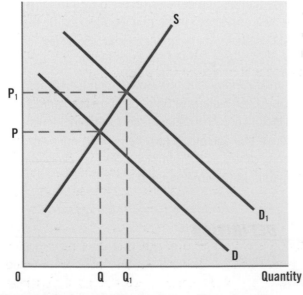

Figure 3.2 Underproduction due to a positive externality

ACTIVITY ⋯⋗

a) The Lancashire resort of Blackpool is known throughout the world for its autumn illuminations. Displays containing millions of lights stretch for around five miles along the promenade. No charge is made to see them, although there is a voluntary contribution scheme. Each day, thousands of visitors see the free show. It is also a tradition for some people to stay in the resort for a short holiday, so filling hotels and guest houses that would otherwise be empty and have to close. Other businesses in the town also benefit from the illuminations.

Explain the private, external and social benefits that occur as a result of the illuminations in Blackpool.

b) In November 2007, it was announced that the residents of Huddersfield are to get a new sports centre .... courtesy of Tesco! This is to replace an existing local authority-owned facility that opened over 30 years ago and that was in urgent need of refurbishment. The new sports centre is to be located on a new site. From Tesco's standpoint, the deal is that they are to be allowed to build an 'Extra' store on the site of the original sports centre and adjacent land which they discreetly bought a few years ago. Two unsightly blocks of flats will have to be demolished to make way for the new store.

Explain the likely private, external and social benefits that will occur as a result of this arrangement.

Merit goods and demerit goods

Markets can fail in the provision of what are known as **merit goods** and **demerit goods**. Merit goods tend

DEFINITIONS

Merit goods: these have more private benefits than their consumers actually realise.

Demerit goods: their consumption is more harmful than is actually realised.

to have positive externalities associated with their consumption, while demerit goods can have negative externalities arising out of their use. As a result of information failure, merit goods are more beneficial than consumers may realise; demerit goods are more harmful than consumers appreciate.

Let us go back to two earlier examples. Most economists agree that inoculations are a merit good, since other people may not catch flu or some other more serious disease as a consequence of a person having a particular inoculation. The excessive consumption of alcohol, which can lead to binge drinking, is seen as a demerit good. This is because it can result in a range of negative externalities as described earlier.

The problem when considering whether certain goods are merit or demerit goods is that value judgements have often to be made. This is because it is very difficult to say specifically that, for example, some people may not catch flu as a result of others having an inoculation. Such a judgement has to be made by someone, usually the government or some governmental agency. The assumption is made that these organisations know better than individuals what is good or what is bad for them. In taking this approach, it is genuinely believed that individuals lack accurate information about the respective positive or negative externalities. In terms of what was described earlier, there is information failure.

Some economists would argue that there is no such thing as merit goods and demerit goods. They take the view that, in cases like inoculations and drinking, it should be the individual and not the government who knows best what is good for them. This contradicts the usual assumption that the government knows better than any individual what is good or bad for them because it has considerable information at its disposal.

A controversial issue is that of the combined MMR (measles, mumps, rubella) inoculation. The government's advice is that all young children should receive this inoculation. Not all parents agree, some arguing that there is evidence that it can produce devastating side effects, such as cerebral palsy, in a minute number of cases. So, not everybody would take the view that the MMR vaccine is a merit good.

So, how might we define a merit good? An accepted definition is that it is a good that is better for a person than that person realises. As referred to earlier, this is because an individual consumer does not have all the information available to make a decision on whether it is a good thing to consume a particular product. This in itself results in merit goods being under-consumed, and under-produced, in a free market situation (see Figure 3.2). Resources are therefore not being efficiently allocated – the market is failing.

Education and health are good examples of merit goods. For the past 60 years, their consumption has been viewed as desirable by successive governments and encouraged. If they were only available on a 'pay as you consume' basis through the market mechanism, their consumption would be vastly reduced compared to when they are provided centrally from tax revenue. The reason for the government's intervention arises from the wider economic and social benefits of a well-educated, healthy population. Although there are private-sector alternatives, the government sees its responsibility as one of providing an effective, well-funded, quality service for all concerned.

Demerit goods are so-called as their consumption is more harmful than consumers may realise. Again, value judgements are involved. For some so-called demerit goods, it is their excessive rather than typical consumption that means they are classified in this way. Certain types of alcohol, red wine for example, can produce positive externalities when consumed in moderation; it is excessive consumption over a short period that makes alcohol a demerit good.

On the other hand, cigarette smoking is generally recognised as a demerit good. Despite very clear and pungent health warnings on cigarette packets, many smokers remain ignorant of the health risks of smoking. In some cases, due to the addictive nature of tobacco, they may choose to ignore such warnings. The outcome therefore is one of over consumption and over provision (see Figure 3.1). It is now agreed that one of the spill-over effects of smoking in public places was that non-smokers, and those who worked in premises where smoking was allowed, experienced negative externalities. These effects consisted of a poor-quality atmosphere or more serious negative health effects due to exposure to cigarette smoke. Smokers also impose considerable costs on the National Health Service. All of this supports the description of smoking as a demerit good.

The case for chewing gum to be classified as a demerit good is less certain, even though the inconsiderate disposal of spent gum produces negative externalities. If manufacturers' claims are to be believed, chewing gum helps promote healthy teeth and gums. Private as well as social benefits therefore accrue. In contrast, there is no argument with respect to the use of illegal drugs, such as heroin and ecstasy, which are clear examples of demerit goods. Their consumption leads to many dangers – the problem is that young users especially do not recognise or choose to not recognise these dangers.

> **learning tip**
>
> Merit goods have positive externalities and demerit goods have negative externalities arising from their consumption.

Public goods

The nature of **public goods**, as their name suggests, is that they are consumed collectively. It is difficult, if not impossible, to charge for them directly, so there is a need for them to be financed by the government from general tax revenue. It is also true that, if left to the free market, most public goods would not be provided, despite the benefits they give to those who consume them.

> **DEFINITION**
>
> **Public goods:** goods that are collectively consumed and have the characteristics of non-excludability and non-rivalry.

Figure 3.3 shows some examples of public goods in terms of their defining characteristics. These are:

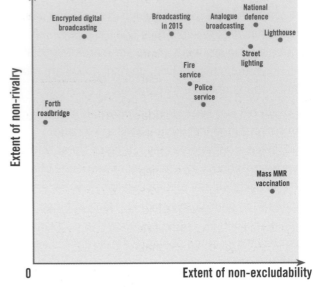

Figure 3.3 Typology of public goods

● **Non-excludability**. This means that individuals cannot be excluded from their consumption. They are provided for all, irrespective of whether they have paid for the product indirectly through taxation. A typical example is the police service. This is available to all residents and visitors to the UK and is funded through local council taxes. Not all residents pay this tax, nor do overseas visitors, yet neither group is denied access to the police if the need arises. Those not paying, but enjoying the benefit of a public good are called **free riders**.

● **Non-rivalry**. This means that consumption by any one person does not affect the consumption of any

> **DEFINITIONS**
>
> **Non-excludability:** situation existing where individual consumers cannot be excluded from consumption.
>
> **Free rider:** someone who directly benefits from the consumption of a public good but who does not contribute towards its provision.
>
> **Non-rivalry:** situation existing where consumption by one person does not affect the consumption of all others.

others. Again, in the case of the police service, if one person is being protected by the police service, this should not affect the local service that is provided to all other members of the community.

These characteristics are ideals of a pure public good, making them the exact opposite of private goods, which are both excludable and rival. (A bottle of Coke *is* excludable, since the person buying it can expect to consume it. It is also rival in the sense that if someone else consumes part of it, there is less Coke available for the person who bought it.) In the real world, not all public goods possess both characteristics to the same extent. A few examples drawn from Figure 3.3 will make this clear.

One of the best examples of a public good is a street light. Once one has been installed, it operates for the benefit of all who pass under it – it is non-excludable. It is also non-rival, since all people benefit in the same way. The other point about a street light is that it would be virtually impossible to collect a form of toll from anyone passing; as a result, there is no way that the private sector would consider its provision.

A further type of public good is called a **quasi-public good**. Quasi-public goods possess some, but not all, of the characteristics of a public good. Most tend to have the non-excludability characteristic, but not that of non-rivalry. They therefore also have some of the qualities of a private good. A few examples will explain these features.

DEFINITION

Quasi-public goods: goods having some but not all of the characteristics of a public good.

A stretch of road or motorway is a particularly good example. Except for the M6 Toll road and some river and estuary crossings, roads in the UK are provided out of tax revenue, at no charge to the user. In principle, any person who can legally drive and own a vehicle can use roads, including overseas visitors. Some element, however, of non-excludability is present. Road space is becoming increasingly rival, as shown by spiralling levels of congestion. If

everyone who was eligible to use their vehicle did so at any one time, gridlock would occur.

A similar example is a holiday beach. In the UK, unlike some other countries, there are no charges levied on those who wish to sit on a beach and enjoy the natural features and sunshine. If, however, hordes of people descend on a beach, then the enjoyment of those who were there first starts to diminish rapidly. (Brighton on a bank holiday is typical.) The result is that the non-rivalry characteristic of public goods does not apply.

The Severn Road Bridge is a different type of quasi-public good. Vehicle users have to pay a toll to travel north from one side of the river to the other. If they do not pay the toll they are excluded. Travel to the south is free, so the few who only travel this way are not actually excluded. Non-rivalry is not always present, due to the level of congestion at busy times.

The Severn Bridge toll crossing

learning tip Examples of pure public goods are rare. Quasi-public goods are more common.

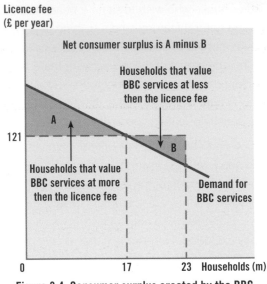

Figure 3.4 Consumer surplus created by the BBC

ECONOMICS IN CONTEXT

MARKET FAILURE IN BROADCASTING

The future funding of the BBC has been the subject of public debate for some time. Exceptionally, in broadcasting, the BBC is funded by an annual licence fee, £121 in 2004 [£135.50 in 2007], consistent with its role as a public service broadcaster. It is widely believed that in the digital age, as more channels become available, existing broadcasters like ITV and Channel 4 will be less inclined to fulfil a public service broadcasting function – they will shift towards a fully commercial approach.

Gavyn Davies, of Fulcrum Asset Management, estimated that, in 2004, the BBC created a public value surplus of about £2 billion [see Figure 3.4]. This serves only to reinforce the view that there is a clear benefit to be derived from the BBC in its current form.

Furthermore, in Davies' view, public service broadcasting will remain a classic public good in a fully digital age. The BBC will still be non-rivalous, as one person's use will not stop others from switching on – the marginal cost of providing its services to extra viewers will remain close to zero. There will not be a charge at the point of use. For this reason, a licence fee system is superior to a 'pay as you view' model. The non-excludability characteristic would remain as it stands, once the annual fee has been paid. Other digital broadcasting providers, such as Sky and Setanta, exclude all or parts of their audience through card and other subscription devices.

The danger in an all-digital age is that there will be more television being produced with negative externalities, such as swearing and violence. Such programmes may appeal more to subscribers than those programmes that generate positive externalities that educate and inform. In turn, the customer for programmes is the advertiser, not the viewer. The incentive for the broadcaster is to produce programmes that maximise advertising revenue and hence profits. News programmes, classic serials, minority drama and specialist sporting events are unlikely to attract the advertising revenue required by pay television providers.

A public-funded broadcaster will provide all types of programme, because it is concerned with whether the social value justifies their cost, not whether the cost will be covered by advertising revenue or subscriptions. This has to be a further over-riding argument for a publicly-funded BBC.

Source: Gavyn Davies, *The BBC and Public Value,* Social Market Foundation 2004

Government intervention to correct market failure

Governments intervene in the workings of the market mechanism to correct market failures in various ways. Some are obvious, others less so. Let us return to some of our earlier examples to show how diverse this intervention is in our own economy.

● *Negative externalities.* Charges are made by local authorities for the safe disposal of tyres and refrigerators; there are laws banning fly-tipping. As regards chewing gum, most effort is geared towards providing information for its safe disposal, for example 'Bin it' posters on bus shelters. For binge drinking, in some parts of the country, the owners of licensed premises are required to pay a local levy to provide for police support workers to control revellers and fund additional street cleaning as well as to employ staff to control their premises.

taxes

● *Positive externalities.* In the case of inoculations, which are free, advertising tends to stress the benefits of a particular form of vaccination. Government provision and funding for education, and training and subsidies for major transport projects such as Crossrail, recognise their wider social and economic value.

● *Merit goods.* The provision of information and state provision from tax revenue are two ways in which the government seeks to address problems of under-consumption.

● *Demerit goods.* The provision of impartial information and indirect taxation are the main ways in which the government hopes to regulate and reduce their consumption.

● *Public goods.* Government or state provision from general tax revenue. In some cases, such as in broadcasting, a charge is made for consumption.

It should be clear from this selective description that a whole range of methods are used by governments to correct market failure. The extent and intensity of such methods depends largely upon how concerned a government is about a particular market failure and whether it believes that intervention will produce a better allocation of resources.

Returning to the methods, it is possible to distinguish between two types of approach. These are:

● methods that involve some manipulation of the market mechanism – subsidies, indirect taxation and the provision of information. These are generally referred to as market-based solutions.

● non-market methods – direct provision and various forms of regulation and control.

These methods, and others that are relevant for the types of market failures explained so far, will now be analysed.

Taxation

A wide range of taxes is levied by central and local government on firms and consumers in the UK. Figure 3.5 shows the main sources of taxation projected for 2007/08. There are two main types of tax:

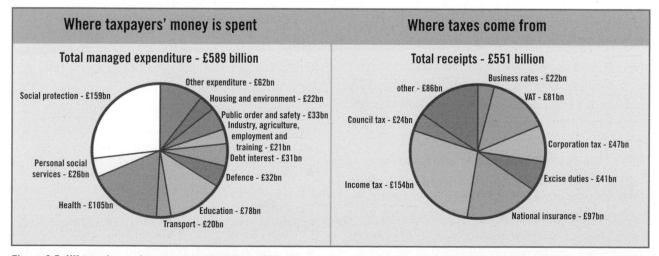

Figure 3.5 UK taxation and government spending, 2007–08   *Source:* HM Treasury. Crown Copyright material reproduced by permission of the Controller of HMSO and the Queen's Printer for Scotland

- **direct taxes**, such as income tax, corporation tax and national insurance contributions, all of which are taxes on the incomes of individuals and firms
- **indirect taxes**, such as value added tax (VAT) and excise duties, that tax the sale of certain products; council tax and business rates are charged locally on the ownership of houses and business premises.

DEFINITIONS

Direct tax: one that taxes the income of people and firms and that cannot be avoided.

Indirect tax: a tax levied on goods and services.

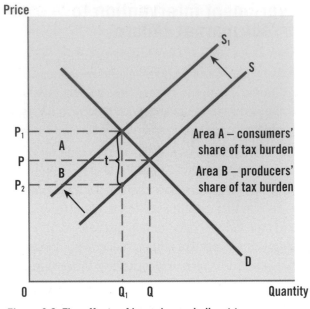

Figure 3.6 The effects of imposing an indirect tax

As Figure 3.5 indicates, the burden of taxation is broadly split equally between the two types of tax. Income tax, though, is by far the largest contributor to the Treasury. All forms of taxation are paid to the government, which in turn allocates tax revenue to various forms of public spending. There is little or no direct hypothecation, the term used to describe a situation where a particular tax is explicitly earmarked for a particular form of government spending.

For reasons explained earlier, a considerable amount of tax revenue is needed to finance merit goods and public goods. Health and education, both merit goods or services, are the second and third largest areas of government spending (see Figure 3.5). Defence and law and order, both public goods, required £65 billion in 2007/08.

Indirect taxes are widely used to discourage production of demerit goods and other goods and services that produce negative externalities. Although imposed on the producer, most forms of indirect tax tend to be passed on, in full or in part, to consumers. This invariably leads to increased prices in the market. Figure 3.6 shows the market outcome when a new tax, t, is introduced on this type of product. As this figure shows, the new tax will lead to a shift to the left of the supply curve from S to S_1. This means that less will now be demanded and supplied as the market price has increased.

In principle, the tax that is imposed should equal the value of the negative externality. When this occurs, the producer is required to pay the tax in full – prices charged therefore fully take into account the cost of the negative externality. In this way, the external cost is internalised to the producer. A tax that works in this way is entirely consistent with the **polluter pays principle**.

DEFINITION

Polluter pays principle: any measure, such as a green tax, whereby the polluter pays explicitly for the pollution caused.

This is fine in theory, but difficult to apply in practice for four reasons:

- There are problems in determining the exact amount of the tax, since it is invariably difficult to estimate the cost of the negative externality.

- Producers may not always pay the full amount of the tax. In Figure 3.6, the producer has had to accept a cut in the price received to P_2 from P, but the burden of the tax is shared with the consumer.

- The price elasticity of demand for many demerit goods is inelastic, meaning that consumption may not be reduced by as much as intended, with the result that production is higher than intended.

● Better quality information for consumers might also be used to further reduce consumption.

> **learning tip**
>
> An efficient way of correcting market failure is to internalise the cost of the negative externality.

Subsidies

A **subsidy** is a direct payment made by government to producers of a good or service or, in some cases, to its consumers. Its purpose is to reduce the cost in order to provide a higher level of production or consumption than would exist if it was left to the free market. Such payments are particularly relevant in

> **DEFINITION**
>
> **Subsidy:** a payment, usually from government, to encourage production or consumption.

the case of merit goods and where products generate positive externalities.

Examples of subsidies are:

● *to producers*: payments to train-operating companies to operate franchised services, payments to local bus companies to run loss-making services in rural areas, payments by the EU to farmers, grants from the UK and EU to firms relocating or setting up businesses in deprived areas.

● *to consumers*: the winter fuel payment to people aged 60 and over, the educational maintenance

ECONOMICS IN CONTEXT

AIR PASSENGER DUTY

An air passenger duty (APD) has been in place since 2001. This is a green tax, the purpose of which is to make airline passengers more aware of the cost of the negative externalities that are associated with flying. From February 2007, the APD was doubled to £10 for a short-haul flight and to £40 for an economy long-distance flight leaving the UK. APD is a blunt tax, in so far as it does not take into account the specific 'carbon footprint' resulting from any person's decision to fly. Like all taxes, revenue goes directly to the Exchequer – it is not invested in a special green fund for the aviation industry, as some experts would like to see.

From November 2009, the way in which the tax is charged will change. It will be explicitly linked to the amount of carbon dioxide produced on each flight.

This should give an incentive to airlines to operate environmentally efficient aircraft and should put pressure on them to increase load factors (the number of seats occupied). The cost to passengers, therefore, will be variable. Flying in a new aeroplane with a high load factor will be cheaper per head than, say, the same flight in an old aeroplane that is only half full.

APD is not without its critics. Most airlines operating from UK airports see the tax as no more than a source of additional tax revenue. The low-cost carrier easyJet, though, has welcomed the change in the basis for the tax, arguing that their passengers would pay less, due to their relatively new aircraft and high load factors. Others have argued that it will actually increase emissions, since some passengers may well decide to make long-haul instead of short-haul flights.

To fly or not to fly is a difficult question to answer. Mark Ellingham, founder of the Rough Guide series of books, believes that 'all of us have a responsibility to inform travellers as clearly and honestly as possible about the environmental cost of their journeys.' He is particularly critical of the trend towards so-called 'binge flying', largely brought about by the expansion of low-cost carriers in Europe. He would like to see APD increased to £100 on flights to Europe and Africa and to £250 on journeys to the rest of the world, and to see a halt to airport expansion. He, like others, takes the view that, even with the changes to APD, there will only be a marginal impact on travel decisions – the projected 6 per cent per annum growth in air travel seems likely to continue unabated.

allowance for 16–18-year-olds in further education, the higher education maintenance grant, payments by local authorities to low-income households for energy conservation improvements.

In all such cases, if left to the free market, there would be under-production and under-consumption.

In some respects, a subsidy works in the opposite way to an indirect tax. Figure 3.7 shows the effect on the market equilibrium following payment of a subsidy. As this shows, introducing a subsidy leads to a shift to the right in the supply curve from S to S_1. This results in a fall in price from P to P_1 and an increase in the quantity demanded and supplied from Q to Q_1.

Allocating subsidies can be controversial. A key consideration in the decision-making process is whether there is an external benefit. Let us consider two examples:

● *University education.* The cost of getting a university degree cannot be understated (no doubt as many of you will soon appreciate). The social benefit of a well-trained and well-educated labour force is central to the government's objective of enhancing our competitiveness. This is why tuition fees are subsidised and modest maintenance grants paid to students from low-income families. Some of the cost, but not all, has to be borne by the student,

on the basis of the private benefit that will accrue through the increased earnings potential arising from a university degree. Some critics would argue that the current system stops some talented students from going to university, particularly students from low- to middle-income families, and that more government support should be provided.

● *Rural bus subsidies.* The operation of public transport in rural areas has never been particularly profitable. This is especially the situation today because of increased levels of car ownership. The consequence is that, for a majority of largely older and poorer people, their only link with the outside is a heavily subsidised bus service. Such services have been cut back and remain under threat due to the small numbers who use them. The issue that local authorities have to address is whether the social need or benefit justifies the level of funding that is made available.

learning tip	A subsidy is designed to keep prices down while increasing production and consumption.

ACTIVITY ···⟫

In November 2007, a report by the Theatres Trust said that a massive £250 million was needed to modernise many of London's less commercial theatres. It further stated that the economics of the theatre made it impossible for the investment to come from owners and producers. Two approaches were suggested. The first was a levy on all West End ticket prices; an alternative approach was for the government to use public money to fund the modernisation in recognition of the 'economic significance of the theatre to culture, heritage and tourism'.

Discuss which one of these two approaches is the most appropriate way of dealing with this problem of market failure.

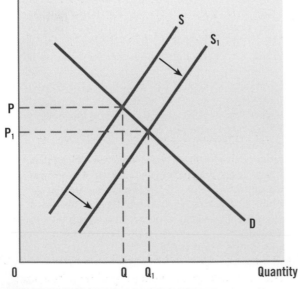

Figure 3.7 The effects of introducing a subsidy

Regulations, standards and legal controls

There are other ways, not involving the direct use of the price mechanism, that are used by governments

Handwritten margin notes:
correct market failure

A of subsidies
● effects the poor

Dif subsidies
● too high subsidy → over production
● hard to calculate the right amount of subsidy

to correct market failure. These take the form of a wide range of regulations, standards and legal controls. There are hundreds of examples. A few to consider are:

● Environmental – legislation relating to the emission of pollutants into the atmosphere, for the handling, storage and disposal of chemicals, noise levels from pop concerts, vehicles, industrial machinery, disposal of asbestos, radioactive waste and certain types of domestic appliance.

● Transport – legislation governing the compulsory use of seat belts, the construction and use of motor vehicles, railway trains and aircraft, vehicle speed limits, licensing of drivers and operators of buses and trucks.

● Professional – regulations relating to the qualifications of doctors, dentists and nurses, academic qualifications and those for lawyers and accountants.

● Use of demerit goods – restrictions on the sale of tobacco products and alcohol, various types of dangerous drugs.

The list is almost endless. All such controls are used by the government in the face of market failure and, if left just to the free market, undesirable market outcomes would occur. The purpose of such controls is to over-ride the workings of the market mechanism.

Let us take the case of environmental regulations and standards. Examples such as those above seek to control pollution of the air and water. Firms and consumers of products that pollute are required to comply with these regulations and standards. If they fail to do so, then a government body such as the Environment Agency or the Department for Transport Vehicle Inspectorate can take action against the polluters. This action can involve anything from a written warning to comply to a heavy fine or even closure of the business. The cost of enforcement is sometimes seen as a possible drawback of this form of government intervention.

In theory, the standards set should achieve what the legislation and standards see as an optimum scale of activity or use. If the standards are too low, the polluter receives benefits that are greater than the external costs of the pollution caused. Where

standards are too severe, there is always a temptation for the polluter to take risks by emitting pollutants into the air or water, particularly if any resulting fines or the risk of detection are low.

Setting standards requires accurate information. This is not always possible. It is also difficult in many polluting situations to clearly identify the source of pollution. Another criticism is that once a standard has been set, there is no incentive for firms or individuals to work in a more environmentally amenable way. Notwithstanding, regulations and standards have been a very important way of reducing many forms of environmental pollution that would otherwise have been unavoidable.

Tradable permits

Tradable permits are a market-based means of correcting market failure. They allow the owner the right to emit a specific level of pollution. The total number of permits is strictly controlled, as a means of limiting the overall level of pollution to what is seen as acceptable. The market aspect of these permits is that they can be bought and sold at a price to be agreed between their owner and purchaser. The incentive is for permit holders to achieve a lower level of pollution; any unused or partly used permits can then be transferred for a price to other firms that are having problems reaching the approved standard. In some respects, therefore, tradable permits combine the benefits of a market solution with those of regulation. If firms do not have sufficient permits to cover their pollution, then they will be prosecuted.

DEFINITION

Tradable permit: a permit that allows the owner to emit a certain amount of pollution and that, if unused or only partially used, can be sold to another polluter.

Figure 3.8 (see over) shows how, in theory, the price of permits is determined. The supply of permits is fixed at Q. When the demand for permits is D, the market

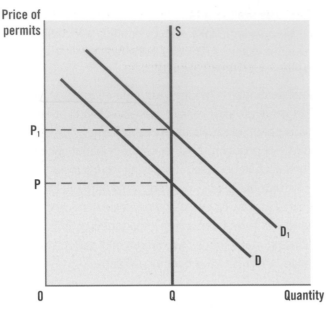

Figure 3.8 Price determination of tradable pollution permits

price is *P*. If more polluters require permits, *D* will shift outwards to D_1, increasing the price to P_1. A tightening of pollution standards can be shown by a shift to the left of *S*, so increasing the price of permits for a given level of demand. Any relaxation in standards will see a fall in the market price of permits.

A serious case of atmospheric pollution

The European Union's Emissions Trading Scheme (ETS) is a practical working example of a tradable permit scheme. The first phase of the ETS covers carbon dioxide emissions – the biggest contributor to climate change – from large firms in a range of polluting industries, such as energy production, metals processing, and paper, glass and cement manufacturing. The ETS gives the firm a form of property right to pollute, but only up to a certain level. In some respects, it is seen as more acceptable to business than a green tax – it is giving them something they can sell for a right that previously cost nothing. From the government's perspective, it is achieving a desired environmental outcome consistent with the country's maximum level of permitted emissions.

There are some disadvantages to the ETS. The most obvious are the problems of calculating and actually distributing permits to polluters. Problems also arise with respect to the market price for traded permits and whether there should be an annual auction for permits that remain unsold. In addition, there is the cost of policing and enforcing such a law to make sure that firms have sufficient permits to cover their pollution.

> **learning tip**
> Watch out for more details of the ETS, as it is planned to extend the scope of the scheme.

Role of government in information provision

Given that information failure is one of the causes of market failure, it seems logical to expect governments to provide information in order to correct market failure. This is particularly, and increasingly, so with respect to the provision of demerit goods. The government has been keen to see information provided on the true social as well as private costs involved in their consumption. Some examples include:

● health warnings on cigarette packets

● advice on the maximum number of units of alcohol that should be consumed

- improved labelling on food products, such as the 'traffic light' system that indicates the fat, sugar and salt content

- advice on the consumption of junk food and on links to child obesity.

In most cases, such information has been accompanied by regulations and laws, such as the smoking bans in public places, advertising restrictions on the promotion of demerit goods and positive measures such as the nutritional requirements for the provision of healthy school meals.

The government also ensures, through the Advertising Standards Agency, that media advertisers are truthful about the claims made about their products, particularly health and beauty products. In this way, it is hoped that consumers will receive truthful and impartial information.

ACTIVITY ⋯⋰

a) Using examples known to you from a variety of different markets, discuss the extent to which the provision of accurate information can be used to combat market failure.

b) A smoking ban is now operating in public places. Discuss the extent to which this may have reduced the negative externalities associated with smoking.

Exam Café
Relax, refresh, result!

Alice

AS Economics is a new subject for me, unlike my other AS subjects that I took at GCSE. My teacher says that we are all going to take the Unit 1 exam in January. She said it is very important we do not fall behind. She also said, if we are not set work in a lesson, that we should make a point of answering the activities that are in the text book. I have found this helps me a lot.

Nick

From what I have learned so far, economics seems a useful subject to study. The examples I have come across in class and in the textbook confirm this. I have now started to read a decent newspaper (some days, not all!) and surf the BBC News website for examples of market situations where the economics I have learned so far can be applied. I have given my teacher some examples and she has referred to these sometimes in her classes.

Emily

In the last month before the exam, I have found it useful to spend time answering the exam practice paper in the text book and the one on the price of oil on OCR's website. It seems these cover the range of topics we have been taught. Although it is difficult, I find it best to shut myself away for 1½ hours and answer these papers under what are close to exam conditions. I turn my iPod off! I have found it helps to answer the same question paper two or three times. My teacher says he has seen an improvement in my answers.

Do you know about …?	turn to page
The basic economic problem	4
Factors of production	4–5
Opportunity cost	6
Production possibility curves	10–15
The determinants of demand	24, 28
The distinction between movements along a demand curve and shifts of a demand curve	26, 31
The determinants of supply	32, 35
The distinction between movements along a supply curve and shifts of a supply curve	36–37
How the market equilibrium is determined	38
How changes in demand and supply affect the market equilibrium	40
Price, income and cross elasticity of demand	42–47
How these are interpreted by businesses	49–53
Allocative efficiency	53–54
Market failure	55
Information failure	55–58
Private costs, social costs, external costs	59–60
Private benefits, social benefits, external benefits	59–60
Merit, demerit and public goods	62–66
The various methods used to correct market failure	67–73

Quick-fire quiz

1. How can a production possibility curve be used to show the possible combinations of output of two products facing a company or economy?

2. What are the main determinants of demand for a product?

3. Should a firm raise or lower its prices when the price elasticity of demand for its product is inelastic?

4. Why are merit goods likely to be underprovided and underconsumed?

5. How might the government correct market failure when negative externalities are present in a market?

Get the result !

Exam question

A firm discharges chemical waste into a nearby river, causing negative externalities.
Discuss whether an indirect tax is the best way of correcting this form of market failure.

Charlotte's answer

Comments on Charlotte's answer

It is clear that Charlotte understands the question. She is aware of the general economics context and its application. Some limited use of concepts is included in the answer. Overall, though, the answer is rather simplistic and lacks adequate analysis. The 'discuss' aspect of the question is ignored.

The answer could be improved through:

- a more explicit definition of negative externality, such as 'where the social costs of an action are greater than the private costs'

- reference in the answer to the diagram; the labelling could also be improved

- using the term 'internalising the cost of the externality' to give more substance to the otherwise correctly made point about the polluting firm bearing the cost

- a discussion of whether an indirect tax or other methods of government intervention, such as regulations or tradable permits, are a better way of tackling pollution problems than an indirect tax.

A negative externality is one where there are external costs. In the case of a firm discharging chemical waste into a river, the negative externalities are not very pleasant. They include fish killed, awful smells and coloured water in the river. The firm gets rid of its waste like this because it is easy and cheap. It is an example of market failure because of this.

An indirect tax is one that could be used to make the firm pay for its pollution. This would mean that it had to pay a sum of money to the government because it was a polluter. This seems right, as it is only fair that it should do this, since other bodies like the local council are faced with having to make good the damage the firm has caused. An indirect tax like this is sometimes called a green tax, since it is being used to improve the quality of the environment.

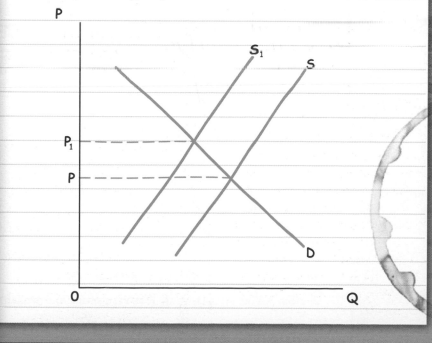

This example of market failure is one that occurs quite regularly. Last week, for instance, my local newspaper in Dewsbury reported a very similar case. The result was that hundreds of river fish were killed, much to the disgust of the local angling club, who had to cancel their medal competition event.

A negative externality arises out of an action which results in the social costs exceeding the private costs. This means that there are external costs that are not paid for by the chemical firm responsible for the negative externality. The effects of this are shown in the diagram below.

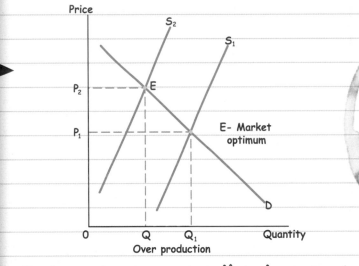

This diagram shows two important effects of a situation where there is a negative externality. First, the price that is paid is below the market optimum, and second, the output that is produced is above what it should be if the market was working efficiently. This is why an indirect tax (green tax) can be applied to correct the negative externality. If this happens in full, the price will rise and the output of chemicals produced will fall to the socially optimum level.

An indirect tax is an obvious way of correcting this form of market failure, since it internalises the cost of the negative externality. This is consistent with the 'polluter pays' principle. Having said this, a pollution tax like this is not easy to calculate and it is very difficult to manage. This is why there are good reasons for the government to look at other means of control, such as regulations and tradable permits. These have certain advantages over a green pollution tax.

Let us start with a telling question. What do you think is the main reason why some students do not do as well in exams as they expect? Is it because:

(a) They have not done enough work or not revised effectively?

(b) They have run out of writing time and not answered all of the questions?

(c) They have not answered some of the questions in the way the examiner has expected?

(d) They have not understood what they have been taught?

All four are possibilities – the most common reason, though, for underperformance in an examination is (c). By this, we mean that you, the candidate, have not answered some of the questions in the way that the examination paper has required you to.

Let us give you a silly example to show what we mean. Suppose you get a question that says

Explain why a chair normally has four legs.

The question is very clear and your answer should concentrate on explaining 'why a chair normally has four legs'. You should stick to this. What is *not* required is for you to say that chairs are made to sit on, are constructed from wood, metal or plastic and that some have fabric covers while others do not, and so on.

All examination questions consist of two elements. These are a *command word* (sometimes called a *directive word*) and the subject you have to write about. The command word is very important, since it gives you explicit advice on the style of answer you should write. The table below

shows the most common command words you will come across in OCR's AS Level Economics and what is required in your answer. *Make sure you really understand this table, in particular the differences between the various command words.*

Common command words in AS Level Economics exam questions

Command word	What's required
AO1	
Define	Give the exact meaning (as in the textbook)
Describe	Give an account of
State/Identify	Given an example or point out
AO2	
Explain	Give clear reasons for
Compare	Give similarities and differences
Account for	Give specific reasons
AO3	
Analyse	Pick out the main parts/points
AO4	
Comment	Give a reasoned opinion
Discuss	Give both sides, for and against

This is not an exhaustive list – but it does contain most of the command words used in OCR's AS Level Economics. The AO1–AO4 headings refer to the particular assessment objectives that these words are assessing.

- If the question says 'Using the information provided...', then there is a very explicit requirement for you to go back to the case material. This reference can be to a specific part of the text, for example lines 8-9, or to a table or figure. You have to use the information in your answer.

- If the question says 'Use a diagram to show ...', then this means that a diagram is the only thing that is required in your answer. If the command is to 'Use a diagram to explain...', then your answer should be in the form of a diagram followed by a short explanation/reasoned account of what is shown on the diagram.

- If the question says 'State and explain ...', then it is asking for two things. The first is a straightforward example or reason, the second is an explanation as to why this is an appropriate answer to the question.

Another piece of advice concerns diagrams. You can pick up a good number of marks for clearly drawn, accurate diagrams. Some questions specifically ask you for a diagram. Sometimes, but not always, a diagram may help to explain your answer to the final question. But, if you do include a diagram here, make sure it is correct and that you actually use it in your answer. This is a common failing for many students.

Good time management is also essential if you are to do well in a written examination. The AS unit examinations last only 1½ hours. *This is not very long, so it is important that you answer all of the questions and that you broadly spend an amount of time on each that is commensurate with the marks allocated.*

Each unit has 60 marks available. One way of looking at this is around 1½ minutes per mark. A better way, though, is:

- to spend about 10 minutes at the start of the examination reading through the case study and the questions that follow. When you do this, why not underline the economic terms that have been used in the case study and the AO3 and AO4 command words that have been used in the questions. These questions are the ones that carry the highest number of marks; you need to score well on them to get a good grade.

- to allow about 5 minutes at the end of the exam to go back to any questions that you could not complete and to re-read your answer to the final question that normally carries 18 out of the 60 marks available.

- to spend 25-30 minutes on this last question. Also, try to make a simple plan or mind map before you actually write your answer.

But remember, if you cannot answer a particular question, move on to the next. Do not waste valuable writing time.

So, OCR examiners are impressed when the answers you write are:

- clearly written to the point of the question

- make full use of economics terminology and concepts

- written in a way that is consistent with the command word

- of a length broadly commensurate with the marks available

- and, if required, contain accurate diagrams.

Exam practice paper

The growing problem of obesity

Obesity, the word used to describe the condition of excessively fat people, is a growing problem in the UK. Its scale is now so great that it affects males and females of all ages in the population. It is particularly prevalent among the lower social classes.

A recent report (2007) for the Department of Work and Pensions stated that around two thousand people were 'too fat to work' and that they had been paid £4.4m in incapacity benefit. This shocking revelation fuelled suspicion over whether these and over 2.6 million other people claiming £7.4 billion incapacity benefits could have been hired for some of the 1 million new jobs that had been taken up by migrant workers from the rest of the enlarged EU.

Child obesity has also attracted considerable media attention. An obsession with high-fat junk food, chips and chocolate coupled with too little exercise and too much time staring at a computer screen are often cited as some of the reasons for the increasing numbers of schoolchildren now classed as obese.

So what can be done about it? Jamie Oliver's campaign to improve the nutritional quality of school meals and improved labelling on offending food packaging can help, but lots more can and should be done. Economists view obesity as a clear example of market failure, largely arising because of information failure. They believe that more can be done to address this failure, including the selective use of market-based solutions.

It is worthwhile to study what is happening in the USA, which has the highest percentage of obese people anywhere in the world. Some states are so concerned about obesity and its wider effects that they are considering slamming a tax on high-fat foods to discourage consumption. If this is successful, economists would be happy, as it would be a typical market solution to a problem of market failure. The challenge is to get the millions of hamburger-munching, pizza-troughing, fizzy drink-guzzling Americans of all ages to change their lifetime habits.

a) i)   Define opportunity cost. (2 marks)
    ii) Use the information provided to explain the opportunity cost to the UK economy of those people claiming incapacity benefit. (4)

b) In recent years, there has been a large increase in the demand and supply of high-fat junk food. With the aid of a demand and supply diagram, explain the effects on the market equilibrium. (4)

c) The price elasticity of demand for a premium grade hamburger meal at a well known fast food outlet has been estimated to be –0.1; for a healthy meal option it is estimated at –0.4 and for icecream sundaes –1.6.

    i)   Explain what these figures mean. (4)
    ii) Comment upon how this data may be used by a fast food outlet. (6)

d) i)   Describe what is meant by a demerit good. (2)
    ii) Explain why there is likely to be information failure in the provision of high-fat fast food. (4)
    iii) Comment on the extent to which high-fat fast food is a demerit good. (6)

e) Use a diagram to explain how a new indirect tax on certain types of junk food would affect the market equilibrium. (10)

f) Discuss the likely effectiveness of **two** methods, including taxation, that are available to governments seeking to reduce the consumption of demerit goods. (18)

PART 2

The national and international economy

INTRODUCTION

This part introduces macroeconomics: the performance of the whole economy. You will explore how the output and the prices in an economy are determined.

Chapter 4 concentrates on aggregate demand and aggregate supply analysis. You will see some similarities with demand and supply analysis, including the widespread use of diagrams. But you will now analyse *total* economic activity and not simply the market for one product. For instance, it is the price of the product that is measured on the vertical axis of a demand and supply diagram, whereas it is the price level that is measured on that of an aggregate demand and supply diagram. On the horizontal axis it is real GDP (Gross Domestic Product, or the output of an economy) that is measured.

Chapter 5 explores indicators of national economic performance. You will explore how economic growth, unemployment, inflation and the balance of payments are measured, what causes changes in the indicators of macroeconomic performance, and consequences of these changes. You will examine how exchange rates are determined and the effect of changes in them.

Chapter 6 focuses on the policies that can be used in the management of the economy. You will explore the nature of these policies, including their effectiveness. You will also examine the nature and the benefits of international trade.

When you have completed this part you should be able to:

- apply aggregate demand and supply to explain current economic issues
- explain how the performance of an economy is measured
- compare the performance of the UK economy with other economies
- explain the causes and consequences of economic growth, unemployment, inflation and balance of payments deficits
- assess fiscal, monetary and supply-side policies
- explain the causes and consequences of exchange rate changes
- describe the nature and benefits of international trade.

4 Aggregate demand and aggregate supply and their interaction

On completion of this chapter you should be able to:

- define aggregate demand and describe the components of aggregate demand and explain what determines each of them
- recognise that aggregate demand and the price level are inversely related
- explain why the aggregate demand curve may shift
- define aggregate supply and explain why the aggregate supply curve may shift
- define what is meant by equilibrium in the macroeconomy
- explain how macroeconomic equilibrium is determined and why it may change
- understand what is meant by the circular flow of income
- show a general awareness of the multiplier effect and the concepts of leakages and injections
- discuss how changes in aggregate demand and aggregate supply may affect output, unemployment and inflation.

Introduction

In Part One, you examined how markets for particular products work and how sometimes they fail to achieve allocative efficiency. In Part Two, attention moves to a study of the whole economy. What is happening in the economy can have a significant impact on all of us. Indeed, the quality of our lives is influenced by, among other factors, how easy it is to find a job and the prices we pay for the products we are able to buy. These factors are, in turn, influenced by the aggregate (total) level of demand and the aggregate (total) level of supply in the countries in which we live.

This chapter will examine the nature of that aggregate demand and aggregate supply and how they interact to affect output, unemployment and inflation.

 learning tip Remember aggregate means *total*. It does not mean average.

Aggregate demand

Aggregate demand (AD) is the total demand for goods and services produced in an economy at a

DEFINITION

Aggregate demand: the total demand for a country's goods and services at a given price level and in a given time period.

given **price level** and in a given time period. This planned expenditure on domestic output comes from households, firms, the government and foreigners. It is made up of **consumer expenditure** (C), **investment** (I), **government spending** (G) and **net exports**, which is **exports** (X) minus **imports** (M).

So, AD = C + I + G + (X − M).

Confident consumers spend more

DEFINITIONS

Price level: the average of each of the prices of all the products produced in an economy.

Consumer expenditure: spending by households on consumer products.

Investment: spending on capital goods.

Government spending: spending by the central government and local government on goods and services.

Exports: products sold abroad.

Imports: products bought from abroad.

Net exports: the value of exports minus the value of imports.

Government spending is spending by the central government and local government on, for example, education, health care and the police service. It does not include **transfer payments** such as housing benefit, **job seeker's allowance** and state pensions. This is because such payments do not involve the government itself buying goods and services. If the government does, for instance, increase job seeker's allowance, this would be reflected in higher consumer expenditure.

Net exports add foreigners' spending on the country's goods and services and deduct spending by the country's population on imports. This component can make a positive or a negative contribution to

The components of aggregate demand

Consumer expenditure is also known as *consumption*. It is, for most countries, the largest component of aggregate demand. It is spending by households on items such as clothing, food and insurance. Investment is the most volatile component of aggregate demand. Spending on capital goods, such as delivery vehicles, machines and office buildings, may rise by 60 per cent one year and fall by 20 per cent the next.

DEFINITIONS

Transfer payments: money transferred from one person or group to another not in return for any good or service.

Job seeker's allowance: a benefit paid by the government to those unemployed and trying to find a job.

aggregate demand. If a country has a **trade surplus**, with exports being greater than imports, then adding net exports to C + I + G will increase aggregate demand. In contrast, the existence of a **trade deficit** would mean that aggregate demand would be lower than total domestic demand.

DEFINITIONS

Trade surplus: the value of exports exceeding the value of imports.

Trade deficit: the value of imports exceeding the value of exports

---

learning tip

Remember, aggregate demand is planned spending on the products produced by an economy and not planned spending within an economy. So, aggregate demand adds spending on exports and deducts spending on imports. In contrast, planned spending within an economy includes spending on imports but not spending on exports.

ACTIVITY ⋯⋮

In 2007, investment in the USA was $1,920 billion, government spending was $2,178 billion, consumer expenditure was $8,199 billion, exports $1,171 billion and imports $1,780 billion.

a) Calculate the aggregate demand of the USA in 2007.

b) Did the USA have a trade deficit or a trade surplus in 2007? Explain your answer.

CONSUMER EXPENDITURE

There are a range of influences on how much households spend. They include:

● *Real disposable income.* This is the main influence on consumer expenditure. Richer households and richer economies tend to spend

---

more in total than poorer ones. They obviously have more money to spend. The proportion of income that is spent, which economists call the **average propensity to consume (APC)** may, however, fall as disposable income rises. A city banker earning a disposable income of £6,000 a week will spend more than a teacher with a disposable income of £700 a week. The city banker, though, is likely to spend a lower proportion as she can enjoy a high material living standard and still be able to save a significant amount. For instance, she may spend £4,500 while the teacher spends £630. In this case, the teacher has a higher APC – 0.90 (£630/£700) – than the banker, who has an APC of 0.75 (£4,500/£6,000).

● **Wealth.** The more wealth people have – in the form of, for example, their home, savings account and shares – the more they tend to spend. Wealth can be spent and can be used to borrow against. It also results in greater **consumer confidence**. A rise in house prices, for instance, would usually make homeowners feel wealthier and encourage them to spend more. Indeed, there are a number of links between house prices and consumer expenditure. A rise in house prices tends to increase activity in the housing market – more people choose to sell and buy houses. When people move they spend more on furniture, carpets, curtains and DIY materials.

● *Consumer confidence and expectations.* This can have a significant influence on consumer expenditure. When consumers are feeling optimistic about the future, expecting their job prospects to be good and their wages to be high, they spend more. This is why sometimes the proportion of income spent can rise as income rises.

● *The rate of interest.* Changes in the rate of interest are another important influence on consumer

DEFINITIONS

Consumer confidence: how optimistic consumers are about future economic prospects.

Rate of interest: the charge for borrowing money and the amount paid for lending money.

expenditure, although they can be overshadowed by the state of consumer confidence. Usually a fall in the rate of interest will stimulate a rise in consumer expenditure. This is for three main reasons. It makes it cheaper for consumers to borrow in order to buy expensive items such as cars. It reduces the incentive to save because by spending now people are giving up less interest. The third reason is that those who are paying interest on a mortgage or on any other type of loan will have more money to spend. Of course, **net savers** (those who save more than they borrow) will lose out if the rate of interest falls. Their ability to spend will fall. Net savers, however, spend a smaller proportion of their income than borrowers do. So the fall in spending from net savers is usually more than offset by the rise in spending from borrowers. There is, nevertheless, the possibility that spending may not rise when the rate of interest falls. This is because people may think that the reduction is only temporary or they may be delaying changing their spending if they think that the rate will fall further. In addition, if people are worried about the future, they may not increase their spending even if the rate of interest falls. (See section on 'Saving', below.)

● *The age structure of the population.* This can affect consumer spending. It is generally thought that the young and the elderly spend a relatively high proportion of their disposable income. This, however, is not always the case (see 'Saving' below).

DEFINITIONS

Average propensity to consume (APC): the proportion of disposable income spent. It is consumer expenditure divided by disposable income.

Net savers: people who save more than they borrow.

Wealth: a stock of assets, e.g. property, shares and money held in a savings account.

● **Distribution of income**. As already noted, poor people spend a higher proportion of their income

than do rich people. So, government measures that redistribute income from the rich to the poor are likely to increase total consumer spending.

● **Inflation**. It is difficult to determine what impact inflation has on consumer spending. If people expect prices to rise rapidly in the future they may increase their spending now. On the other hand, there have been periods when inflation was high and accelerating when people increased their saving rather than their spending. This may have been because people were trying to maintain the real value of their saving.

DEFINITIONS

Distribution of income: how income is shared out between households in a country.

Inflation: a sustained rise in the price level.

ACTIVITY ····

Consumer expenditure in Venezuela increased considerably in 2007. This change in consumer expenditure was driven by three main factors. One was rising wealth due to the higher price of oil (Venezuela is an oil-producing country). Another factor was inflation outstripping interest rates so that most Venezuelan people chose to spend rather than save. The third factor was that banks were providing cheap loans.

a) Define consumption.

b) Identify two other components of aggregate demand.

c) Explain one of the causes of an increase in consumer expenditure mentioned in the passage.

SAVING

Saving is not a component of aggregate demand but it is useful to discuss it here. This is because saving influences the spending undertaken by households, firms, the government and foreigners. For the moment, we will concentrate largely on saving by households. Influences on saving include:

ECONOMICS IN CONTEXT

CONSUMER EXPENDITURE IN THE USA

Between 2004 and 2006, US consumer expenditure rose at a steady 3 per cent per year. In these years most US households were confident about the future. Unemployment was low and falling. It was easy to borrow from US banks. Optimism about the future encouraged US households to build up debt, which grew to 130 per cent of their annual income.

Then, in mid-2007, the situation changed. Unemployment rose as the economy grew more slowly. US banks, which had lent to borrowers with a poor credit record in what is called the sub-prime market, got into difficulties when some people were unable to keep up with their mortgage payments. The sub-prime mortgage crisis resulted in a 'credit crunch' with banks becoming more cautious in their lending policies and making their lending criteria more stringent.

House prices fell by 5 per cent. This lowered the value of household wealth and reduced the amount against which households could borrow. 2007 also witnessed a significant drop in consumer confidence. The University of Michigan's index of consumer

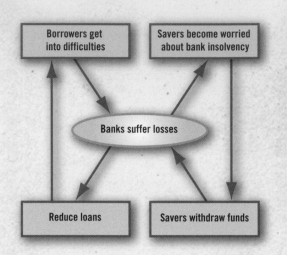

confidence was at its lowest level in 15 years.

The rise in unemployment and difficulty in borrowing reduced house prices and the fall in consumer confidence led some economists to anticipate the first fall in consumer expenditure since 1991.

● *Real disposable income.* This is the main influence on saving. As real disposable income increases, households usually not only save more but also save a higher proportion of their income. Their **average propensity to save** rises.

● *The rate of interest.* A rise in the rate of interest increases the reward for saving and so usually encourages people to save more. There are some people, though, who are **target savers**. They are saving to achieve a particular sum in savings. In their case, higher interest rates would reduce the amount they have to save.

● *Confidence and expectations.* Households and firms also tend to save more when they are uncertain or concerned about the future. If, for instance, people are worried that they may lose their jobs, they are likely to save now as a precaution against a sudden drop in income.

● *Saving schemes.* Some saving is contractual, when people agree to save a certain amount on a regular basis in insurance and pension schemes.

DEFINITIONS

Saving: real disposable income minus spending.

Average propensity to save (APS): the proportion of disposable income saved. It is saving divided by disposable income.

Target savers: people who save with a target figure in mind.

● *Range of financial institutions.* Saving can be affected by the range of well-respected financial institutions in the country. In those countries with a high number of established and trusted financial institutions, people will find it straightforward to save and will have the confidence to place their savings with these institutions. In practice, however, it has been found that as a financial system becomes more developed and sophisticated, saving rates may fall. This is because people find it easier to borrow.

● *Government policies.* A decision by the government to introduce tax-free saving schemes will encourage people to save more. In contrast, a government decision to raise state pensions may reduce the incentive for people to save for retirement.

● *The age structure of the population.* It has been found that people usually save very little when young but increase their saving in their middle years. It also used to be assumed that the elderly **dissave**, drawing on their savings to maintain their living standards when they retire. In some cases this is true and is one reason for the decline in the national **savings ratio** in the rapidly ageing countries of Italy, Japan and South Korea. Some pensioners, however, continue to save. Their motives may include the desire to be able to pay for care or medical treatment should the need arise, and a desire to pass on something to their children.

DEFINITIONS

Dissave: spending more than disposable income.

Savings ratio: savings as a proportion of disposable income.

ACTIVITY ····⋮

The Chinese are among some of the biggest savers in the world. On average, in 2007 Chinese households saved 40 per cent of their disposable income. Most Chinese do not have a pension or medical insurance. In the same year, UK households had a savings ratio of 3 per cent.

a) Explain one possible reason why the UK savings ratio was so low in 2007.

b) Analyse one reason why, in the future, the Chinese savings ratio may:

i) decrease

ii) increase.

ECONOMICS IN CONTEXT

WHY DO THE GERMANS SPEND MORE THAN THE BRITISH?

Germany's savings ratio averaged 10 per cent in the period 2000–07. This was relatively high by EU standards and was significantly higher than the UK's 4 per cent average for the same period.

In recent years, Germany's unemployment rate has been double that of the UK. This has made Germans more anxious about their job security than their British counterparts.

In addition, in the period 2000–07, while the UK government was increasing its spending on health care, the German government was cutting it. Some Germans, as a result, were saving more in order to cover possible medical costs. The German government also cut state benefit and pension provisions, which again encouraged Germans to keep their savings ratio high.

There is a chance that things might change. German unemployment fell in 2007 and there are signs of changes in the German housing market. Traditionally, home ownership in Germany has been low. Recent years have, however, seen an increasing number of Germans buying their homes. If this trend continues, German spending may rise, at the expense of saving. Germans are likely to feel wealthier and are likely to spend more on furniture and fittings.

INVESTMENT

Firms invest when they expect the returns from the capital goods that they buy to be greater than their cost. In other words, they will invest if they anticipate that such spending will be profitable. Influences on investment include:

● *Changes in real disposable income.* If real disposable income is increasing, demand for consumer goods and services is also likely to be rising. This may encourage firms to expand their capacity. In itself, however, a rise in disposable income may not be sufficient to encourage firms to invest. Firms would also have to believe that the rise in demand will last and that their existing capital goods are not sufficient to produce the extra output.

● *Expectations*. Firms are much more likely to invest if they feel optimistic about future economic prospects. The extent and speed of changes in expectations are the main reasons for the volatility of investment.

● **Capacity utilisation**. Firms are also more likely to invest if they are currently operating close to full capacity. In contrast, if they have considerable spare capacity (unused capital goods), they may be able to increase output without having to buy new capital goods.

● *Current profit levels*. High profit levels can encourage investment in two ways. They provide the finance to invest, and they are likely to contribute to firms' optimism about the future.

● **Corporation tax.** Corporation tax, also known as corporate tax, is a tax on firms' profits. A cut in corporation tax increases the amount of profit firms can keep and so can result in an increase in investment. A government can also stimulate investment by providing investment subsidies.

● *The rate of interest*. As with consumer expenditure, investment is influenced by changes in the rate of interest. A rise in the rate of interest would be likely to reduce investment for four main reasons. First, it will increase the opportunity cost of investment. A firm can use its profit for a number of purposes, including investment, placing it in financial institutions to earn interest or distributing it to shareholders in the form of dividends. Opting to buy capital goods when the rate of interest rises would involve forgoing more money on, for instance, a saving account in a bank. Although most investment is financed out of **retained profit**, some is financed by borrowing. Second, a higher interest rate would make it more expensive to borrow and so may discourage some investment projects. Third, as well as affecting the cost of investment, a change in the rate of interest will affect the expected return on the investment. A higher rate of interest is likely to reduce investment, as firms will anticipate that consumer spending will fall. Finally, in addition, a rise in the rate of interest tends to reduce the demand for shares. This is because some people, who might have bought shares, may now place their money in an interest-bearing account instead. Lower demand for shares will reduce their price level and so decrease the funds that firms can raise for investment.

● *Advances in technology*. A firm may buy new capital equipment if it thinks that it will produce better quality products or produce products more cheaply. In either case, it would expect to earn a higher profit. In the first case, this would be because it would anticipate higher demand and, in the second case, it would anticipate that its **unit cost** would fall. If other firms are adopting advanced technology, a firm may be forced to follow suit just to stay competitive and maintain its profit level.

● *Price of capital equipment*. A reduction in the price of capital equipment may also increase investment. Such a fall may make it viable for more firms to use the equipment or for those firms already using the equipment to expand their capacity.

DEFINITIONS

Capacity utilisation: the extent to which firms are using their capital goods.

Corporation tax: a tax on firms' profits.

Retained profits: profit kept by firms to finance investment.

Unit cost: average cost per unit of output.

ACTIVITY ····⑈

India's rapid increase in output in recent years has been driven by increases in investment and consumption. In 2007 a survey, carried out by Grant Thornton, a London-based accounting firm, found that Indian entrepreneurs were the most optimistic among those in 32 countries. Changes in the Indian interest rate have also stimulated investment.

a) Distinguish between investment and consumption.

b) What is the relationship between business optimism and investment?

c) Explain what is likely to have happened to the Indian interest rate in the period discussed.

learning tip

Be careful not to confuse investment and saving. Remember, investment is spending on capital goods, whereas saving is disposable income minus consumer expenditure. A rise in the rate of interest usually causes a fall in investment and a rise in saving.

GOVERNMENT SPENDING

Government spending decisions are influenced by a number of factors. These include:

● The government's view on the extent of market failure and its ability to correct it. In countries where there is a high level of state intervention, government spending usually forms a higher proportion of aggregate demand than in those countries where free market forces play a greater role. For example, government spending in 2007 accounted for 27 per cent of aggregate demand in Sweden but only 12 per cent of aggregate demand in Chile.

ACTIVITY ····⋮›

Government spending, as a proportion of aggregate demand, is higher by 2 percentage points in Canada than in the USA. The USA tops the table for health care spending as a proportion of **real GDP**, although most of this spending comes from the private sector.

a) In which country does the government spend the most? Explain your answer.

b) Explain two factors that influence how much a government spends on health care.

DEFINITIONS

Real GDP: the country's output measured in constant prices and so adjusted for inflation.

Gross domestic product (GDP): the total output of goods and services produced in a country.

● The level of economic activity in the economy can influence government spending. If there is a high level of unemployment, a government may raise its spending in a bid to increase aggregate demand and the output of the economy. In contrast, if there is a high inflation rate, a government may reduce its spending.

● A desire to please the electorate. Voters can put pressure on the government to spend money improving education, health care and transport infrastructure. A government may increase its spending before a general election in an attempt to win political support.

● War, terrorist attacks and rising crime, or their threat, can also increase government spending.

NET EXPORTS

Among the influences on export revenue and import expenditure are:

● *Real disposable income abroad.* A rise in income abroad is likely to result in more exports being sold. For example, the USA is one of the UK's main trading partners. If people in the USA enjoy higher disposable income, they will buy more goods and services, some of which will come from the UK.

● *Real disposable income at home.* In contrast, a rise in income at home may result in a fall in exports. This is because firms may divert some products from the export market to the home market to meet the rising domestic demand.

● *The domestic price level.* The value of exports may fall and the value of imports rise if the domestic price level rises relative to the price levels in the country's trading partners. If domestically produced products become more expensive, firms and households at home and abroad will switch from them to products made in other countries.

● **The exchange rate**. As well as being influenced by the inflation rates, the price of exports and imports

DEFINITION

Exchange rate: the price of one currency in terms of another currency.

are also affected by exchange rate changes. A fall in a country's exchange rate will reduce the price of exports and raise the price of imports. This, in turn, is likely to result in a rise in export revenue and a fall in import expenditure. A rise in the exchange rate, on the other hand, is likely to result in a fall in net exports. (See pages 135–137 for a more detailed explanation of the effects of a change in the exchange rate.)

● *Government restrictions on free trade.* A country's net exports may rise if other countries' governments remove trade restrictions. China, for instance, might be able to export more steel to the USA if the US government removed **tariffs** on Chinese steel. Such a move would lower the price of Chinese steel on the US market and so make it more price competitive.

> **DEFINITION**
>
> **Tariff:** a tax on imports.

> **ACTIVITY ⋯⋅**
>
> Throughout most of the 1990s, Germany imported more than it exported. In 2001, the position changed and from then up to 2007, export revenue exceeded import expenditure by increasing amounts. In contrast, in the period 2001–07, the UK imported more than it exported.
>
> a) Identify whether Germany's or the UK's trade position made a positive contribution to the country's aggregate demand in the period 2001–07. Briefly explain your answer.
>
> b) Explain two causes of an increase in exports.

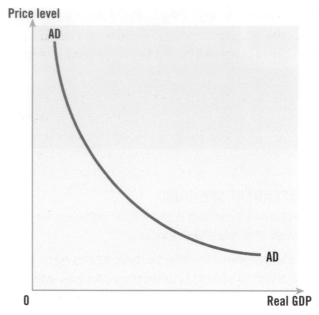

Figure 4.1 **An aggregate demand curve**

The relationship between aggregate demand and the price level

In November 2007, Turkey was experiencing an 8 per cent inflation rate. The Turkish government expressed concern that this relatively high rate of increase in the Turkish price level would have an adverse effect on demand for the country's products. It was right to be worried. Aggregate demand (AD) is inversely related to the price level. A rise in the price level causes a fall, or contraction, in aggregate demand and a fall in the price level results in a rise, or extension, in aggregate demand.

The relationship is shown in Figure 4.1. The vertical axis is labelled the price level and the horizontal axis is labelled real GDP (which represents the output of the economy). The aggregate demand (AD) curve slopes down from left to right.

> **learning tip**
> Remember that spending on imports reduces a country's aggregate demand (AD). This is because the spending is going on foreign and not domestically produced products.
>
> Be careful when answering questions on factors influencing any of the components of AD. For example, check whether they are asking why a country's exports are at a high level or asking why they have increased. In the former case, you might write about a low exchange rate and low inflation, whereas in the latter case, you should write about a fall in the exchange rate and a fall in the inflation rate.

The reasons why AD and the price level move in opposite directions are different from the inverse relationship between the demand for a product and its price.

On a demand diagram, it is only the price of the product itself that is changing – the price of all other products are held constant. In this case, a fall in price makes the product cheaper relative to other products. In the case of an AD curve, there is no relative price change among domestic producers.

There are three effects which explain why the AD curve is downward sloping:

● *The wealth effect.* This relates to changes in households' and firms' real wealth when the price level changes. A fall in the price level increases the amount of goods and services that wealth, kept in the form of money in bank accounts and other financial assets, can buy. On the other hand, a rise in the price level reduces the purchasing power of wealth and so causes aggregate demand to contract.

● *The rate of interest effect.* A rise in the price level means that some people will sell financial assets, such as **government bonds**, to obtain more money to pay the higher prices. The resulting increase in the supply of government bonds reduces their price. Such a change in the price of bonds raises the percentage rate of interest. This is because the amount paid in interest on a bond stays the same when its price alters. So, for example, a bond may pay £5 interest. If initially it is sold for £100, the rate of interest paid is 5 per cent. A fall in its price to £50 would increase the interest rate to 10 per cent. A higher interest rate is likely to reduce consumption and investment. In contrast, a fall in the price level will reduce the interest rate and cause an extension in AD due to higher consumption and investment.

DEFINITION

Government bond: a financial asset issued by the central or local government as a means of borrowing money.

● *The international trade effect.* This is relatively straightforward. A rise in the price level, assuming no change in foreign prices and the exchange rate, will make the country's products less internationally competitive. This would cause households and firms to buy more from foreign producers and less from domestic producers. Net exports would fall and aggregate demand would contract.

So the AD curve slopes down from left to right, since a rise in the price level would reduce monetary wealth, raise the interest rate and reduce the country's international competitiveness.

> **learning tip**
>
> Do not confuse an AD curve diagram with a demand curve diagram. An AD curve shows total demand altering as the price level changes. A demand curve shows the demand for a single product altering as its relative price changes.

ACTIVITY ····⁝>

In 2006 the price level in Argentina rose by 12.3 per cent, while that in Japan fell by 0.4 per cent.

a) Which country experienced a contraction in its AD?

b) Which country is likely to have become more internationally competitive? Briefly explain your answer.

Shifts in the aggregate demand curve

While a change in the price level causes a *movement along* the AD curve, a change in any other influence on AD will cause a *shift of* the AD curve. Figure 4.2 (see over) shows an increase in AD with the AD curve moving out to the right.

A change in any of the determinants of any of the components of AD will cause a shift of the AD curve. Such changes include, for example, changes in

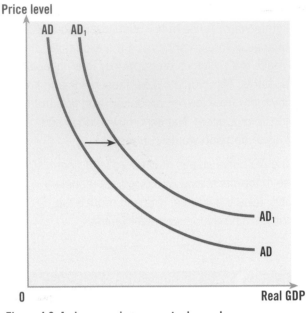

Figure 4.2 An increase in aggregate demand

expectations, changes in government policy, changes in the exchange rate and a change in population size. If households and firms become more optimistic about economic prospects, consumer expenditure and investment will increase, thereby shifting the AD curve to the right. A cut in income tax would raise real disposable income and so would again probably increase consumption and investment. A rise in the interest rate, independent of a change in the price level, would, on the other hand, reduce consumption and investment. A fall in the exchange rate would be likely to increase AD as a result of increasing net exports. A rise in population size would increase consumption and would be likely to stimulate an increase in investment and government spending.

A decrease in AD may be caused by a fall in share prices on global markets. This is because wealth would decline, which would be likely to reduce consumption, and if firms find it more difficult to raise finance, investment may decline.

Aggregate supply

Aggregate supply (AS) is the total output of goods and services that producers in an economy are willing and able to supply at different price levels in a given time period.

The shape of the AS curve is influenced by the level of the capacity existing in the economy. When output is low and unemployment is high, as shown over the range O to Y in Figure 4.3, AS is perfectly elastic. This means that more can be supplied without raising the price level. Any increase in output can be achieved by offering unemployed workers jobs at the going wage rate and paying the going price for raw materials and capital equipment. Between Y and Y_1, AS is at first elastic and then it becomes increasingly less responsive to changes in the price level. As resources become scarcer, producers have to employ less efficient workers and machinery. This pushes up unit costs of production and the price level. At Y_1 all resources are employed and AS becomes perfectly inelastic. At full capacity it is not possible to produce any more, irrespective of how high the price level rises.

ACTIVITY ···⋗

Between 2004 and 2007, the external sector made an increasingly negative contribution to French AD growth. Domestic demand increased at a relatively slow rate. Consumer expenditure grew at an annual rate of only 1.8 per cent, largely due to relatively high unemployment, weak wage growth and a lack of consumer confidence. Government spending rose at a slightly more rapid rate, approximately 2.4 per cent.

a) Explain what is meant by 'the external sector made an increasingly negative contribution to AD growth'.

b) Which component of AD is not mentioned in the above passage?

c) Using an AD diagram, illustrate the effect of an increase in consumption.

DEFINITION

Aggregate supply: the total amount that producers in an economy are willing and able to supply at a given price level in a given time period.

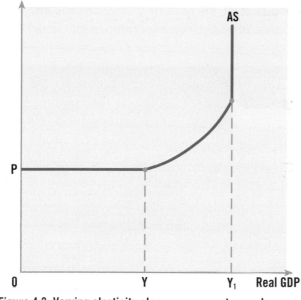

Figure 4.3 Varying elasticity along an aggregate supply curve

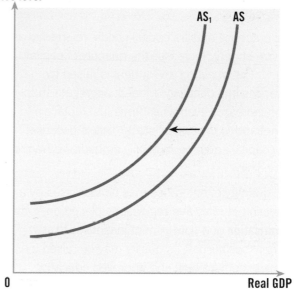

Figure 4.4 A decrease in aggregate supply

ACTIVITY ⋯⋮

In recent years inflation in the UK has remained low even though the economy has been operating close to full capacity. Draw a diagram to illustrate how the shape of the AS curve may have changed.

SHIFTS IN THE AGGREGATE SUPPLY CURVE

A change in AS means that the total output that producers are willing and able to supply at any given price level alters. A decrease in AS is represented by a shift to the left of the AS curve whereas an increase in AS is shown by a shift to the right.

The main causes of changes in AS in the short run are changes in the costs of production. The economy's costs of production may fall, and so AS increases, as a result of a fall in raw material costs and a fall in wages. In contrast, a rise in the costs of production will cause a decrease in AS. For example, an increase in the price of oil may raise the costs of many producers in an economy, by increasing the costs of both producing products and transporting them. Figure 4.4 shows AS decreasing.

In the longer run, the two main causes of shifts in the AS curve, which alter productive capacity, are changes in the quantity and quality of resources.

These causes can be further broken down by examining how the quantity and quality of particular resources can be affected.

The quantity of labour may increase as a result of net immigration of people of working age, a higher proportion of women entering the labour force and a rise in the retirement age. Improvements in education and training will improve the quality of labour and raise **productivity**. Figure 4.5 shows an increase in

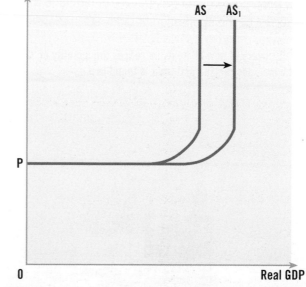

Figure 4.5 An increase in aggregate supply which increases productive capacity

AS, with the productive capacity of the economy increasing.

The purchase of extra capital goods, referred to as net investment, increases the quantity of capital goods. The *quality* of investment is raised by advances in technology. Indeed, aggregate supply often increases even when firms just replace and do not add to the capital stock. This is because new capital equipment usually embodies advanced technology.

The quantity of enterprise may be increased by a reduction in rules and regulations placed on firms, **privatisation** and government incentives to start up new businesses. Its quality may be raised by management training and improved education.

DEFINITIONS

Productivity: output, or production, of a good or service per worker per unit of a factor of production in a given time period.

Privatisation: transfer of assets from the public to the private sector.

There are a variety of ways that the quality of land may be improved. The productivity of farmland may be raised by the application of fertilisers and rivers

The discovery of new oil fields increases the quantity of 'land', which includes the sea and what is found in it

may be cleaned up. The discovery of new oil fields would increase the quantity of land whereas the depletion of gold mines would reduce it.

learning tip

Remember that a shift of the AS curve to the left represents a decrease in AS. It might appear that AS is higher, but when you compare it against real GDP, you can see that at any price level the economy's output is lower.

The vertical part of the AS curve is equivalent to a production possibility curve (see page 10) and the factors that shift a PPC also cause the vertical part of the AS curve to shift.

A fall in unemployment does not in itself increase aggregate supply. It will cause a rise in actual, but not potential, output unless the lower unemployment encourages more people to enter the labour force.

ACTIVITY ····⟩

A number of changes have affected the US economy in recent years. In each case, decide whether the change would cause:

i) a decrease in AD

ii) an increase in AD

iii) a decrease in AS

iv) an increase in AS.

The changes are:

a) a fall in house prices in 2007

b) a fall in the size of the labour force in 2007

c) a rise in the interest rate in 2006

d) a rise in labour productivity in 2006

e) a loss of lives and widespread damage to buildings caused by hurricanes Katrina, Rita and Wilma in 2005

f) a fall in the value of the dollar in 2005.

Macroeconomic equilibrium

Macroeconomic equilibrium occurs when aggregate demand and aggregate supply are equal, as shown in Figure 4.6. When aggregate demand and aggregate supply are equal, there is no reason for the economy's output and price level to change. Total domestic output and the price level will be stable.

If, however, aggregate demand was higher than aggregate supply, there would be a shortage of goods and services. Firms would find their stocks declining. The excess aggregate demand would encourage them to expand their output. The surplus AD may also push up the price level, depending on the level of capacity.

Aggregate supply exceeding aggregate demand would also lead to pressures that would move the economy back to equilibrium. This time, the existence of unsold goods and services would cause aggregate supply to contract. The price level may fall but again this would depend on the level of capacity. In practice, prices can be 'sticky', that is, inflexible downwards, largely because workers resist cuts in their wages.

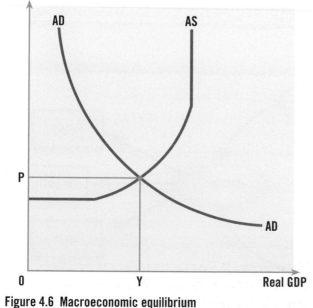

Figure 4.6 Macroeconomic equilibrium

Anything that causes aggregate demand or aggregate supply conditions to change will move the economy to a new macroeconomic position.

learning tip

Always remember to use macro labels on AD/AS diagrams i.e. AD not D, AS not S, price level and not price, real GDP and not quantity, and Y not Q.

ACTIVITY ····

Figure 4.7 shows the AD and AS conditions of an economy.

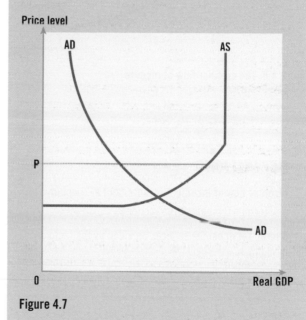

Figure 4.7

a) Why is the economy not in macroeconomic equilibrium?

b) Explain what will happen to the price level and real GDP in the future.

The circular flow of income

The circular flow of income is a model that seeks to explain how the economy works and how changes in AD occur. In the simplified version shown in Figure 4.8 (see over), there are two sectors, households and firms. Between these two sectors are the flows: income, products and **factor services**. Households

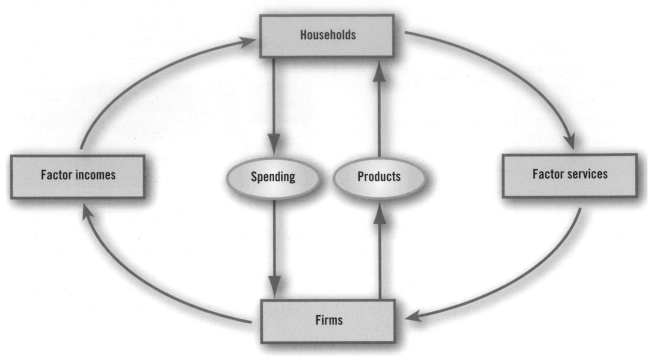

Figure 4.8 The circular flow of income

provide factor services and in return receive incomes. They use these incomes to buy products produced by firms.

In practice, not all the income that is earned is spent. There are also additional forms of spending that do not arise from the circular flow. Income that is not spent on domestic output is said to leak out of the circular flow. There are three **leakages** (or withdrawals). These are taxes (T), saving (S) and spending on imports (M). Leakages reduce aggregate

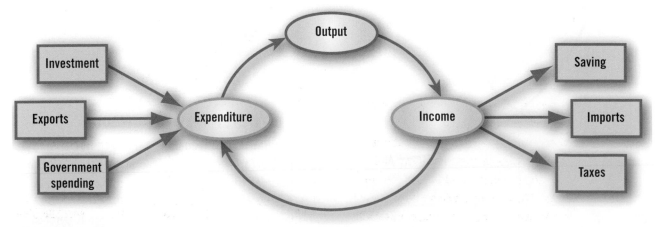

Figure 4.9 Injections and leakages

demand. In contrast, **injections** increase aggregate demand, injecting extra spending into the economy. Investment (I), government spending (G) and exports (X) are all injections. These are additional forms of spending, arising from outside the circular flow. Figure 4.9 shows another version of the circular flow, incorporating injections and leakages.

When the value of injections equals the value of leakages, output will not be changing and there will be macroeconomic equilibrium.

The multiplier effect

When injections exceed leakages, aggregate demand will increase. The rise in AD will have a greater final effect on the economy. This **multiplier effect** occurs because when people spend money, that expenditure becomes the income of those who sell them the products. They, in turn, will spend some of the money they receive. So there is knock-on effect, with AD rising by more than the initial amount. For

example, the government may increase its spending on education, raising the wages of teachers. The teachers are likely to spend more on, for instance, entertainment, housing and holidays. Those selling these products will receive more income. Some of the income will be spent and some will leak out of the circular flow. Spending will continue to rise until leakages match the initial injection.

Figure 4.10 shows the initial increase in AD of £5 billion from a rise in government spending, and the final increase in AD of £15 billion. The existence of the multiplier effect means that a government has to recognise that any change in government spending or taxes will have a knock-on effect on the economy. So that, for instance, if the government wants to raise real GDP by £10 billion and the multiplier has been estimated at 2, it would have to raise its spending by £5 billion.

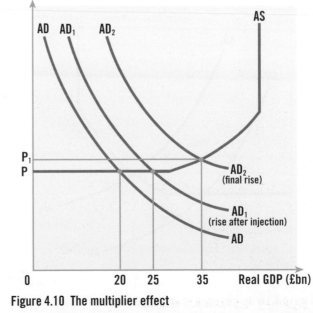

Figure 4.10 The multiplier effect

ACTIVITY ⋯⦂

a) If the multiplier is 2½ and the government wants to raise real GDP by £150 billion, how much would it have to raise its spending by?

b) If export revenue falls by £8 billion and as a result real GDP declines by £12 billion, what is the size of the multiplier?

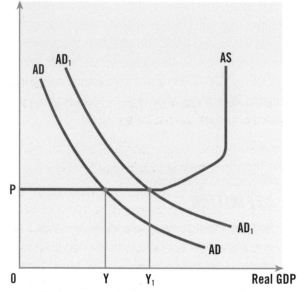

Price level

Figure 4.11 An increase in aggregate demand raising the country's output but leaving the price level unchanged

Changes in aggregate demand

The three key influences on the effect of a change in AD on the output of an economy, unemployment and inflation are: the size of the initial change, the size of the multiplier and the original level of economic activity.

A large change in AD with a large multiplier effect will, not unsurprisingly, have a much larger impact on the economy than a small change in AD with a small multiplier effect.

If the economy is initially operating with considerable spare capacity, an increase in AD is likely to raise the output of the economy, reduce unemployment and leave the price level unchanged. Figure 4.11 shows that the rise in AD causes output to increase from Y to Y1 and leaves the price level unchanged at P.

A rise in AD may increase both output and the price level. This outcome will occur if either the economy moves from a position of significant spare capacity to one where there are shortages of resources, or it moves from one where shortages are already being experienced to one where there are even greater shortages. Figure 4.12 illustrates these possibilities, with the increase in AD raising real GDP from Y to Y_1 and causing the price level to rise from P to P_1.

Finally, if the economy is already operating at the full employment level, with no spare capacity, an increase in AD will be purely inflationary. Figure 4.13

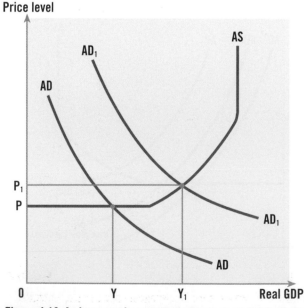

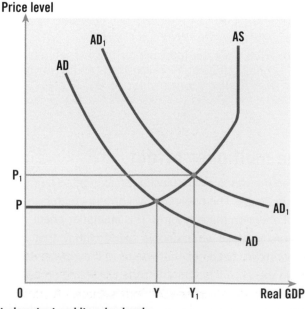

Figure 4.12 An increase in aggregate demand raising both the country's output and its price level

Price level

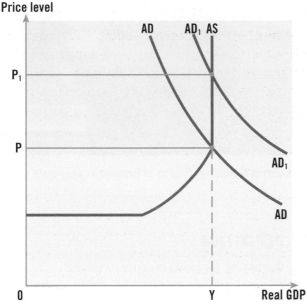

Figure 4.13 An increase in aggregate demand raising the price level but having no effect on the country's output

shows an increase in AD pushing up the price level from *P* to *P₁* but leaving the output of the economy unchanged at *Y*.

Price level

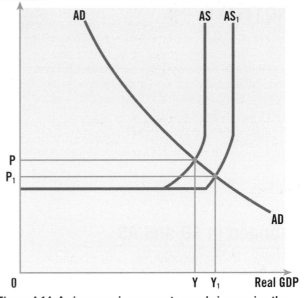

Figure 4.14 An increase in aggregate supply increasing the country's output and lowering the price level

raise the output of the economy and lower the price level. This outcome is shown in Figure 4.14.

There is the possibility, however, that an increase in AS may have *no* impact on the economy. This situation would occur if the economy was initially operating at a low level of output with a high level of unemployed resources. In this case, the increase in AS will increase potential output but not actual output and will leave the price level unchanged as shown in Figure 4.15.

Price level

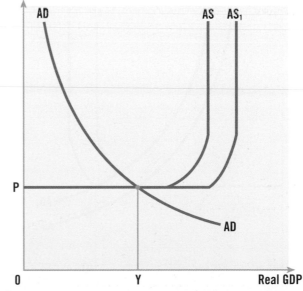

Figure 4.15 An increase in aggregate supply raising potential output but having no effect on the country's output or price level

ACTIVITY ⋯⋗

A number of economic changes have occurred in recent years in Mexico. In 2006, the rate of interest fell, which stimulated more households to take out mortgages. The boom in house construction caused a number of firms, including Cemex, Mexico's largest cement company, to expand. The Mexican government in 2004 and 2005 raised its spending on infrastructure, education and health. It was anxious to improve the performance of the economy, in part to discourage its young people leaving to live and work in the USA. In 2007, the Mexican government raised taxes in order to reduce inflation.

From the passage above, identify and explain:

a) one cause of an increase in AD.

b) two causes of a decrease in AD.

Changes in aggregate supply

As with changes in AD, the effects of changes in AS will depend on the size of the change and the initial level of economic activity. An increase in AS occurring when the economy is at, or close to, full capacity will

ACTIVITY ····⦂

In 2007, Chinese firms were expanding and new businesses were being set up. Some economists expressed concern that Chinese productive capacity was growing much more rapidly than demand for Chinese products.

a) Draw an AD/AS diagram to illustrate the state of the Chinese economy in 2007.

b) Explain two factors that would encourage firms to expand.

Advances in technology lead to an increase in aggregate supply

Changes in AD and AS

Over time, in most economies, both AD and AS increase. In most years, consumption and investment increase. AS rises mainly due to advances in technology and improved education.

If increases in AS can match increases in AD, the economy can enjoy higher output without encountering inflationary pressures. Figure 4.16 shows the economy's output rising to Y_1 but the price level staying at P.

If, however, AD grows more rapidly than the growth in productive capacity, inflation will occur. Figure 4.17 shows an economy **overheating**. It is experiencing higher output, but this rise is coming at the cost

DEFINITION

Overheating: the growth in aggregate demand outstripping the growth in aggregate supply, resulting in inflation.

of inflation and will not be sustainable unless AS increases at a more rapid rate.

Some changes can affect both AD and AS. A decision by firms to spend more on capital goods will increase both total spending and productive capacity. Immigration of people of working age and government spending on training that raises workers' productivity will also shift both curves.

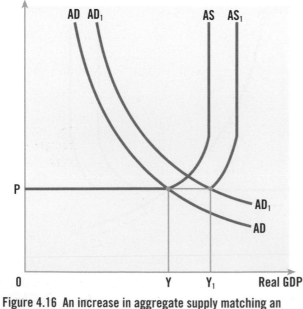

Figure 4.16 An increase in aggregate supply matching an increase in aggregate demand

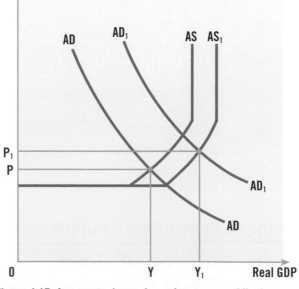

Figure 4.17 Aggregate demand growing more rapidly than aggregate supply

learning tip

In analysing the effects of changes in AD and/or changes in AS on a country's economy, consider the impact on real GDP, the price level and output.

ECONOMICS IN CONTEXT

THE BRICS

The Brics is a term used to cover four economies that are emerging to become major producers. These are Brazil, Russia, India and China. All three have witnessed significant increases in their aggregate output, pushing them up the league table of countries in terms of the size of their economies.

Table: World rankings of countries based on real GDP in 2006

1	USA	8	Spain
2	Japan	9	Canada
3	Germany	10	India
4	China	11	Brazil
5	UK	12	South Korea
6	France	13	Mexico
7	Italy	14	Russia

Both aggregate demand and aggregate supply have been increasing in these countries. One reason for this is that the Brics continue to experience increasing investment. Higher investment increases both demand for capital goods and the country's productive capacity.

Output gap

An **output gap** is said to exist when an economy is not producing at full capacity. A negative output gap

DEFINITION

Output gap: the difference between an economy's actual and potential real GDP.

ACTIVITY ····⫶·

At the start of 2007, Algeria had an unemployment rate of 17 per cent. During 2007 the Algerian government increased its spending to improve the country's roads and railways.

a) Using an AD/AS diagram in both cases:

  i) illustrate Algeria's macroeconomic position at the start of 2007

  ii) analyse the impact of the increase in government spending.

b) Discuss one other cause of a change in a country's real GDP.

occurs when the economy's actual output is below its potential output. Figure 4.18 illustrates an economy operating with unemployed resources and an output gap of *ab*.

A positive output gap arises when an economy's actual output is above that of its potential output. This might seem to be impossible and indeed in the long run an economy cannot produce more than its productive capacity allows. For a short time, however, an economy may be able to produce more if workers work overtime, some people who are not usually in the labour force enter it, and machinery is used flat

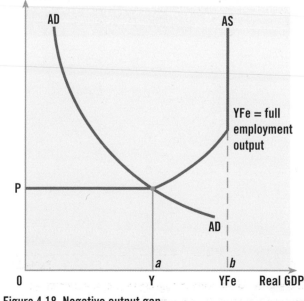

Figure 4.18 Negative output gap

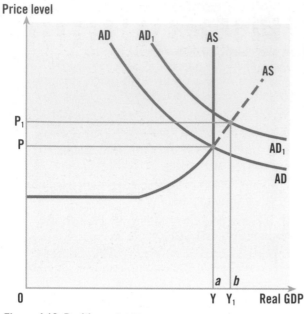

Figure 4.19 Positive output gap

out. It will not be possible to sustain this output in the long run, unless AS increases. Figure 4.19 shows an increase in AD stimulating a rise in AS beyond potential output and the price level increasing from P to P_1. Indeed, countries with positive output gaps usually experience inflation.

> *learning tip*
> For ease and speed, it is acceptable to draw AD curves as straight lines. This is the approach we have taken in the next two chapters.

> *learning tip*
> AD/AS analysis is an important tool in understanding and evaluating changes in the economy. Practise using it by assessing macroeconomic changes such as reported in the newspapers, economic magazines and on the BBC News and other websites. For the BBC News website, go to www.heinemann.co.uk/hotlinks, insert the express code 2209P and click on 'BBC News'.

5 Government economic policy objectives and indicators of national economic performance

On completion of this chapter you should be able to:

- define economic growth, unemployment, inflation, the balance of payments, income distribution and economic stability
- show an awareness of trends in economic growth, in unemployment, inflation and the current account of the balance of payments
- understand the objectives of government policy in terms of economic growth, employment, balance of payments, economic stability and income distribution
- define GDP and real GDP
- explain how economic growth, unemployment and inflation are measured in the UK and discuss the difficulties of measuring them
- outline the structure of the current account of the balance of payments account of the UK economy
- explain the causes of economic growth, unemployment, inflation, and a deficit or surplus on the current account of the balance of payments, and discuss their consequences
- outline how exchange rates are determined by the demand and supply of currencies
- recognise that a fall in the exchange rate will lower export prices and raise both import prices and aggregate demand (and vice versa)
- explain how changes in the exchange rate may affect the macroeconomy.

Introduction

The previous chapter examined how changes in aggregate demand and aggregate supply affect the level of output in an economy, the price level and unemployment in an economy. This chapter examines in more detail macroeconomic performance and government macroeconomic policy objectives.

Key performance indicators

In assessing how well an economy is performing, there are certain indicators that economists examine.

One of the most significant of these is **economic growth**. Short-run, or actual, economic growth is said to occur when an economy increases its output. For an economy to continue to increase its output, its productive potential must increase. If it does not, the economy will hit a supply constraint, unable to produce any more with its given quantity and quality of resources (factors of production). Long-run, or potential, economic growth, takes place when the productive capacity of the economy increases.

When a country's output increases, **unemployment** usually falls. An economy is thought to be doing well if its unemployment is low. Unemployment exists when people who are willing and able to work are without jobs. Some people aged between 16 and 65 are not in the **labour force** because, for example, they are homemakers, disabled or have retired early. These people are said to be **economically inactive** and are not regarded as unemployed.

Another indicator of economic performance is inflation. This is a sustained rise in the price level. A country may also experience **deflation** which is a sustained fall in the price level, although this is less common.

A country's external performance can be assessed by examining its **balance of payments**. This is a record of a country's economic transactions with the rest of the world. It contains a fascinating collection of information and enables us to see, for example, which products the country buys and sells, which countries it trades with, and which countries it is investing in and receiving investment from.

Economists may also examine how evenly income is distributed. If a government is concerned that income is too unevenly distributed, it may decide to redistribute some income from rich households to poor households. This would involve taxing the rich and providing state benefits for the poor.

Increasingly in recent years, governments have been concerned to promote economic stability. They try to prevent significant fluctuations in output, employment and inflation. This is because such fluctuations can create uncertainty and make it difficult for households, firms and the government to plan ahead. These effects can, in turn, discourage workers from improving their skills, firms from investing and the government from undertaking major reforms. So, reducing economic fluctuations should increase an economy's long term growth potential.

DEFINITIONS

Economic growth: in the short run, an increase in real GDP, and in the long run, an increase in productive capacity, that is, in the maximum output that the economy can produce.

Unemployment: a situation where people are out of work but are willing and able to work.

Labour force: the people who are employed and unemployed, that is, those who are economically active.

Economically inactive: people of working age who are neither employed nor unemployed.

Deflation: a sustained fall in the general price level.

Balance of payments: a record of money flows coming in and going out of a country.

learning tip In assessing how well an economy is performing, it is useful to examine a range of information about the economy over a period of time, and to compare its performance with other economies. This comparison is more valid if the economies are using similar measures of inflation and unemployment.

ACTIVITY ····

In 2007, India had 36 dollar billionaires and 100,000 dollar millionaires. Its economy has been growing at an annual average of 8 per cent in recent years. Despite its economic boom, a significant proportion of its population still live in poverty. Asia's biggest slum, called Dharawi, which is home to more than a million people, is located in Mumbai (also known as Bombay).

a) What evidence is there here that income is unevenly distributed in India?

b) Identify a government objective referred to in the passage.

c) Explain how achieving one other government objective could reduce poverty.

Current trends

Between 1992 and 2007, the UK experienced the longest period of continuous economic growth on record. This economic growth has been relatively stable and it is predicted that the UK economy will continue to grow, setting new records.

This stable economic growth has been combined with low unemployment and low and stable inflation. This has led some economists to suggest that the shape of the UK's aggregate supply curve may have changed, becoming more **elastic** up to the full capacity level. Figure 5.1 shows that aggregate supply can be close to the full employment level without causing inflation.

The UK has been enjoying an unemployment rate lower than most other European Union (EU) countries. Aggregate demand has been relatively high in the UK. The country also has a more flexible

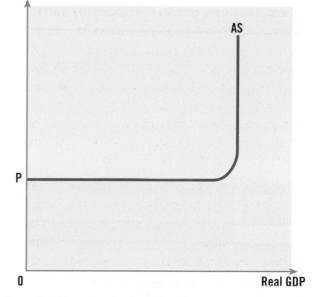

Figure 5.1 Changing shape of the AS curve

labour market. It is easier for firms to 'hire and fire' workers in the UK than it is in most other EU countries. This means that firms are more willing to recruit new workers when demand is increasing.

There are thought to be a number of reasons why the **inflation rate** has fallen and stayed relatively low. These include a reduction in inflationary expectations resulting from the success of the government's monetary policy, a high value of the pound and increased global competition putting pressure on firms to keep their costs and prices low. Advances in technology and the immigration of workers from the enlarged EU have also helped to increase aggregate supply (AS) in line with increases in aggregate demand (AD).

The UK has been experiencing a current account deficit, caused largely by a deficit in trade in goods. Trade in services has been doing well and is expected to continue to do so. As a number of other

DEFINITION

Elastic: responsive to a change in market conditions.

Inflation rate: the percentage increase in the price level over a period of time.

economies, including China and India, continue to grow, the UK is likely to be able to sell more financial, business, educational and other services.

The UK economy does, however, face a number of challenges. UK economic performance would be improved by a better transport infrastructure, a higher economic activity rate, better education, higher productivity, more spending on research and development and more innovation.

> **learning tip**
> Be careful when examining economic growth and inflation rates. For instance, a country's economic growth rate may be 3 per cent in 2008 and 2 per cent in 2009. This does not mean that output fell in 2009. It means that output rose but rose at a slower rate than in 2008. Similarly a fall in the inflation rate from, for example, 6 per cent to 4 per cent occurs when the price level rises more slowly – the price level does not fall.

ACTIVITY ····⫶

In 2007, the US housing market ran into difficulties. American banks had lent to low-income families, some of whom were unable to keep up with their mortgage repayments. These defaults on payments led to a slowdown in activity in the housing market and a greater reluctance of banks to lend. Both these effects reduced aggregate demand and led economists to predict a reversal in the generally good economic performance that the US had been enjoying.

a) Explain why a 'slowdown in activity in the housing market and a greater reluctance of banks to lend' reduced aggregate demand.

b) Describe what is meant by a 'good economic performance'.

Objectives of government economic policy

Governments have always had general policy objectives for the macroeconomy but in recent years many have set more specific targets.

ECONOMIC GROWTH

Governments want to achieve economic growth because of the benefits it brings, including increasing material living standards. Governments now also stress the importance of achieving steady and sustainable economic growth. Steady economic growth avoids harmful fluctuations in economic activity.

Sustainable economic growth is growth which can continue over time. It can be taken to mean both economic growth that can be maintained year after year and economic growth that can be enjoyed generation after generation. The first type of sustainable economic growth is achieved if increases in aggregate supply match increases in aggregate demand. Governments talk in terms of trying to achieve actual economic growth matching **trend growth**. Such economic growth should avoid the costs which arise from a negative output gap (with unemployment) and a positive output gap (with inflation).

DEFINITIONS

Sustainable economic growth: economic growth that can continue over time and does not endanger future generations' ability to expand productive capacity.

Trend growth: the expected increase in potential output over time. It is a measure of how fast the economy can grow without generating inflation.

Wind farms are a possible source of sustainable economic growth

To sustain economic growth from one generation to another, the methods used to raise productive potential and output must not endanger future generations' ability to grow. This means avoiding depleting non-renewable resources and damaging the environment. Most governments are now seeking to reduce pollution and are searching for cleaner sources of energy; some are trying to conserve non-renewable resources.

EMPLOYMENT AND UNEMPLOYMENT

Another government policy objective is high employment and low unemployment. Some governments state that their objective is **full employment**. This term is somewhat misleading as it does not mean zero unemployment. It is often taken to be 3 per cent unemployment. Even during periods of high economic activity, some people will be out of work. They will have left one job and be seeking a new job (people in-between jobs).

DEFINITION

Full employment: a situation where those wanting and able to work can find employment at the going wage rate.

As well as trying to ensure that those who are able and willing to work have jobs, governments are increasingly trying to encourage more people of working age to enter the labour force. Having a higher proportion of economically active people should raise the productive potential of the economy and reduce the cost of state benefits.

INFLATION

A third macroeconomic policy objective is low and stable inflation. This can also be referred to as price stability, although it does not actually mean a zero inflation rate with the price level remaining unchanged. What price stability does mean is a low and consistent rate of inflation. The UK government, for instance, has set the Bank of England the target

of achieving a 2 per cent inflation rate. The reason governments do not aim for zero inflation is because measures of inflation tend to overstate price rises and because a low level of inflation can bring advantages. For example, it may enable firms to reduce their costs by not raising wages in line with inflation rather than by making some workers redundant.

BALANCE OF PAYMENTS

In the past, governments placed considerable emphasis on achieving a satisfactory balance of payments position, particularly with respect to trade in goods and services. Nowadays, a government may not be too concerned in the short term if import expenditure exceeds export revenue, if the deficit is likely to be self-correcting. This will be the case, for example, if a deficit is arising from the import of raw materials that will be converted into finished products, some of which can be exported. They may also not be too concerned if a **current account deficit** is offset by a net inflow of direct and portfolio investment. In the longer term, however, a government is still likely to want to see an increase in the international competitiveness of its producers, in order to keep aggregate demand and output high in the economy.

DEFINITION

Current account deficit: when more money is leaving the country than entering it, as result of sales of its exports, income and current transfers from abroad being less than imports and income and current transfers going abroad.

ECONOMIC STABILITY

While a satisfactory balance of payments position has been somewhat downgraded as an objective, economic stability has become more significant as an objective. As already indicated, governments want to avoid significant fluctuations in the economy. An economy which experiences periods of 'boom and bust', with rapid, unstable increases in aggregate demand and then periods of falling aggregate demand, are likely to suffer from periods of inflation and unemployment and will underperform in terms of economic growth.

INCOME REDISTRIBUTION

At any particular time, a government may also seek to redistribute income. This may be done in order to ensure everyone has access to basic necessities and/or to correct what is seen as an inequitable distribution of income. In transferring some income from the rich to the poor, it will, however, be keen not to damage incentives. It will not want to tax workers and firms too much so that work and enterprise are discouraged. It will also not want to make state benefits so generous nor so easy to obtain that living off benefits is made more attractive than working.

> **learning tip**
>
> Try to keep up to date with the news. Read quality newspapers, watch television news, listen to the news on the radio and/or access news online. This will help you evaluate whether the government is achieving its objectives and if it is placing more emphasis on a particular objective.

ACTIVITY ····⫶

The Brazilian government's main objective in recent years has been to achieve a low and stable inflation rate. In the 1980s, the country experienced **hyperinflation**. In the 1990s inflation was lower but still in double figures. Between 2003 and 2007 the inflation rate fell from 17 per cent to 3.7 per cent. The fall in inflation and its greater stability have stimulated an increase in investment.

a) What is meant by a 'low and stable inflation rate'?

b) Identify two other objectives of government policy.

c) Explain the likely effect of an increase in investment on one of these objectives.

> **DEFINITION**
>
> **Hyperinflation:** an inflation rate above 50 per cent.

GDP and real GDP

We have already seen that changes in aggregate demand and aggregate supply affect a country's output, as measured by real GDP.

Economists first calculate what is called money or **nominal GDP**. This is output measured in terms of the prices in the year in question. They then convert nominal into real GDP (GDP adjusted for inflation). It is important to make use of real GDP figures when assessing an economy's output performance. This is because nominal GDP figures can be distorted by inflation. For example, the GDP of a country measured in the prices in the year in question (current prices) may rise from, for example, £800 billion in 2008 to £880 billion in 2009. This would appear to suggest that output has risen by:

£80 billion/£800 billion x 100% = 10%

Nominal GDP has risen by 10 per cent. But at least part of this increase may be due to a rise in the price level. So, to calculate the rise in the volume of output, the effects of changes in the price level are taken out by multiplying GDP by the base year index divided by the current year price index.

$$\frac{\text{GDP figure x base year price index}}{\text{current year price index}}$$

So, if the price index in 2008 was 100 and 104 in 2009, real GDP was:

$$\frac{\text{£880 billion x 100}}{104} = \text{£846.15 billion}$$

In real terms, GDP has risen by £46.15 billion /£800 billion x 100% = 5.77 per cent.

> **DEFINITION**
>
> **Nominal GDP:** output measured in current prices and so not adjusted for inflation.

ACTIVITY ⋯⟩

Between 2000 and 2006 the UK's GDP measured in current prices increased from £1,003,297m to £1,299,622m. Over this period the price index rose from 100 to 116.

a) Calculate the percentage increase in nominal GDP.

b) Calculate the real GDP for 2006.

c) Calculate the percentage increase in real GDP.

Measuring economic growth

Economic growth is usually measured by the annual percentage change in real GDP. As just mentioned, this is the change in the country's output.

The circular flow of income (see page 95) shows that a country's output is equal to the country's income and its expenditure. So, real GDP can be calculated by totalling up the output, income or expenditure of the country and economic growth can be calculated by changes in any of these. In each case, care has to be taken. When using the output method, it is important to avoid double counting, that is, counting the same output twice. For instance, it is important not to count the output of raw materials and then include them again in the value of finished products. In the income method, only incomes that have been earned in return for providing goods and services are included. Transfer payments are not. So, for instance, job seeker's allowance and pensions are not included. With the expenditure method, it is important to remember to include exports (as they are made by producers in the country) and to exclude imports (as they are made by producers in other countries).

PRODUCTION AND PRODUCTIVITY

Production is what is produced. So, when real GDP increases, it means that output has risen. **Labour productivity**, in contrast, is output per worker hour. Changes in productivity are another factor that can be examined to assess a country's economic performance. If productivity rises by more than wages, then labour costs will fall and a country can become more price competitive.

DEFINITION

Labour productivity: output per worker hour.

It is possible for production and productivity to move in opposite directions. When an economy is expanding, production will rise. If less skilled workers have to be recruited to make the extra output, productivity may fall. This may indicate that, while an economy may appear to be doing well, its ability to sustain rises in output may be in doubt.

ACTIVITY ⋯⟩

Germany's economic growth rate has fluctuated in recent years (see Figure 5.2). In contrast, its productivity growth has remained strong.

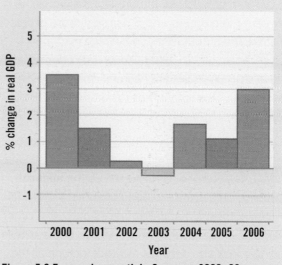

Figure 5.2 Economic growth in Germany 2000–06

a) In which year was output lowest?

b) Apart from output, identify another way of measuring GDP.

c) What is meant by 'productivity growth'?

DIFFICULTIES IN INTERPRETING CHANGES IN REAL GDP

On the surface, an increase in real GDP suggests that living standards are improving, as more goods and services are being produced. This may, however, not always be the case.

Some street traders are part of the informal economy

One problem of interpretation that economists can eliminate is that a rise in output may be exceeded by a rise in population. If there is, for example, 3 per cent more output and 5 per cent more people to share the output, then on average each person will be worse off. So, what economists often assess is real GDP per head (sometimes called real GDP per capita). This is found by dividing real GDP by population.

In comparing a country's real GDP over time and between countries, other problems can occur. One is the existence of what is known as the **informal economy**. This is unrecorded economic activity. Its existence means that the country's output is higher than official real GDP figures suggest. Some people selling goods and services may not include all the money they have earned on tax returns and those engaged in illegal activities will not declare any income they earn in such pursuits.

DEFINITION

Informal economy: economic activity that is not recorded or registered with the authorities in order to avoid paying tax or complying with regulations, or because the activity is illegal.

In the UK, building, electrical installation and repairs, car repairs and plumbing are important areas of the informal economy.

The existence of an informal economy has a number of consequences. One is that it distorts a range of economic data. The rate of inflation in the informal economy is usually much lower than that in the rest of the economy. This means that official measures overstate inflation. The work undertaken in the informal economy also means that official data, as well as understating real GDP, also understates employment.

Tax revenue is lower than would be possible if all economic activity were taxed. This can have consequences for tax rates and government spending. An informal economy can also result in lower productivity. Firms in the informal economy tend to stay small to avoid attention from the authorities. This limits their ability to use advanced technology and take advantage of **economies of scale**.

DEFINITION

Economy of scale: the advantage of producing on large scale, in the form of lower long-run average cost.

In deciding how the level of, and changes in, real GDP affect people's living standards, it is important to consider the composition of real GDP. If more is produced but the extra output consists of capital goods, people will not immediately feel better off, although they will be in the long run.

Output may also rise because of an increase in what economists call 'regrettables'. If, for example, the rise in real GDP has been accounted for by increasing the police force to match rising crime, people may actually feel worse off.

A rise in real GDP may not benefit many of the population if income is very unevenly distributed, or if they are working longer hours, or working under worse conditions. In addition, the official figures do not include positive and negative externalities. So, for example, if pollution rises, real GDP does not fall, even though people will experience a lower quality of life.

Recent work by Professor Richard Layard of the London School of Economics has found two reasons to explain why people do not seem to get happier as they get richer. One is that people quickly get used to an improvement in their living standards. For example, some years ago, a home computer was regarded as a luxury. Now it is increasingly becoming a necessity.

The second reason is that people's happiness appears to be closely related to their income relative to others rather than to their absolute income. For instance, a study asked Harvard University students whether they would prefer $50,000 a year while other people got half that income or $100,000 a year while others earned twice that income. Most chose the first option.

On a macro level, national surveys of happiness have found that it has hardly changed at all over the last fifty years. The rich are generally happier than the poor but rich countries do not seem to get happier as they get richer.

MEASURING UNEMPLOYMENT

Economists measure the number of people who are unemployed and from this find the **unemployment rate**. This is the percentage who are jobless, available to work and are actively seeking employment. It is calculated as:

$$\frac{\text{the unemployed} \times 100\%}{\text{labour force}}$$

In practice, it can be difficult to decide who is unemployed.

DEFINITION

Unemployment rate: the percentage of the labour force who are out of work.

In the UK there are two main measures used. The government's preferred measure is what is known as the **Labour Force Survey (LFS)**. This is based on the International Labour Organisation's definition of unemployment and, as its name suggests, uses a survey of the labour force to collect the information. The **International Labour Organisation (ILO)**, which is

ACTIVITY ···⋗

Mexico has a huge informal economy of unregistered businesses. The World Bank estimated in 2006 that the informal economy accounts for slightly more than half of total employment in Mexico.

It has been calculated that the size of the informal economy in Mexico has not changed over the last 13 years. Over this period, Mexico has experienced an average annual economic growth rate of 3 per cent.

Productivity is low in this part of the economy. The skills of those working in the informal economy tend to be low, with many of the workers lacking basic skills. The firms operating in this sector also find it difficult to expand.

The Mexican government is currently seeking to reduce the size of its informal economy by cutting down on the rules and regulations that

firms have to comply with and by reducing the tax firms have to pay.

a) Does Mexico's real GDP figure reflect the true level of output in the country? Explain your answer.

b) Why is productivity low in Mexico's informal economy?

c) Explain:

   i) how the measures that the Mexican government is using may transfer activity from the informal economy to the formal (recorded) economy.

   ii) how one other policy measure could achieve the same objective.

d) Analyse the possible effect on Mexico's economic growth rate of moving activity from the informal to the formal economy.

an agency of the United Nations, defines someone as unemployed if they are:

> 'out of work, want a job, have actively sought work in the last four weeks and are available to start work in the next two weeks or are out of work, have found a job and are waiting to start it in the next two weeks.'

To find out how many people are unemployed according to the ILO definition, the Office for National Statistics (ONS) carries out the LFS. This is a survey of 60,000 households that collects a range of information on the labour force, including type of employment, earnings and educational qualifications of the labour force, as well as unemployment. The ONS publishes in the middle of each month the number of people unemployed on the LFS measure. This is an average for the latest three month period.

At the same time it publishes unemployment figures based on the **claimant count**. This is a monthly count of those claiming unemployment-related benefits. Most are claiming job seeker's allowance (JSA). A few do not claim JSA but sign on at Job Centre Plus local

offices to claim national insurance credits in order to maintain pension eligibility. Claimants 'must declare that they are out of work, capable of, available for and actively seeking work in the week in which their claim is made'.

learning tip Remember, the labour force includes both the employed and the unemployed.

DIFFICULTIES OF MEASURING UNEMPLOYMENT

There is no perfect measure of unemployment. Both the LFS measure and the claimant count measure have their advantages and disadvantages.

The LFS measure is thought to capture more of those who are unemployed. Some people can be actively seeking work but not be entitled to claim unemployment-related benefits. Such people include those whose partner is working or claiming benefits, and young people who are under 18 and are looking for work. These people would not appear in the claimant count but would appear in the LFS measure.

The LFS measure is also widely used by the Statistical Office of the European Union and by the Organisation for Economic Co-operation and Development (OECD) and most countries. This widespread international use is very suitable for international comparisons. The LFS also provides a range of information, including changes in economic activity. It is, however, more expensive to collect than the claimant count. There is also a risk that it may be subject to sampling errors.

The claimant count measure is relatively cheap, as the data is a by-product of administrative records of people claiming benefits. It is also relatively quick to compile and is available earlier than the LFS-based unemployment data.

Some people claiming benefits may not be actively seeking work – they may be claiming benefits on false pretences. These fraudsters, though, are thought to be outnumbered by those genuinely seeking work who are either not entitled to benefits or choose not to claim them.

Another disadvantage of the claimant count is that it is not suitable for international comparisons. This is because the categories of people entitled to benefits varies over time and between countries.

ACTIVITY ····⦂

UK unemployment rate

Year	LFS measure (%)	Claimant count measure (%)
2000	5.5	3.6
2001	5.0	3.2
2002	5.2	3.1
2003	4.9	3.0
2004	4.8	2.7
2005	4.8	2.7
2006	5.5	3.0

a) Compare the trend in unemployment as measured by the LFS and by the claimant count.

b) Explain why the claimant count produces a lower percentage than the LFS measure.

MEASURING INFLATION

There are a number of measures of inflation. The main measure of inflation is the **consumer prices index** (CPI). It forms the basis for the inflation target that the government requires the Bank of England's Monetary Policy Committee to achieve. It is also the main measure used in the rest of the European Union, where it is often referred to as the harmonised index of consumer prices (HICP), and in most other countries in the world. The CPI and most other measures of inflation are weighted price indices.

DEFINITION

Consumer prices index: a measure of changes in the price of a representative basket of consumer goods and services. Differs from the retail prices index (RPI) in methodology and coverage.

There are various stages in constructing a weighted price index. The first stage is to select a base year. This should be a relatively standard year in which nothing unusual happened. The variable being measured is given a value of 100 in the base year and other years are compared to it. In the UK, statisticians employed by the ONS seek to find out what people spend their money on by carrying out the Family Expenditure Survey. This involves sampling more than 6,000 households, which are asked to keep a record of their expenditure.

From the information gathered, the statisticians decide which items to include in the price index. In effect a 'shopping basket' is created. This is a representative sample of about 650 goods and services. These products have weights attached to them. The weights reflect the proportion spent on the different items. If it is found, for instance, that 10 per cent of people's expenditure goes on food, this will be given a weighting of 10/100 or 1/10.

Table 5.1 gives the categories of products in the UK's CPI and their weights.

Table 5.1 The categories of products and their weighting in the UK's CPI in 2007

Category of item of expenditure	Weight
Food and non-alcoholic beverages	103
Alcoholic beverages and tobacco	43
Clothing and footwear	62
Housing, water, electricity, gas and other fuels	115
Furniture, household equipment and maintenance	68
Health	24
Transport	152
Communication	24
Recreation and culture	153
Education	18
Restaurant and hotels	138
Miscellaneous goods and services	100
Total weighting	1,000

Expenditure weights are held constant for a year. Then the items in the shopping basket and their weights are reviewed and changed in the light of changes in household spending patterns.

After assigning weights to the items in the different categories, the next stage is to find out how the items have changed in price. Officials visit a range of outlets throughout the country and gather approximately 120,000 price quotations for their 650 different items. They do this each month. Finally, the weights are multiplied by the new price index for each category in order to find the change in the price level. For instance, households may spend £10 on food, £30 on housing and household goods, £20 on clothing and footwear, £15 on transport and £25 on entertainment. This would give a total expenditure of £100. Food may have fallen in price by 2 per cent, housing and household goods may have risen in price by 10 per cent, clothing may have increased by 4 per cent, transport by 4 per cent and entertainment by 8 per cent.

Table 5.2 shows how this information would be used to calculate a weighted price *index.*

In this example the price level has risen by 6.35 per cent.

Another way of finding the percentage change in the price level is to work out the weighted price change for each category. This is shown in Table 5.3, using the same information as in Table 5.2.

> **learning tip**
>
> Remember, index numbers are very useful, as they enable us to see percentage changes at a glance. To convert figures into index numbers, the calculation is:
>
> $$\frac{\text{Actual figure} \times 100}{\text{Base year figure}}$$

Table 5.2 Weighted price index

Category	Weight	Price index	Weighted price index
Food	1/10	x 98	= 9.8
Housing and household goods	3/10	x 110	= 33.0
Clothing and footwear	1/5	x 104	= 20.8
Transport	3/20	x 105	= 15.75
Entertainment	1/4	x 108	= 27.0
Total			106.35

Table 5.3 Weighted price change

Category	Weight	Price change (%)	Weighted price change (%)
Food	1/10	x –2	= –0.2
Housing and household goods	3/10	x 10	= 3.0
Clothing and footwear	1/5	x 4	= 0.8
Transport	3/20	x 5	= 0.75
Entertainment	1/4	x 8	= 2.0
Total			6.35

ACTIVITY ⋯⋮

In January 2007, the ONS announced changes to the basket of goods and services to apply from February 2007 to January 2008. DVD recorders, satellite navigation (satnav) systems, digital (DAB) radios, ringtones and digital photograph processing were included for the first time. In contrast, blank VHS tapes and video cassette recorders were removed from the basket.

In terms of food items, changes in consumption patterns led to broccoli and olive oil replacing Brussels sprouts and vegetable oil in the new basket. It was also decided to collect changes in the price of strawberries every month.

a) What is the 'basket' referred to here?

b) What would have caused the ONS to replace video cassette recorders with DVD recorders?

c) What is suggested here about the availability of strawberries throughout the year in the UK?

THE CPI AND OTHER MEASURES OF INFLATION

Another measure of inflation used in the UK is the **retail prices index (RPI)**. This measure is the one used for adjusting pensions and other benefits to take account of changes in inflation and is frequently used in wage negotiations. It is the one which has been used for the longest time in the UK and data go back to June 1947. In contrast, the official CPI series started in 1996, although estimates for earlier periods are available back to 1988.

The CPI and RPI are calculated using the same underlying price data. They are both measures of

DEFINITION

Retail prices index (RPI): measure of inflation that is used for adjusting pensions and other benefits to take account of changes in inflation and frequently used in wage negotiations. Differs from the consumer prices index (CPI) in methodology and coverage.

the average change from month to month in the prices of consumer goods and services bought in the UK. Where they differ is in their coverage and methodology. The CPI, unlike the RPI, excludes all housing costs including mortgage interest payments and council tax. It also excludes the road fund licence and television licence. It does, however, include university accommodation fees, foreign students' university tuition fees and stockbrokers' charges, which are not included in the RPI.

The CPI weights are based on spending by all private households, foreign visitors to the UK and residents of institutional households. In contrast, the RPI weights are based on expenditure by private households only, excluding the highest income households and pensioner households mainly dependent on state benefits. The CPI also uses a geometric mean in constructing the index whereas the RPI uses an arithmetic mean.

From the RPI, two other measures of inflation are constructed. These are RPIX and RPIY. These seek to provide a picture of the inflationary pressures building up in the economy. RPIX is RPI minus mortgage interest payments. RPIY is RPI minus not only mortgage interest payments but also indirect taxes. RPIX was the government's initial target measure for inflation.

There is a case for excluding mortgage interest payments. This is because otherwise, when the Bank of England raises the rate of interest to reduce inflation, it will actually increase it as measured by the RPI. The counter argument is that changes in mortgage interest payments can make a noticeable difference to people's cost of living.

Governments also measure core inflation by constructing a core consumer price index. This excludes energy and food prices. Changes in the price of energy and food can be one-off or seasonal changes, and so removing them from a price index can further highlight the underlying trend in the price level.

DIFFICULTIES OF MEASURING INFLATION

The CPI and the other measures of inflation mentioned aim to give a representative picture of what is happening to prices in a country. This may, however, not be a totally accurate picture. To assess whether prices are rising, the prices of the same goods and services should be compared. In practice, though, goods and services change, often improving in quality. So, for example, if the price of a vacuum cleaner rises by 6 per cent, this may reflect a higher charge to cover improvements in the model rather than the same cleaner becoming more expensive. It has been estimated that, if the price changes that reflect improvements in quality were to be removed, the inflation rate would be reduced by 1.1 per cent.

Measures of inflation also tend to overstate inflation, as they measure the price of a fixed basket of products. Although the weights are revised each year, the measures do not take into account people's ability to alter what they buy during the year. People usually move away from buying products that are becoming relatively more expensive towards those that are becoming relatively cheaper.

Recently the UK has spent more on imports than it has earned from exports

ACTIVITY ···⫶

Economists from the International Monetary Fund found in 2007 that Brazil's consumer prices index overstates the rise in the country's price level. The opening up of the country to international trade in the 1990s has continued to increase the quality and availability of products to Brazilian consumers. These changes are still not fully reflected in the country's CPI.

a) Outline the stages involved in constructing a CPI.

b) Explain why a rise in the quality of products consumed means that a CPI will overstate inflation.

The structure of the current account of the balance of payments

The main elements of the balance of payments are the current account, the capital and financial accounts and net errors and omissions.

The *current account* receives most media attention. It includes trade in goods, trade in services, income and transfers. Trade in goods records the earnings

from exports and the expenditure on imports of goods, for example, cars, food and chemicals. In recent years the UK has had a deficit in trade in goods. This means that it has spent more on imports of goods than it has earned from selling goods to other countries. Trade in goods used to be known as, and is still sometimes referred to, as the *visible balance*. This term emphasises that the items in this section can be seen and touched and have a tangible existence.

Trade in services includes, for instance, travel (tourism), insurance, financial and computer and information services. This part is also sometimes called the *invisible balance*. This reflects the fact that services cannot be seen. The UK performs well in services. Since 1966 it has recorded a surplus in the invisible balance every year.

The income part of the current account covers largely investment income. The UK usually has a surplus on income. This means that its residents earn more in terms of profit, interest and dividends on their investments abroad than foreigners do on their investments in the UK.

Transfers cover the transfer of money made and received by the government and individuals, for example, government payments to and from the EU and money sent out of the UK by foreigners working in the UK to relatives abroad.

The *capital and financial accounts* show the movement of direct investment – for example, the purchase or setting up of a factory, and portfolio investment – for example, the purchase of shares, and bank loans between the country and abroad.

The last section, *net errors and omissions*, is added to ensure that the balance of payments does balance. As the balance of payments is based on information relating to a vast number of transactions, it is not surprising that some mistakes are made and some items are initially left out.

> **learning tip**
>
> You need to take a broad overview of the balance of payments, but the section you need to devote most attention to is the current account, particularly the trade in goods, trade in services and income parts.

ACTIVITY ⋯⋰

In 2006, the UK had a current account deficit of £47,781m. Its trade in goods was –£83,631m, income was £18,555m and current transfers was –£6,759m.

a) Calculate the value of trade in services in the 2006 current account.

b) Apart from the current account, identify another section of the balance of payments.

The causes of economic growth

In the short run, an economy with spare capacity can experience economic growth as a result of an increase in aggregate demand. For example, a fall in the exchange rate may increase net exports and result in export-led growth, as shown in Figure 5.3.

There may also be consumption-led growth, which may be caused by, for instance, a cut in income tax or a rise in consumer confidence. Of course, aggregate demand and hence short-run economic growth may also occur, as a consequence of an increase in government spending or net investment.

An advantage of net investment is that it increases both aggregate demand and aggregate supply. For an economy to experience economic growth in the long run, its productive capacity has to increase. So the essential causes of long-run economic growth are increases in the quantity and/or quality of resources.

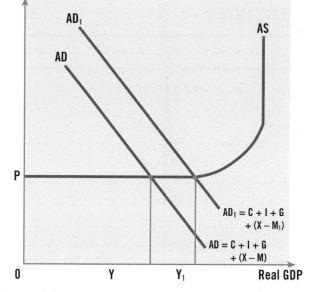

Figure 5.3 Export-led growth

As well as through net investment, an economy's resources may be increased as a result of the size of the labour force rising. Figure 5.4 shows economic growth occurring as a result of, for instance, more women entering the labour force.

The main causes of an increase in the quality of an economy's resources, and hence its ability to produce products, are advances in technology and improvements in education and training.

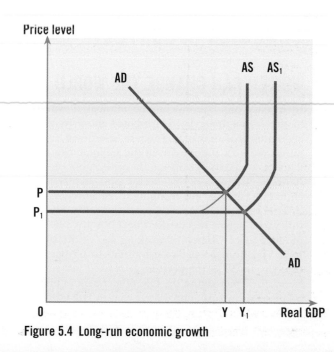

Figure 5.4 Long-run economic growth

ACTIVITY ⋯⋯✦

The Indian economy grew at an average annual rate of 8 per cent between 2003 and 2007. It is predicted that it will emerge as one of the world's biggest economies over the next 30 years. The country has a growing number of ambitious graduates, many of whom are skilled in IT and English. It is attracting a large amount of investment from abroad, encouraged by the high number of skilled, low-cost professionals. Services, the main source of economic growth, account for more than half of India's output. The service sector, however, employs less than a third of the country's labour force. Most people still work in agriculture and many of them still live in poverty. A significant proportion of the country's city slum dwellers are desperately seeking work.

a) Is the Indian economy working at full capacity? Explain your answer.

b) Using an aggregate demand and aggregate supply diagram, explain one reason why the Indian economy is growing rapidly.

The unemployed may lack the skills for the job vacancies available

DEFINITION

Cyclical unemployment: unemployment arising from a lack of aggregate demand.

THE CAUSES OF UNEMPLOYMENT

The causes of unemployment can be examined from the demand side and the supply side. **Cyclical unemployment**, which can also be called demand deficient unemployment, arises due to a lack of aggregate demand. In this case demand for most products will be low and unemployment may be high.

ECONOMICS IN CONTEXT

WOMEN CAN CHANGE THE WORLD

In recent years, the rise in the number of women in the labour force has contributed more to global economic growth than increases in investment, rises in productivity or the growth of the Chinese economy. This rise is due to a change in the type of jobs on offer (with an increase in service sector jobs), an increase in child care facilities and changing social attitudes.

The proportion of economically active women still varies across the world. The USA has seen the proportion of women of working age in the labour force rise from 33 per cent in 1950 to 65 per cent in 2006. In 2006, the percentage was 72 per cent in Sweden, 67 per cent in the UK, 60 per cent in France, 57 per cent in Japan and 50 per cent in Italy.

The economic activity rate of women is highest in East Asian economies and lowest in some Arab countries. For instance, in Saudi Arabia women form only 5 per cent of the labour force. Even here, though, things are changing. In part, this is because of a need for a larger labour force in order to expand productive capacity. In 2004, the Saudi Arabian government lifted a ban on women holding a wide range of jobs. Women now account for more than half of university students in the country. Even if only half of these enter the labour force when they graduate, there will be a considerable increase in the country's ability to produce goods and services.

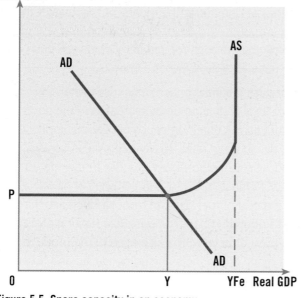

Figure 5.5 Spare capacity in an economy

unemployment are technological and international unemployment. Technological unemployment, as its name suggests, arises when workers lose their jobs because of advances in technology. International unemployment occurs when jobs are lost because firms decide to carry out some of their work abroad (outsourcing) or because households and firms decide to buy imports rather than domestically produced products.

Immobility of labour also contributes to **frictional unemployment**. This form of unemployment occurs when workers are in-between jobs. It is less serious than structural or cyclical unemployment. This is because it lasts for a shorter period than the other two. Some level of frictional unemployment is always likely to exist in an economy.

Figure 5.5 shows an economy operating with spare capacity and cyclical unemployment.

Unemployment can also arise due to problems with the supply of labour. Although there may be job vacancies, employers may not be willing to employ those people who apply because they lack the right skills. It might also be that there are job vacancies in one part of the country but the unemployed live in another part. These problems of occupational and geographical immobility are characteristics of what is called **structural unemployment**. This unemployment is usually caused by the decline of certain industries and occupations due to changes in demand and supply.

> **DEFINITION**
>
> **Frictional unemployment:** short term unemployment occurring when workers are in-between jobs.

As with structural unemployment, frictional unemployment can be broken down into a number

> **DEFINITION**
>
> **Structural unemployment:** unemployment caused by the decline of certain industries and occupations due to changes in demand and supply.

Structural unemployment that is concentrated in a particular geographical area is sometimes called regional unemployment. Other forms of structural

ACTIVITY ····

In the period 2000 to 2006, unemployment in South Africa averaged 28 per cent. The South African government was increasing aggregate demand to reduce the country's negative output gap. It was also concerned about the country's severe skills shortage.

For example, in 2002 a South African bank estimated that 300,000 to 500,000 vacancies throughout the country, including in accountancy, banking and engineering, remained unfilled because there were not enough skilled people to recruit.

a) Draw an aggregate demand and aggregate supply diagram to illustrate the state of the South African economy in the period described.

b) What evidence is there here that South Africa was suffering from structural unemployment? Explain your answer.

of categories, depending on what is causing the time gap between leaving one job and taking up another one. One category is search unemployment. Some unemployed people do not take the first job offered to them but spend time searching around for what they consider to be a good job. Other people may be seasonally unemployed because their labour is only demanded at certain times of the year, for example, ice cream sellers and fruit pickers. Yet others may experience casual unemployment. This means that they are out of work in-between irregular periods of employment. Two groups of workers who suffer from this type of frictional unemployment are actors and building workers.

THE CAUSES OF INFLATION

As with unemployment, inflation can arise from both the demand side and the supply side. In analysing its causes, inflation can be put into two categories – demand-pull and cost-push inflation. **Demand-pull inflation** arises from aggregate demand increasing at a faster rate than aggregate supply. When the economy is producing at or near its productive capacity, increases in aggregate demand are likely to push up the price level, as shown in Figure 5.6.

One reason why there may be an excessive growth in aggregate demand is the money growing faster than real output. In this case, consumption may rise more rapidly than productive capacity, which will push up the price level as shown in Figure 5.7.

Cost-push inflation, in contrast, arises when the price level is pushed up by increases in the costs of production. A common cause of cost-push inflation is a rise in wage rates above increases in costs of production. Another cause is a rise in raw material costs. For instance, a rise in the price of oil will push up the cost of fuel. This, in turn, will increase the cost of distributing products, household heating costs and the price of travel. Oil is also used in the production of a range of products, including plastic and textiles, and to run capital equipment.

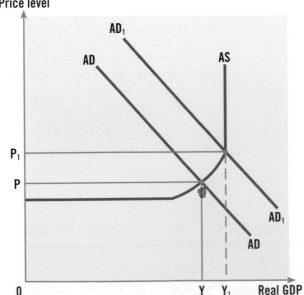

Figure 5.6 An increase in AD pushing up the price level

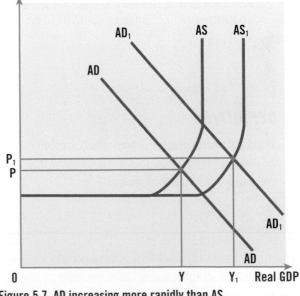

Figure 5.7 AD increasing more rapidly than AS

Price level

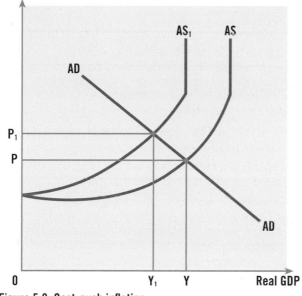

Figure 5.8 Cost-push inflation

In the case of cost-push inflation, it is the decrease in aggregate supply that causes the price level to rise and real GDP to fall, as shown in Figure 5.8.

> **learning tip**
>
> In practice, once inflation is under way, it can be difficult to determine whether it is caused by cost-push or demand-pull factors. One can lead to the other. For example, an increase in aggregate demand, causing demand-pull inflation, may cause workers to press for wage rises. If firms give workers wage rises this, in turn, can cause cost-push inflation.

ACTIVITY ···▷

In 2007, Venezuela experienced an annual inflation rate of 17.2 per cent. Prices were driven up by rising consumption. Venezuelans spent more, in part, because of a fall in the rate of interest.

a) Define inflation.

b) Explain what type of inflation Venezuela was experiencing in 2007.

c) Explain:

   i) why a fall in the rate of interest would be likely to increase consumption

   ii) another cause of an increase in consumption.

THE CAUSES OF A DEFICIT ON THE CURRENT ACCOUNT OF THE BALANCE OF PAYMENTS

A deficit on the current account occurs when the country's expenditure abroad exceeds its revenue from abroad. The two main reasons why this situation can arise are a) because the country's inhabitants have spent more on goods and services from abroad than overseas residents have spent on the country's products and/or b) because there has been a net outflow of investment income.

Among the causes of a deficit on the trade in goods and services are: changes in income at home and abroad, and changes in the exchange rate and structural problems. If incomes are falling abroad, demand for the country's exports is likely to fall. A rise in incomes at home would also contribute to a deficit. This is because the country's inhabitants are likely to buy more products. Some of these will be imports. Some may also be domestically produced products originally intended for the export market.

A rise in the exchange rate may also result in a deficit, as it will raise export prices and lower import prices.

A deficit caused by changes in income (sometimes called a cyclical deficit) or by a change in the exchange rate will be of less concern to a government than one caused by structural problems. This is because income and the exchange rate are likely to change in the future. In contrast, if the deficit is caused by the country's firms charging too much for their products, producing poor quality products or not picking up on changes in demand, the deficit may persist.

An outflow of investment income will occur if the investments that foreign residents have made in the country earn more than investments the country's inhabitants have made in other countries. Whether this happens will be influenced by a number of factors, including the relative volume of investments made and the level of profit, interest and dividends earned on the investments.

THE CAUSES OF A SURPLUS ON THE CURRENT ACCOUNT OF THE BALANCE OF PAYMENTS

A surplus on the current account is experienced when a country's revenue from abroad is greater than its expenditure abroad. It may occur due to

ACTIVITY ···✦

Education is becoming one of the UK's most important export industries. In 2005 the economy earned £13 billion from exports of tuition services, training, examinations, publishing and educational programmes for foreign students. This figure was higher than export earnings from the sale of cars, from food, beverages and tobacco, and from computer services.

The UK is currently attracting a quarter of all students studying outside their country of origin. It is the second most popular destination for foreign students after the USA. Foreign students are attracted to the UK by the good reputation of the degrees and what is seen as an attractive lifestyle.

However, the UK is facing increased competition. A number of countries, including Australia, India, Malaysia, New Zealand and Singapore, are advertising their courses more extensively and France and the Netherlands are offering more degree courses in English.

a) In which section of the balance of payments does education appear?

b) Explain two reasons why the UK is so successful in selling education to other countries.

c) Discuss the economic factors that will influence whether the UK will continue to be 'the second most popular destination for foreign students'.

the country's revenue from exports exceeding its expenditure on imports and/or because the country is a net earner of investment income.

Care has to be taken in interpreting a surplus on trade in goods and services. This is because it may arise from the strength of the economy, from a change in its exchange rate or from a weakness of the economy.

The country is likely to have a surplus if its products are of a high quality, are produced at a low cost and reflect what households and firms at home and abroad want to buy. A fall in the exchange rate can also give rise to a surplus, for at least a time. This is because a reduction in the value of the currency lowers export prices and raises import prices.

There may also, however, be a surplus because the economy is in a recession. In such a situation, a country's inhabitants may not be buying many products, including imports, and its firms, finding it difficult to sell at home, may be competing more vigorously in export markets.

THE CONSEQUENCES OF UNEMPLOYMENT

Unemployment can have a number of consequences for the economy, for the unemployed and for other economies.

Lost output

One of the most significant costs of unemployment is lost output. Having people who are willing and able to work without jobs is a waste of resources. If these people were in work, the country would produce more goods and services, and so material living standards would be higher. For instance, more houses might be built, more films made and more banking services provided if more of the labour force were employed.

Figure 5.9 shows an economy producing inside its production possibility curve. Actual output is below potential output.

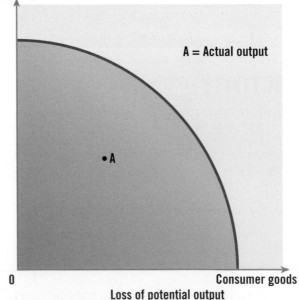

Figure 5.9 Economy producing inside its production possibility curve

Lost tax revenue

Unemployment results in tax revenue being lower than possible. If more people were in work, incomes, spending and possibly profits would be higher. This would mean that the government would collect more revenue from income tax. This higher tax revenue could be spent, for instance, on education, health care and transport. Such spending might improve the quality of people's lives and increase the country's productive capacity. If a government wants to maintain a given level of spending in the face of rising unemployment, it will have to either raise tax rates or borrow. Higher tax rates will reduce people's disposable income and their spending power. A rise in government borrowing may push up the rate of interest, which in turn will also reduce their spending power.

Government spending on unemployment benefits

If unemployment rises, the government will have to spend more on unemployment related benefits, principally job seeker's allowance. This may mean that it has to reduce its spending on other areas, such as education, or will have to raise its borrowing or tax rates.

So the money spent on unemployment benefits has an opportunity cost – it could have been used for other purposes or it could have meant lower tax rates and/or lower government borrowing.

Pressure on other forms of government spending

As well as affecting the amount the government spends on unemployment-related benefits, rising unemployment can put upward pressure on a variety of other forms of government spending. When people are unemployed they are more likely to suffer health problems, including mental health problems, marital difficulties and some may even turn to crime.

More health problems will mean higher waiting lists for health care, unless the government spends more on the sector or raises the sector's productivity. Marital break-ups can increase the need for housing benefits and the provision of social housing. If rising unemployment does lead to increasing crime, the government will have to spend more on the police and judicial system.

Costs to the unemployed

As mentioned above, the unemployed may suffer from poor health and family break-ups. They are also likely to experience a loss of income. Most unemployed people usually earned more than they receive in job seeker's allowance. The loss of income is particularly acute in the case of those not entitled to unemployment benefit. Work also provides some people with a sense of purpose and worth and some experience a loss of status when they become unemployed.

Children with unemployed parents can also suffer. Unemployment is one of the main causes of poverty, and children from poor households tend to suffer worse health and perform less well at school. They may have fewer educational tools at home, be less likely to have their own bedroom to study in, and usually have lower expectations.

Hysteresis

One of the costs of unemployment can be unemployment itself. This is known as **hysteresis.** The longer people are out of work, the more difficult it can be for them to gain another job. The problems arise in terms of both the demand for and the supply of labour. Employers may be reluctant to take on someone who has been out of work for a long time for two main reasons. One is that the length of time they have been out of a job may indicate that they are not good workers. The other is that the longer someone is unemployed, the more rusty their skills become and the more out of touch they become with advances in working methods and technology.

On the supply side, the **long-term unemployed** may tend to seek work less actively over time. They may lose the work habit and get used to being at home. Perhaps more significantly, they may become discouraged by rejection after rejection.

DEFINITIONS

Hysteresis: unemployment causing unemployment.

Long-term unemployment: unemployment lasting for more than a year.

THE COSTS FOR OTHER ECONOMIES

Unemployment in a country's trading partners is likely to reduce demand for its exports. This, in turn, will reduce the country's aggregate demand and may cause some unemployment. A country may also experience immigration from countries with high and rising unemployment. This can be beneficial if the country has an ageing population and a shortage of

labour, but it may place a burden on the country's housing stock.

ACTIVITY ⸱⸱⸱⸱

Unemployment (%) (LFS measure)

Country	April 2007	April 2006
France	8.4	8.2
Germany	9.2	9.6
Japan	4.0	4.1
UK	5.5	5.0
USA	4.4	4.8

a) Compare the unemployment rate in the countries in April 2007.

b) Compare the change in the unemployment rate in the countries between April 2006 and April 2007.

c) Were there more people unemployed in France or in the USA in April 2007? Explain your answer.

learning tip In assessing economies' unemployment performance, it is more informative to use unemployment rates than the number unemployed (think about your answer to question c) above). Where possible, use figures based on the same measure of unemployment.

THE BENEFITS OF UNEMPLOYMENT

There are a few possible benefits of unemployment. For a few people, it may give them time to search for a more rewarding job. The existence of unemployment makes it easier for firms, wishing to expand, to recruit workers. It can also reduce demand-pull and cost-push inflation. Figure 5.10 shows that when the economy moves from producing at full employment to a lower level of output and some unemployment, the pressure on the price level falls.

The existence of a relatively high level of unemployment may discourage workers from seeking

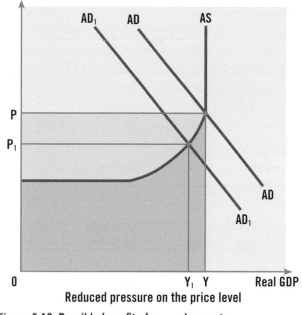

Price level

Reduced pressure on the price level

Figure 5.10 Possible benefit of unemployment

wage rises and may dissuade them from taking industrial action.

> **learning tip**
>
> Students often assert that a rise in unemployment will lead to a deterioration in the current account of the balance of payments, as less will be produced and exported. The effect is more complex, and rising unemployment may be associated with an improving current account position. This is because, with higher unemployment, there will be less spending in the economy. This should mean less is spent on imports. Some products intended for the home market might also be diverted to the export market. So, if you are going to refer to the impact on the current account, you need to recognise that the effect is uncertain.

THE OVERALL EFFECT

It is generally agreed that the costs of unemployment above a certain level exceed any benefits. This is why low unemployment or full employment is one of the main macroeconomic objectives pursued by governments.

THE SIGNIFICANCE OF UNEMPLOYMENT

How significant the consequences of unemployment are depends on how much unemployment there is, how long on average people are unemployed, the benefits provided to the unemployed, the type of unemployment and the distribution of unemployment.

The higher the rate of unemployment, the more serious the costs are likely to be. A 3 per cent unemployment rate is not considered to be a problem. This is because there will always be some people in-between jobs. Indeed, frictional unemployment exists even in a booming economy. In contrast, a 10 per cent unemployment rate, for instance, would involve a greater loss of output, higher government spending on benefits and a greater loss of tax revenue.

The comments above depend on the 3 per cent unemployment and the 10 per cent lasting for the same length of time. It is important to consider not only the rate of unemployment but also the duration. A 6 per cent unemployment rate with people on average being out of work for two years would have more harmful effects than a 10 per cent rate with people being out of work on average for only three months. This is because costs tend to build up over time and when people have been out of work for more than a year, they often find it difficult to get a job.

Generous unemployment benefits reduce the costs of unemployment but they have an opportunity cost for the economy. The costs of unemployment benefits and other costs of unemployment will also tend to be high if the unemployment is cyclical unemployment. This is because such unemployment is widespread and can be on a significant scale. Cyclical unemployment tends to have the highest costs and frictional unemployment the lowest costs. Structural unemployment is more serious than frictional and is likely to cause problems in particular areas of the country.

The costs of unemployment are not usually borne evenly. This is because particular groups, including young men, tend to be more susceptible to unemployment. This uneven distribution of unemployment can be socially divisive.

ACTIVITY ···→

In May 2007, unemployment reached 53 per cent in Zimbabwe. The high rate of unemployment has contributed to rising malnourishment and a smaller proportion of children going to school. It has also led to between 3 and 4 million of the country's population leaving the country.

a) Explain how a high rate of unemployment can result in 'malnourishment and a smaller proportion of children going to school'.

b) Using a production possibility curve, analyse the effect on the Zimbabwean economy of the events explained above.

---

learning tip

In the exam, be prepared to discuss the benefits of a fall in unemployment as well as the consequences of unemployment.

THE CONSEQUENCES OF INFLATION

There are a number of effects that may arise as a result of inflation.

Fall in the value of money

The one certain consequence is a fall in the value of money. With the price level rising, each pound coin and other unit of the country's money will buy less. The purchasing power of money falls. Of course, whether a household experiences a loss in its purchasing power as a result of inflation will depend on whether their disposable income rises by more or less than, or the same amount as, inflation. If its disposable income rises by more than inflation, its real income will rise.

Menu costs

Menu costs get their name from the need for restaurants to print new menus on a frequent basis

---

DEFINITION

Menu costs: the costs of changing prices due to inflation.

---

during times of high inflation. The term now has a wider meaning. It is applied to the need for firms in general to alter their prices in, for instance, catalogues, newspaper advertisements and websites. This can involve considerable time and effort and can increase labour costs. It can also be expensive to print and distribute new catalogues.

Shoeleather costs

Shoeleather costs relate to the costs involved in reducing holdings of cash and money in current accounts and seeking the highest rate of interest. During periods of inflation, households and firms cannot afford to have money lying idle, not earning interest, as it will be losing value. They have to place it in financial institutions and have to search out the most rewarding rate of interest. The term gets its name from the need for people to walk to the bank more frequently to withdraw or move money, which causes their shoes to wear out more frequently. Of course, nowadays, most money is withdrawn or moved electronically. It does, nevertheless, involve time and effort. For instance, when inflation is low, a firm receiving revenue into its current account that it plans to pay out in wages the next week can leave it in its current account for this short period. When inflation is high, however, staff time and effort will have to be involved in finding where the money could earn the most interest in a savings account and making the necessary arrangements to open such an account and then move the money out of it.

DEFINITION

Shoeleather costs: costs in terms of the extra time and effort involved in reducing money holdings.

Administrative costs

As well as shoe leather and menu costs, inflation can impose other administrative costs on firms. Staff time may have to be devoted to adjusting accounts, assessing raw material costs, negotiating with unions about wage rises and estimating appropriate prices.

Inflationary noise

Inflationary noise refers to the distorting effect that inflation causes. It means that market prices do not signal the relative scarcity of products efficiently. Without inflation, if the price of, for example, one model of television rises, it can be concluded that it has become relatively more expensive. With inflation, however, consumers will be uncertain whether the rise in price does actually reflect a relative price rise or whether it is just in line with inflation.

> ### DEFINITION
> **Inflationary noise:** the distortion of price signals caused by inflation.

Random redistribution of income

Inflation increases the cost of living, as people have to pay more to buy the same basket of goods and services. As noted above (see page 126), the purchasing power of money falls. This does not necessarily mean that people's ability to buy products will fall. What will determine the outcome for a household will be the relationship between the change in its income and the price level.

Inflation can cause some people to gain and some people to lose in a way that is not based on economic or social merit. For instance, some workers with weak bargaining power may not receive wage rises which keep pace with inflation. Borrowers will gain and lenders will lose if inflation reduces the **real interest rate**. If, for example, the rate of interest is 6 per cent and there is 2 per cent inflation, someone lending £100 would expect that the £106 they would receive at the end of the loan period would buy them approximately £4 more goods and services than they could have bought before lending the money.

> ### DEFINITION
> **Real interest rate:** the nominal interest rate minus the inflation rate.

If, however, inflation rises to 8 per cent the £106 will actually buy less, about what £98 would have previously have bought them, when the lender is repaid.

Fiscal drag

One specific form of redistribution of income that can occur as a result of inflation is from taxpayers to the government. If tax brackets are not adjusted in line with inflation, people's income will be pushed into higher tax bands. Taxpayers will pay a higher proportion of their income in tax and so experience a fall in their disposable income. The government will receive more tax revenue. This tendency is referred to as **fiscal drag**.

> ### DEFINITION
> **Fiscal drag:** people's income being dragged into higher tax bands as a result of tax brackets not being adjusted in line with inflation.

Uncertainty

One of the most serious disadvantages of inflation, especially if it is unexpected, is the uncertainty it creates. If firms are uncertain about what their costs will be and what prices they will receive from selling their products, they may be reluctant to invest.

Inflation also complicates household financial planning, making it difficult for people to decide how much to save and where to place their savings.

Inflation causing inflation

The experience of inflation can lead people to behave in a way which causes inflation to continue. If households expect prices to rise in the future, they may seek to buy more items now, thereby increasing aggregate demand. If workers think that inflation will be a problem, they will ask for pay rises just to protect their current real earnings. Inflationary expectations will also cause firms to raise their prices in order to protect their real profit levels.

Loss of international competitiveness

Inflation can have a harmful effect on a country's international trade position. If the country's inflation rate is above that of its main competitors, its goods and services will become less price competitive. This is likely to result in fewer exports being sold and more imports being purchased.

THE BENEFITS OF INFLATION

There is a possibility that inflation can bring benefits to an economy. If it is a low and stable rate and is demand-pull inflation, the higher aggregate demand and steady rise in the price level may encourage firms to increase output.

Workers also like rises in their pay, even if these are matched by higher prices, with their real pay remaining the same. Psychologically, we like to feel that we are being appreciated and that our employers think that we are doing well – even if the pay rise is only in money terms.

The ability that inflation gives firms to alter workers' real pay can help labour markets operate more efficiently and reduce unemployment. Workers usually resist cuts in their money (nominal) wages. If demand is falling, firms will have to cut their costs. Inflation enables firms to reduce their real wages. This can be achieved by either keeping money wages the same or raising them by less than inflation. In the absence of inflation it is difficult to cut real wages, and firms might make some of their workers redundant in order to reduce their costs.

DEFLATION

It is also possible that a country may experience deflation. This tends to occur less frequently than inflation, but perhaps more frequently than many people think, since measures of inflation tend to overstate price rises and sometimes mask a fall in the price level.

Deflation arising from the supply side can be beneficial. A fall in the price level arising from a cut in the costs of production will enable consumers to enjoy more goods and services and will increase the country's international competitiveness.

In contrast, deflation caused by a fall in aggregate demand may result in a harmful deflationary spiral. Lower aggregate demand will cause firms to cut back production. This will lead to higher unemployment. Households are likely to reduce their spending, for fear that they may experience unemployment and because they will expect prices to be even lower in the future. This, in turn, will reduce aggregate demand further.

THE SIGNIFICANCE OF INFLATION

The impact of inflation on an economy and its households, firms and government will depend on a number of factors. These are the rate of inflation, its cause, whether it is fluctuating, whether it was correctly anticipated and its rate relative to that of other countries.

A low rate of inflation, especially if it is stable, is unlikely to cause significant problems for an economy. Indeed, as previously mentioned, a lower rate of demand-pull inflation may bring some benefits for an economy.

Cost-push inflation tends to be more harmful for an economy than demand-pull inflation. This is because cost-push inflation is often accompanied by a fall in real GDP (check back to Figure 5.8) and a rise in unemployment.

In contrast to a low rate of inflation, a high rate is likely to cause a number of problems for an economy. The higher the rate, the more serious the problems. For example, hyperinflation leads to very significant menu, shoeleather and administrative costs and considerable inflationary noise. Firms will have to devote a large amount of time and effort to managing their money. This involves an opportunity cost. The time could be used instead on, for instance, planning and costing new products. High inflation may mean that prices are changing so often that firms cannot publish prices. In Argentina in the first half of the first decade of 2000, books did not have prices on them. People visiting a bookshop had to ask an assistant to check on a website for the latest price.

If prices are rising rapidly, it becomes difficult for people to judge what are the best buys. There is also a risk that people will stop being prepared to accept money in payment and will resort to barter.

Fluctuating inflation can be destabilising as, again, it creates inflationary noise and it makes it difficult for the government, firms and households to plan ahead. If, for example, inflation was 8 per cent two years ago, 1 per cent last year and is 4 per cent this year, it will not be easy to assess what it will be next year.

Unanticipated inflation, a situation where people are surprised by the inflation rate, has more harmful effects than anticipated inflation. Unanticipated inflation causes uncertainty and can result in a random redistribution of income. For instance, if workers had expected an inflation rate of 5 per cent, they may have asked for a wage rise of 8 per cent in order to get an increase in their real pay of 3 per cent. If, however, inflation turns out to be 10 per cent, then, even if their wage is raised by the full amount they asked for, they will be worse off. In contrast, if inflation had been correctly forecasted, people will feel more confident and measures can be taken to prevent the random redistribution of income. For instance, interest rates, state pensions and tax bands can be raised in line with inflation.

Even if inflation is stable and has been correctly anticipated, it can still have a have a harmful effect on an economy. As previously indicated, if a country has a higher inflation rate than the main countries it trades with, its current account position is likely to deteriorate. On the other hand, a country may be experiencing an inflation rate of even 10 per cent, but its products will be becoming more internationally

ECONOMICS IN CONTEXT

HYPERINFLATION IN ZIMBABWE

Food shortages in Zimbabwe have accelerated hyperinflation

Hyperinflation brings enormous costs to an economy and, indeed, can lead to a breakdown in the economic and social structure of an economy. When there is a huge rise in the price level, people tend to lose confidence in their currency. Households and firms spend it as quickly as possible, afraid that it will lose value. The extra spending causes prices to rise, which further reduces confidence and stimulates a further increase in spending.

A number of countries have experienced hyperinflation in the past. In 1923 Germany's consumer prices multiplied 7.2 billion times in 16 months. Hungary holds the world record for inflation. In its 1945–46 economic crisis, the country recorded inflation of 4.19 quintillion per month. In the 1980s, Argentina's inflation reached 5,000 per cent and Serbia and Brazil had inflation rates above 4,000 per cent. In the mid-1990s Zaire's inflation rate reached 13,773 per cent. In each of these cases, the government involved had been increasing their spending by a significant amount and financing the extra spending by printing more notes.

The most recent example of hyperinflation has been in Zimbabwe. In October 2007 the country's inflation rate reached 8,000 per cent. The external value of the Zimbabwean dollar, which in 1980 had equalled one US dollar, fell to 1 million Zimbabwean dollars equalling one US dollar.

A number of factors gave rise to the problem. The government had encouraged violent seizures of farmland. This resulted in a decrease in agricultural production, a fall in exports and a reduction in foreign investment in the country. The government resorted to printing money to finance its spending. The country experienced a rise in aggregate demand, but a fall in real output. The government reacted to the inflation by imposing price controls. This made the situation worse. It drove a number of firms, including retail outlets, out of business, further increasing shortages and accelerating the inflation rate.

The hyperinflation has had disastrous consequences for the economy. The collapse of a whole range of businesses has seen unemployment reach unprecedented levels. The poor have been particularly badly hit. Some have even not been able to afford to bury their dead relatives and have had to resort to burying them in fields at night.

competitive if its trading partners have inflation rates of 12 per cent.

Of course, it has to be remembered that the significance of inflation varies between people, as it affects them in different ways. Indeed, different people experience different inflation rates within the same economy. This is because people have different spending patterns and experience different prices in different areas of the country. Young people, for example, may experience lower inflation than the economy's inflation rate suggests if electronic goods rise in price at a lower rate than the price level. Electronic goods may even fall in price due to advances in technology. Young people spend a higher proportion of their disposable income on such goods than on most other goods. The Bank of England now runs a website that allows people to calculate their own inflation rate.

Prices and price rises tend to be lower, for instance, in the north-east of England than in London. It has been estimated by the ONS that, in recent years, there has been a difference in prices of 8 per cent between the two areas.

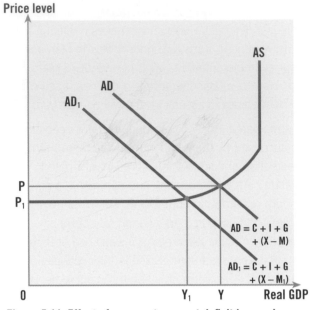

Figure 5.11 Effect of a current account deficit increasing

output, however, is going to people abroad. If a deficit increases, it will reduce aggregate demand in the economy, as shown in Figure 5.11. This will lower the economy's output, be likely to raise unemployment and may put downward pressure on the price level. A rise in the deficit is also likely to lead to a fall in the exchange rate (see below, page 134) and increase the debt of the country.

In contrast, a surplus means a country is consuming less than it is producing and is experiencing a net inflow of money and income. The increase in the money supply will mean that banks will have more money, which can increase bank lending. A rise in a surplus will mean that net exports are increasing. This will raise aggregate demand and be likely to push up the exchange rate.

ACTIVITY ····⫶

In 2006, Bulgaria's CPI rose by 4.8 per cent. In 2007, when the country's inflation rate accelerated to 8.5 per cent, particular groups in the country were unhappy about it. For example, teachers went on strike, complaining against their 5 per cent pay rise, although the government was promising to give them a 30 per cent pay rise in 2008. Exporters were also not happy and the country experienced a trade in goods deficit of $9.1 billion in 2007.

a) i) What happened to teachers' purchasing power in 2007?

ii) What would determine teachers' purchasing power in 2008?

b) Explain why inflation may harm exporters.

THE CONSEQUENCES OF A DEFICIT AND A SURPLUS ON THE CURRENT ACCOUNT OF THE BALANCE OF PAYMENTS

A deficit means that a country is consuming more than it is producing. The income from this extra

---

learning tip

In assessing the significance of a country's current account deficit or surplus, it is useful to consider it in terms of what percentage it is of GDP. The US may have a larger deficit than the UK, but this may just reflect the larger size of the US economy. More significant would be if the USA's deficit was a larger percentage of its GDP than the UK's.

ACTIVITY ⋯⃗

In the first decade of the 2000s, Australia had large deficits on its current account of the balance of payments. Indeed, in 2007, its deficit, as a percentage of GDP, was second only to that of the USA.

There were a number of reasons why the country was importing more than it was exporting. These included a reduction in the tax on imports and the Australian economy growing more rapidly than its trading partners, including Japan and the USA.

One consequence of the deficit was a fall in the value of the Australian dollar. The deficit was also thought to have contributed to Australia's actual output being below its potential output during this period.

a) What is the difference between exports and imports?

b) Explain why 'Australia growing more rapidly than its trading partners' contributed to the country's current account deficit.

c) Analyse how a current account deficit can contribute to a country's 'actual output being below its potential output'.

THE SIGNIFICANCE OF A CURRENT ACCOUNT DEFICIT

How significant a current account deficit is depends on its size, duration, cause and what is happening in the capital and financial account.

A deficit that forms a small percentage of real GDP or one that lasts a short time is unlikely to be very significant. For instance, a deficit equivalent to 2 per cent of GDP that continues for several years or a deficit equal to 5 per cent of GDP that lasts two months will not have much impact on the country's aggregate demand.

As already suggested (see page 121), a deficit may indicate a growing and, indeed, healthy economy, or it may indicate an economy with structural problems. If the output of an economy is increasing, it is possible that, for a time, more foreign raw materials will be bought by firms and the higher income may result in more imports of finished goods. An economy with a high inflation rate and low productivity is also likely to have a deficit, but this time it may continue

for some time unless there is a change in economic performance. A government is likely to try to increase the country's international competitiveness. The effect of a current account deficit on an economy is also influenced by what is happening to the other main sector of the balance of payments. In 2006 the UK had a current account deficit of £47,781m. However, the country had no difficulty in attracting foreign direct investment (FDI). Indeed, it was the main destination in the EU for FDI and also had a net inflow of portfolio investment. These movements in capital and financial capital meant that, despite the current account deficit, the value of the pound remained high and stable.

THE COSTS OF ECONOMIC GROWTH

Economic growth can have costs. If an economy is currently using all of its resources, and thus producing on its production possibility curve, the only way it can increase its output is to switch resources from making consumer goods to making capital goods. Figure 5.12 shows that the opportunity cost of producing an extra 20 billion capital goods is 40 billion consumer goods. In the long run, though, the extra capital goods will enable more consumer goods to be made.

If economic growth is achieved in a way that is not sustainable, for example, by the expansion of heavy

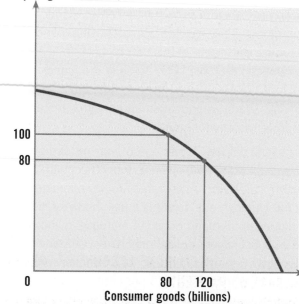

Figure 5.12 Opportunity cost of economic growth

industry without regard to controls on pollution, there will be damage to the environment. There is also the risk that economic growth may result in the depletion of non-renewable resources.

In addition, economic growth may reduce the quality of some people's lives. A growing economy is one that requires some people to adopt new skills and some to change jobs. The pace of work may also increase. Some people may find these changes stressful. For example, the increase in the number of cars has increased people's flexibility of travel but has also resulted in more congestion, more accidents and an increase in breathing-related diseases and more noise.

THE BENEFITS OF ECONOMIC GROWTH

Although there can be costs of economic growth, most governments believe that the benefits of economic growth outweigh the costs. This is why economic growth is a key macroeconomic objective.

The main benefit of economic growth is likely to be a rise in people's material standard of living. If real GDP per head rises, the population can enjoy more goods and services. Of course, whether they all do so will be influenced by the distribution of income.

Another benefit is that economic growth enables poverty within a country to be reduced without having to redistribute existing income. Higher output raises tax revenue without having to increase tax rates, and some of this can be used to finance schemes to help the poor. Some of the higher tax revenue can also be used to improve public services, such as education and health care, and to improve the environment.

An additional way higher output may reduce poverty is by increasing employment. Indeed economic growth can help a government achieve its objective of full employment. There is a risk, however, that, if aggregate demand does not increase in line with production, higher output may be accompanied by higher unemployment. If, for example, workers' productivity increases by 5 per cent and aggregate demand increases by 2 per cent, firms may be able to produce more output with fewer workers.

Actual economic growth raises the level of a country's real output and can thereby increase its status and power in international organisations and in international negotiations. The USA, which has a very high level of real GDP per head, is a very powerful member of the United Nations (UN), the **International Monetary Fund (IMF)** and **World Trade Organisation (WTO).**

DEFINITIONS

International Monetary Fund (IMF): an international organisation that helps co-ordinate the international monetary system.

World Trade Organisation (WTO): an international organisation that promotes free international trade and rules on international trade disputes.

THE SUSTAINABILITY OF ECONOMIC GROWTH

One of the crucial factors that has to be taken into account in deciding whether economic growth is beneficial or not is whether it is sustainable.

ACTIVITY ····⦂

Between 2003 and 2007, Pakistan's economy grew at a rate of 6.4 per cent per year. This relatively rapid rise in the country's output was the result of economic reforms, low interest rates and increased foreign aid. These changes increased investment and exports.

The economic growth has helped to reduce poverty, although the reduction has been accompanied by a rise in income inequality. Some of the extra tax revenue and foreign aid has been spent on increasing the size of the country's armed forces and on the purchase of weapons.

a) Identify two components of aggregate demand mentioned.

b) What evidence is there here that the rich benefited more than the poor from the economic growth in Pakistan?

Governments are becoming increasingly concerned to promote stable economic growth in both the short term and the long term. In the next chapter, we shall examine some of the policies governments use to encourage increases in both aggregate demand and aggregate supply. There are regular meetings of governments at which they seek to reduce climate change and pollution, and meetings that try to promote greater economic stability. These meetings recognise that an individual country's ability to grow now and for generations to come is affected by what is happening in other countries.

Determination of exchange rates

An **exchange rate** is the price of one currency in terms of another currency or currencies. The Bank of

> ### DEFINITIONS
>
> **Exchange rate:** the price of one currency in terms of another currency or currencies.
>
> **Monetary Policy Committee (MPC):** a committee of the Bank of England with responsibility for setting the interest rate in order to meet the government's inflation target.

England **Monetary Policy Committee's** main indicator of the pound's value is the Bank's trade-weighted index. This measures the pound's exchange rate against a basket of currencies, giving each country's currency a weight in proportion to the amount of

ECONOMICS IN CONTEXT

IS CHINA PAYING TOO HIGH A PRICE FOR ECONOMIC GROWTH?

The Chinese economy has grown more rapidly than most over the last two decades. Between 1987 and 2007 its growth rate has averaged 9 per cent. This rapid growth has increased and continues to increase the living standards of the Chinese. Indeed, between 1978 and 2007, China's income per head increased sevenfold and more than 400 million people were lifted out of severe poverty.

However, China's economic growth is coming at a cost. This cost is coming in a number of forms, including high levels of air pollution and water pollution, farmland erosion and desertification. Air pollution is increasing as China's rising energy needs

are being supplied by coal-fired power stations, more factories are operating and more and more cars, with low emissions standards, are being driven on Chinese roads. The country suffers from the world's highest emissions of sulphur dioxide and a quarter of the country suffers from acid rain.

Chemical and other factories are disgorging waste, including toxic waste, directly into rivers. This is contaminating the water, depressing people's immune systems and causing cancer. Between 2005 and 2007, the incidence of cancer rose by 23 per cent in rural areas and 19 per cent in urban areas. The ability of river water to clean itself is being reduced by the excessive amount that is being taken for industrial use. Some factories are having to close down due to a lack of water, and more than 75 per cent of river water flowing through urban areas is unsuitable for drinking or fishing.

The deforestation and loss of agricultural land is causing more cities, including Beijing, to be hit by sand storms and more of the country to turn into desert. The desertification of parts of the country is encouraging migration into already overcrowded cities.

This environmental damage is costing lives, reducing output and endangering China's ability to sustain its impressive growth record.

trade, both in goods and services, that the country has with the UK. So, for instance, the US dollar has a greater weighting than the Swiss franc. The currency weights are regularly updated to reflect changes in the pattern of trade.

Most countries' exchange rates are determined by the market forces of demand and supply. If demand for the currency rises, this will increase the exchange rate (see Figure 5.13), whereas if the supply of the currency increases, the exchange rate will fall.

A rise in the exchange rate of a currency means that each unit of the currency will buy more units of another currency or currencies. It also, of course, means that more units of the other currency will have to be paid to buy the currency. For instance, the exchange rate of the pound may rise from £1 = $1 to £1 = $2. In this case the value of the pound has risen. Each pound now buys more dollars. In turn, more dollars have to be sold to buy £1.

A number of factors influence the demand for and supply of a currency and so its exchange rate.

● The demand for pounds is likely to be high and supply is likely to be low if UK products are internationally competitive. Foreigners would be wanting to buy pounds to buy UK products, while UK citizens will not be selling many pounds to buy imports. Among the key factors that influence

international competitiveness are labour productivity, investment and relative inflation rates.

● Changes in income abroad influence the exchange rate. If, for instance, incomes are rising abroad, then foreigners are likely to buy more UK exports. This will increase demand for pounds and cause a rise in the value of the pound.

● Rising incomes at home may put downward pressure on the value of the pound. This is because the supply of pounds on foreign exchange markets will increase as pounds are sold to get the foreign currency to purchase more imports. Figure 5.14 shows how an increase in the supply of pounds pushes down the price of the pound.

● A rise in UK interest rates, relative to other countries' interest rates, will be likely to increase demand for pounds. Foreigners will want to buy pounds in order to open accounts in UK financial institutions to benefit from the higher interest rates.

● Pounds are also bought and sold by those wishing to undertake foreign direct investment (FDI). For instance, a Japanese firm will buy pounds if it wants to buy a UK car company or to build a new car factory in the UK. FDI in the UK will be attracted by a strong UK economic performance, a skilful labour force and favourable government policies, including

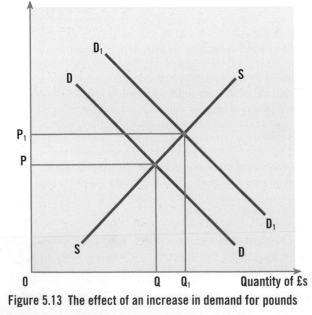

Figure 5.13 The effect of an increase in demand for pounds

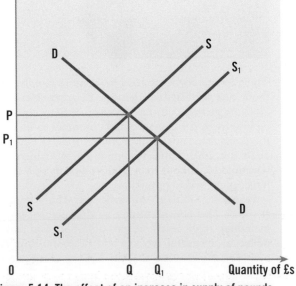

Figure 5.14 The effect of an increase in supply of pounds

regional development grants available to incoming foreign firms.

● Speculation is now an important influence on the exchange rate. A high percentage of the dealing in foreign exchange markets is accounted for by speculation. Speculators buy and sell currency, hoping to make a profit from movements in interest rates and exchange rates. Speculation can have a stabilising or destabilising effect on exchange rates. If speculators respond to a falling exchange rate by selling some of their holdings of the currency, this will drive the rate down even further. If, however, they think this rate will soon start to rise they will purchase the currency now, thereby preventing a large fall.

Speculation is something of a self-fulfilling

principle – by their action speculators bring about what they expect to happen.

ACTIVITY ···⫶

In August 2007, the Singapore dollar climbed to a ten-year high of $1.465 against the US dollar. The Singaporean economy at the time was booming, growing at an impressive rate of 9.4 per cent. The central bank of Singapore, however, was worried about inflation. The country was growing at a faster rate than its trend growth rate and its inflation rate had hit a twelve-year high of 2.9 per cent. It was expected that the central bank would raise its interest rate.

a) Does the information indicate that more or less Singaporean money had to be given in exchange for a US dollar?

b) Explain two reasons for the rise in the value of the Singaporean dollar.

The relationship between the exchange rate and the interest rate

Changes in the exchange rate and interest rate are closely linked. If, for instance, the UK's exchange rate rises, export prices expressed in terms of foreign currencies will rise. Demand for exports will fall and this will reduce aggregate demand (AD). Lower AD will reduce inflationary pressure. This may mean that the MPC will reduce the interest rate.

A reduction in the interest rate will tend to reduce the exchange rate. This is because it will reduce the return on money kept in UK financial institutions. There will probably be an outflow of funds from the UK to other countries. These funds are sometimes referred to as hot money flows. This is because these funds are moved quickly to take advantage of changes in interest rates and exchange rates. An outflow of funds will mean that more of the currency is being sold. The increase in the supply of the currency will reduce the exchange rate.

While a change in the interest rate usually causes the exchange rate to move in the same direction, this is not always the case. This is because a cut in the UK interest rate might make foreigners more confident about the prospects of economic growth in the UK. In this case, they are likely to buy pounds and so push up the value of the pound.

The effect of a change in the exchange rate on export and import prices

A fall in the exchange rate, called a depreciation if caused by market forces, will reduce the price of exports in terms of foreign currencies. For example, initially £1 may equal $2. In this case, a £100 export would sell in the USA for $200. If the value of the pound then fell to £1 = $1.50, the export would sell in the USA for $150.

Most exporters would be likely to let their export prices fall in line with the change in the exchange rate. Selling at a lower price in their export markets should enable them to increase their sales. Those exporters facing inelastic demand for their products may decide to leave their prices unchanged abroad. This would still enable them to earn more revenue, since they will gain more money when they convert their foreign earnings back into pounds. For example, an exporter may decide to keep the price of its £100 product at $200 in the USA when the exchange rate changes to £1 = $1.50. This would mean that the exporter would now receive £133.33 for the product.

ACTIVITY ⋯⁚⟩

On 21 September 2007, the Canadian dollar rose in price against the US dollar to one Canadian dollar = one US dollar. This was the highest value of the Canadian dollar (known as the 'loonie' after the bird, the Common loon, that appears on the dollar coin) since 1976. In 2002 Canadians needed C$1.6 to buy $1 and in 2005 they had to pay C$1.25.

The rise in the value of the loonie was due to an increase in demand for Canada's oil, gas, minerals, metals and farm products, resulting in an increase in Canada's current account surplus.

There was an outpouring of national pride when the parity was reached. Students held parity parties, as did some business groups. Currency

traders at the Royal Bank of Canada in Toronto stood on their desks and clapped and cheered. Exporters, however, did not celebrate. For most countries, the currency remains a symbol of national identity, but a rise in the value of the currency is a mixed blessing.

a) What is meant by 'the Canadian dollar rose in price against the US dollar'?

b) Explain how an increase in Canada's current account surplus could cause a rise in the price of the Canadian dollar.

c) Discuss why there were different responses among Canadians to the exchange rate change.

While a fall in the exchange rate causes a fall in export prices, it will increase the price of imports in terms of domestic currency.

Again, if initially £1 = $2, a $30 US import would sell in the UK for £15. A fall in the value of the pound to $1.50 would lead to the price of the import rising to £20. If US producers decide to keep the price of their products unchanged in the UK, they would experience a reduction in revenue per unit. In this case, selling a product in the UK for £15 would mean a revenue of $22.50.

In contrast to a fall in the exchange rate, a rise in the exchange rate increases export prices and lowers

> **learning tip**
>
> import prices. If the exchange rate rises from £1 = $2 to £1 = $2.50, a £50 UK export would rise in price from $100 to $125. The appreciation would cause a $60 US import to fall in price from £30 to £24. Again, firms may choose not to follow the exchange rate change, but in

most cases they will.

Changes in the exchange rate and the macroeconomy

A reduction in the exchange rate is likely to improve the current account position of the balance of payments. A fall in the price of exports will result in a rise in export revenue if demand is elastic. A rise in import prices will reduce expenditure on imports, again if demand is elastic.

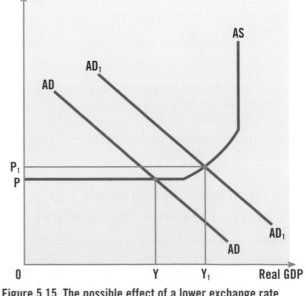

Figure 5.15 The possible effect of a lower exchange rate on the economy

A lower exchange rate, by boosting exports and reducing imports, will also increase aggregate demand. If the economy was previously operating below full capacity, such an increase will also raise employment and real GDP, as shown in Figure 5.15. More workers will be taken on in order to produce more products, both for export and for the home market.

There is a risk, however, that a lower exchange rate will put upward pressure on inflation. This is because the price of imported raw materials will rise, thereby increasing the cost of production and the price of imported finished products that count in the calculation of the country's inflation rate. In addition, domestic firms\facing more expensive imported rival products at home, the prospect of their products being cheaper abroad and higher demand in both markets, will be under less pressure to keep their

costs and prices low.

A rise in the exchange rate, on the other hand, is likely to increase a current account deficit. It is also likely to be deflationary, reducing aggregate demand, which in turn will reduce real GDP and employment. One possible advantage of a higher exchange rate is the downward pressure it is likely to put on inflation. It would also be welcomed by those firms importing products either as raw materials or to sell, and by people travelling abroad, who will find that the currency will buy them more.

ACTIVITY ⋯⟶

6 The application of macroeconomic policy instruments and the international economy

On completion of this chapter you should be able to:

- define fiscal, monetary and supply-side policies

- discuss, using the AD and AS model, the ways in which fiscal, monetary and supply-side policies can affect unemployment, inflation, economic growth and the current account position of the balance of payments

- discuss how effective fiscal, monetary and supply-side policies are in achieving the government's macroeconomic objectives

- discuss the reasons for, and consequences of, possible conflicts between policy objectives

- show an awareness of changes in the UK pattern of international trade since 2000

- explain the advantages that may be gained from international trade

- explain tariff and non-tariff methods of protection.

Introduction

A government can use a range of policy instruments (also called policy measures or policy tools) to achieve its macroeconomic objectives. Which combination it uses is determined by what it is trying to achieve and by how it views the likely effectiveness of the different measures.

Of course, the level of economic activity in one country is also affected by what is happening elsewhere in the world. The UK trades in a vast range of products with countries throughout the world. With other members of the European Union it does not impose and does not face restrictions on what it buys and sells. This, however, is not the case with some of its other trading partners.

Fiscal policy

Fiscal policy is one of the three main economic policies that governments use to influence economic activity and to achieve their macroeconomic policy objectives. The other two are **monetary policy** and **supply-side policies**.

Fiscal policy covers the taxation and spending decisions of a government. The government can change tax rates, the types of taxes it imposes and what it taxes, and the composition, amount and timing of government spending.

The key aim of fiscal policy is to influence aggregate demand (AD). The government can raise AD either by increasing its own spending and/or by reducing taxes. Government spending is a component of AD.

DEFINITIONS

Fiscal policy: the taxation and spending decisions of a government.

Monetary policy: central bank and/or government decisions on the rate of interest, the money supply and the exchange rate.

Supply-side policies: policies designed to increase aggregate supply by improving the efficiency of labour and product markets.

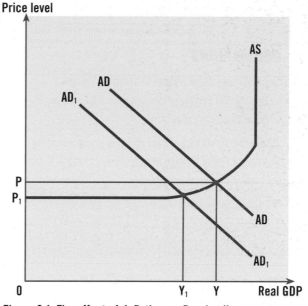

Figure 6.1 The effect of deflationary fiscal policy

Its spending on, for example, computers in schools will directly increase AD. This higher spending will also be likely to have a multiplier effect, causing AD to rise even further.

A cut in income tax will increase people's disposable income. This will raise consumption and again AD. Lower corporation tax (also known as corporate tax) would tend to increase the ability and willingness of firms to invest, thereby increasing another component of AD.

Rises in government spending and cuts in taxes designed to increase AD are referred to as **reflationary**, expansionary or loose fiscal policy. In contrast **deflationary**, contractionary or tight fiscal policy involves measures that reduce AD, that is, cuts in government spending and/or rises in taxes. Figure 6.1 illustrates the effect of deflationary fiscal policy.

Changes in government spending and taxation may be implemented for reasons other than influencing the level of AD. These include encouraging the consumption of merit goods and discouraging the consumption of demerit goods, altering the distribution of income, altering incentives and simplifying the system.

THE NATURE OF FISCAL POLICY

A government may seek to influence aggregate demand to ensure that it matches aggregate supply (AS) and so avoid both unemployment and inflation. If private sector demand (C + I + (X – M)) is low, a government may try to increase AD, whereas if it is considered to be too high, it may try to reduce AD. Taking such action can be referred to as acting counter-cyclically – the government is seeking to create greater economic stability by offsetting changes in private sector spending.

To achieve this objective, a government can use what is called **discretionary fiscal policy** or allow **automatic stabilisers** to operate. Discretionary fiscal policy is used when a government actively influences AD by changing its expenditure or taxes.

In contrast, automatic stabilisers are forms of government spending and taxation that change automatically to dampen down economic fluctuations

DEFINITIONS

Reflationary: of policy measures designed to increase aggregate demand.

Deflationary: of policy measures designed to reduce aggregate demand.

without any deliberate change in government policy. For instance, government spending on the job seeker's allowance falls when economic activity rises. Less is spent on the benefit, not because the government changes the benefit rate but because fewer people will claim it.

Similarly, the government will receive more income tax revenue when real GDP rises, without any change in tax rates. This is because more people will be employed and some people will be earning higher wages. The fall in government spending and rise in tax revenue will reduce the growth in AD and may help to prevent inflation. Of course, some forms of government spending and taxation are not automatic stabilisers. For instance, spending on child benefit is not linked to the **economic cycle**.

A number of governments, including the UK government, are now using fiscal policy rules. These are designed to create greater certainty and stability. The UK introduced fiscal policy rules in 1998. One, known as the golden rule, states that over the economic cycle the government should only borrow to pay for investment spending. This means it has to finance its current spending out of taxation. It will not borrow to fund current spending. The other rule is called the sustainable investment rule. This requires the government to keep public sector debt over the economic cycle at a 'stable and prudent level'.

ACTIVITY ⋯⋗

In March 2006, the Chinese government announced a number of tax changes. These included an increase in the tax on large cars, such as sport utility vehicles. This measure was introduced largely to limit the environmental damage and energy demand arising from the large increase in the number of cars on the roads.

New consumption taxes were applied to golf balls and equipment, some luxury watches and yachts. The taxes on skin care and shampoo products, however, were removed. These products had once been seen as luxurious but are now considered to be everyday necessities.

The tax change that received the most publicity outside China was the imposition of a 5 per cent tax on disposable wooden chopsticks. The government said that this was designed to reduce the use of timber.

a) Identify two different reasons for imposing a tax on a product.

b) Explain what is likely to happen to the tax revenue the Chinese government will collect in the future.

c) Discuss the likely impact on the distribution of income of the changes in taxes that the Chinese government made in 2006.

TYPES OF TAXES

The single most important source of tax revenue in the UK is income tax, and the second most important is value added tax (VAT). Income tax is a direct and **progressive tax**. As a person's income rises, both the amount and the percentage that a person pays in tax rises. VAT is an indirect and largely **regressive tax**. It is imposed on the sale of goods and services at different rates. The standard rate is 17.5 per cent, but a few items, including sanitary protection, are taxed at 5 per cent and some, such as most foods, children's clothing, prescriptions medicines, books and newspapers, do not have VAT charged on them.

Other taxes include excise duty, capital gains tax, corporation tax and inheritance tax. Excise duty is an indirect tax imposed on specific products. These are mainly alcohol, tobacco and petrol. The rate varies depending on the product. Capital gains tax is a tax on the increase in the value (the difference between purchase and selling price) on items such as shares, second homes and paintings. A large number of assets are exempt, including agricultural property, private motor cars and winnings from gambling. As we have already seen, corporation tax is a tax on the profits of firms. Inheritance tax is a tax on transfers of wealth above a certain amount.

GOVERNMENT SPENDING

Government spending, which can also be called public spending or public expenditure, can be divided into:

- capital expenditure – on, for example, hospitals, schools, roads

- current spending – on the running of public services and including, for example, teachers' pay and the purchase of medicines to be used in the NHS

- transfer payments – money transferred from taxpayers to recipients of benefits, for example, pensioners and the unemployed

- debt interest payments – payments made to the holders of government debt, for example, interest paid to holders of National Savings certificates.

The five most important individual areas of government spending in the UK recently have been social protection, health, education, defence and debt interest. The amount and proportion spent on different areas is influenced by a number of factors. For example, spending on social protection is influenced by benefit rates and by the level of economic activity. As indicated earlier (see page 140), it rises during periods of increasing unemployment and falls during periods of falling unemployment.

Expenditure on health and education is affected by government priorities, government policies, and changes in the age composition of population among other factors. The UK's ageing population is putting upward pressure on government spending on health. With people living longer, there is an increasing demand for National Health Service treatment and residential care. Other pressures include increased expectations in relation to the range and quality of health care treatment and advances in technology that have increased the number and complexity of operations that are possible.

Defence spending has been high recently because of the UK's military involvement in Iraq and Afghanistan.

ACTIVITY ⋯⋗

In the first eight months of 2007, Italy's income and corporate tax receipts increased by 21 per cent. The government attributed this to its campaign against taxation evasion. Economists, however, argued that the reduction in tax evasion accounted for only about half of the revenue increase. They identified two other causes. One was the economic growth that the country was experiencing and the other was the rise in the top rate of income tax.

a) What does the above suggest happened to the size of Italy's informal economy in 2007? Explain your answer.

b) Analyse the connection between economic growth and tax revenue.

c) Explain two possible reasons for the change in income tax that the Italian government introduced.

Military involvement abroad increases public expenditure

Debt interest payments are affected by the level of government debt and the rate of interest.

ACTIVITY ····❖

In March 2007, the Chancellor of the Exchequer announced that spending on health care in the UK would rise in cash terms over the financial year by 10 per cent and in real terms by 7 per cent. He also said that spending on defence would increase. In 2007–08, spending on defence was planned to be £32 billion out of total government spending of £587 billion. In the USA in the same period, defence was expected to account for 17 per cent of total government spending.

a) Explain why a rise in government spending may be different in cash and real terms.

b) Analyse the effect of an increase in government spending on health care on:

   i) AD

   ii) AS

c) i) How did planned government spending on defence in the UK compare with that of the USA?

   ii) Discuss whether an increase in government spending on defence will increase people's living standards.

THE BUDGET

In the UK, the Chancellor of the Exchequer outlines government spending proposals in three-year spending reviews and any tax changes are announced in the annual budget. The budget also provides information on the budget position in the past year and predictions for future years.

The Chancellor presents the budget each March

The budget position shows the relationship between government spending and tax revenue. A balanced budget occurs when the two are equal. In practice, budget deficits and budget surpluses are more common. A budget deficit arises when government spending exceeds tax revenue. In this case, the government will have to borrow to finance some of its spending. In contrast, a budget surplus occurs when tax revenue is greater than government spending. Such a surplus will allow a government to repay some of its debt.

A budget deficit or surplus may be the result of cyclical or structural factors. If there is a **recession**, tax revenue is likely to fall and government spending on benefits is likely to rise, due to the operation of automatic stabilisers. The government may also use discretionary fiscal policy in a bid to increase economic activity. In this case, the deficit may disappear as the economy grows.

DEFINITION

Recession: a fall in real GDP over a period of six months or more.

If, however, a budget deficit occurs when there is a high level of economic activity, it may suggest that there is something wrong with the structure of government spending and taxation. There may be an imbalance between the two, with the government being committed to spending too much relative to tax revenue. In this situation, the only way to eliminate the deficit is to cut government spending and/or raise tax revenue.

> **learning tip**
>
> Be very careful to avoid confusing a budget deficit and a current account deficit. Remember a budget deficit arises when government spending exceeds tax revenue. In contrast, a current account deficit is caused by import expenditure exceeding export revenue.

ACTIVITY ····⫶

The Czech Republic in 2007 had a relatively low corporate tax rate of 24 per cent. Some Czech politicians argued in favour of cutting the rate. Others, however, expressed concern that such a cut would increase the size of the country's budget deficit. The table below shows the budget position of a number of countries.

Budget balance as % of real GDP in 2007

Country	Budget balance
Czech Republic	−4.1
UK	−2.7
Italy	−2.5
USA	−1.6
Germany	0.4
Norway	18.9

a) Identify from the table a country that had a budget surplus in 2007.

b) Using an AD/AS diagram, analyse the effect of a cut in corporation tax on an economy.

c) Discuss whether a cut in the corporate tax rate would increase a budget deficit.

Monetary policy

Fiscal policy and monetary policy are sometimes referred to as demand-side policies as both seek to influence AD. Monetary policy instruments or measures include the rate of interest, the money supply and the exchange rate.

The main monetary policy instrument currently being used in the UK, the rest of Europe, the USA and many other countries is the rate of interest. When a central bank raises its official short-term interest rate, known as the base rate (but also sometimes called the bank or the repo rate), commercial banks usually increase their interest rates too. A higher interest rate tends to reduce consumption and lower firms' investment. It is also likely to encourage foreigners to place more money into UK financial institutions because of their higher return. This rise in demand for pounds will push up the value of the pound. A higher exchange rate will make exports more expensive and imports cheaper. This is likely to reduce net exports. So, a rise in the interest rate is likely to decrease AD by reducing consumption, investment and exports minus imports.

There is a chance, however, that a rate rise may not significantly affect consumption and investment. It may, though, cause foreigners to become concerned about the economy's growth prospects. In this case foreigners may move their funds to other countries and so the exchange rate may fall.

Changes in the money supply can also be used to influence AD. An increase in the money supply is likely to increase AD. If the government prints more money or makes it easier for banks to lend more money, people will have more money to spend. Changes in the money supply and interest rates are inversely related. A rise in the money supply, by increasing the amount that banks have to lend, reduces the interest rate.

Some economists define monetary policy to cover only changes in the rate of interest and the money supply. Others, however, also include changes in the exchange rate. A central bank can seek to influence the value of the currency by changing the interest rate and/or by dealing in the foreign exchange market. If it wants to reduce the exchange rate, it

Price of £s in euros

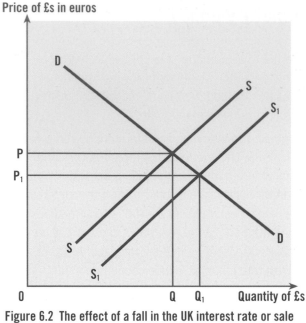

Figure 6.2 The effect of a fall in the UK interest rate or sale of pounds

can lower the interest rate or sell pounds. Figure 6.2 shows the effect that these measures may have on the value of the pound. A central bank may want to reduce the exchange rate in order to improve the current account position of the balance of payments and to stimulate economic activity.

In contrast, if the central bank wants to raise the exchange rate, it can increase the rate of interest and/or buy foreign currency. This would be an example of a deflationary or contractionary monetary policy. Such a policy aims to reduce AD, usually in a bid to lower inflation. A reflationary or expansionary monetary policy, on the other hand, seeks to stimulate a growth in AD.

THE MONETARY POLICY COMMITTEE

The Monetary Policy Committee (MPC) of the Bank of England sets the rate of interest with the main objective of achieving the government's target annual rate of inflation of 2 per cent, as measured by the consumer prices index. It is accepted that the inflation rate may fluctuate around the target. Trying to achieve exactly 2 per cent every month would be very difficult and would involve frequent interest rate changes. For this reason there is a 1 percentage point margin set either side of the central target. Subject to meeting the inflation target, the MPC has

been instructed to support the economic policy of the government, including its objectives for employment and economic growth.

The MPC consists of five members drawn from employees of the Bank of England, including the governor and the two deputy governors, and four economists appointed by the Chancellor of the Exchequer for three-year terms. It meets monthly to review evidence on the performance of the economy and indicators of changes in inflationary pressure. This information includes figures on the current and predicted growth of the money supply, changes in the exchange rate, wage rates, mortgage lending, share prices, productivity, retail sales and surveys of business and consumer confidence. A government official attends the meetings to keep the members informed about government spending and tax plans.

The MPC considers whether it needs to change the rate of interest now to hit the inflation target in two years' time. It has to look this far ahead because it takes that long for changes in the interest rate to have their full impact on the price level. In the light of the information it examines, the MPC votes on whether to change the rate, and if so, by how much.

The Bank of England sets interest rates in the UK

Each month, check the decision made by the MPC. Newspapers and the Bank of England's website (www.bankofengland.co.uk/monetarypolicy/overview.htm) provide detailed information. Consider whether you would have come to the same decision. (For the Bank of England website you can go to www.heinemann.co.uk/hotlinks, insert the express code 2223P and click on 'Bank of England'.)

ACTIVITY ·····

In October 2007, Sweden's central bank, the Riksbank, raised its interest rate from 3.75 per cent to 4 per cent to achieve its inflation target of 2 per cent. The Riksbank's governor, Stefan Ingves, said it was a difficult decision, as the information available to the bank was somewhat contradictory. Sweden was experiencing falling unemployment, but economic growth in the USA, Sweden's third largest export market, was slowing down.

In the same month, India's central bank, the Reserve Bank of India (RBI), sought to restrict the growth of the money supply by reducing the amount commercial banks can lend. At the time the money supply was growing at an annual rate of 22 per cent. The RBI also lowered its inflation target to 3 per cent from 4–4.5 per cent.

a) In October 2007, were Sweden and India pursuing a reflationary or deflationary monetary policy?

b) Using the information provided, explain why the Swedish inflation rate might:

i) have risen

ii) have fallen.

c) Which of the two central banks referred to was seeking to achieve the lowest rise in the price level? Explain your answer.

Supply-side policies

While fiscal and monetary policies seek to influence aggregate demand, supply-side policies aim to influence aggregate supply. Fiscal and monetary policies may try to increase or decrease AD, depending on the level of economic activity. In contrast, supply-side policies always aim to increase AS. They are never designed to reduce AS.

If they are successful, supply-side policies will increase productive potential and can help prevent inflation, reduce structural and frictional unemployment and improve the country's trade position.

There are a range of supply-side policies. These try to lower firms' costs of production and increase productive capacity by increasing the efficiency of labour and product markets. This indicates another difference between fiscal and monetary policies and supply-side policies. The first two seek to improve macroeconomic performance by influencing the whole economy. In contrast, supply-side policies often aim to raise macroeconomic performance by improving the performance of particular markets.

This is why they are sometimes referred to as microeconomic policies.

Some supply-side policies, such as privatisation and deregulation, are based on reducing government intervention in the economy to enable markets to work more efficiently. Others, such as government financed education and training, involve government intervention. Such intervention may increase productive potential in cases where there is market failure.

In deciding whether a change in government spending or taxation is an example of fiscal policy or a supply-side policy, consider whether its main objective is to influence AD or AS. For example, a government may cut income tax rates in order to increase AD or to raise AS.

EXAMPLES OF SUPPLY-SIDE POLICIES
Education and training

Government investment in education and training and government encouragement to firms to increase their training should raise the occupational mobility of labour and labour productivity. If output per worker hour does increase, the potential output of the economy will rise. This will shift the AS curve to the right as shown in Figure 6.3 (see over).

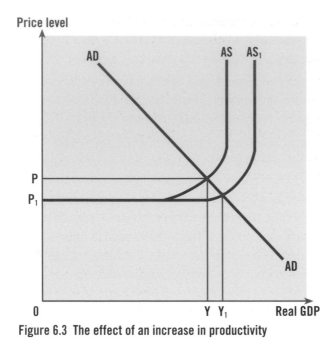

Figure 6.3 The effect of an increase in productivity

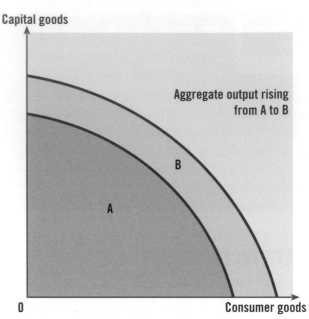

Figure 6.4 The effect of a rise in both the size of the labour force and its utilisation

A government may insist that those who are unemployed undergo training. The UK government's 'welfare to work' approach encourages those who have been unemployed for some time to take up a subsidised job, a place on an educational or training course, or voluntary work. The idea behind this is to develop skills, confidence and work experience.

Government assistance to new firms

New, small firms provide employment, develop entrepreneurial skills and introduce new ideas. They may, however, find it difficult to break into established markets. A government may help by providing them with grants and charging them a low rate of corporation tax.

Reduction in direct taxes

As well as increasing AD, lower direct taxation may also increase AS. This is because lower direct taxes increase incentives to firms, workers and potential workers. A cut in corporation tax will increase both the funds that firms have available to invest and the return from any investment undertaken. If investment does increase, the productive capacity of the economy will rise.

Some economists believe that a cut in income tax will encourage some existing workers to work

overtime, be more willing to accept promotion, stay in the labour force longer, or enter or re-enter the labour force. Such a measure may, as well as increasing the size of the labour force, also increase its use. This will be the case if it persuades more of the unemployed to accept employment at the going wage rate, as their disposable income will now be higher.

Figure 6.4 shows both an economy's productive capacity increasing and its use of that capacity increasing.

Some economists, however, argue that lower income tax rates may encourage some workers to take more leisure time, as they can now gain the same disposable income by working fewer hours. It may also be the case that what is stopping the unemployed from gaining employment is not a lack of willingness to work at the going wage rate but a lack of jobs.

National minimum wage (NMW)

There is some debate about whether the introduction of a national minimum wage or the removal of an NMW is a supply-side policy. The key determinant is whether an NMW encourages people to enter the labour force or whether it reduces the efficiency of the labour market.

Reduction in unemployment benefit

A reduction in job seeker's allowance will widen the gap between income from employment and the benefit. This may force some of the unemployed to seek work more actively and to accept employment at lower wage rates. If this is the outcome, greater use will be made of the labour force. This in itself does not increase productive capacity. What it does do, is to reduce a negative output gap and move output closer to full capacity.

There is a risk, however, that cutting unemployment benefit may increase unemployment. If the unemployment is of a cyclical nature, there will be no jobs available for the unemployed. Cutting their benefits will reduce consumption. This, in turn, will lower AD and cause firms to cut back their output and probably make some workers redundant. In addition, cutting benefits is likely to widen income inequality.

Reduction in other benefits

Reducing other benefits that support people who are economically inactive will increase the productive capacity of the economy if it does encourage them to enter the labour force. If, however, these people are unable to seek work, then all such a measure will do is to reduce the income of benefit recipients.

Reduction in trade union power

A reduction in trade union power may increase the efficiency of labour markets. This will be the case if trade unions reduce employment by pushing wage rates above the equilibrium level and encouraging workers to engage in restrictive practices. In such a situation, reducing the power of trade unions will increase labour productivity and reduce the cost of employing labour. As a result, firms will be encouraged to employ more workers and raise output.

Trade unions, however, may actually help labour markets work efficiently. They may act as a counterbalance to the market imperfection of very powerful employers. They may also reduce firms' costs by acting as a channel for communication between employers and workers on issues, since it is cheaper to negotiate with one body than with individual workers. If this is the case, reducing trade union power may actually raise firms' costs and unemployment.

Privatisation

Some economists argue that government intervention should be reduced. They believe that private sector firms are in the best position to make decisions about what to produce, how to produce and what to charge. This is because they are subject to the discipline of the market. If they do not provide the products that consumers want at competitive prices, it is argued, they will go out of business. So, these economists favour the transfer of firms from the public to the private sector.

Other economists, however, disagree. They argue that government ownership of firms is beneficial in a

ACTIVITY ····⁝⁝

In January 2006, the UK government announced a crackdown on benefits. This was prompted by its concern about the rise in the number of people living on benefits rather than being in the labour force. For example, the number of people claiming incapacity benefit (IB) had risen from 740,000 in 1979 to 2.7m in 2005. The UK had a higher percentage of long-term sick people than any other EU country, apart from Poland.

The changes outlined by the government included replacing IB by an employment support allowance from 2008. This benefit requires claimants to undergo a new medical assessment to determine whether they are able to work and,

if so, what kind of work they can do. Among the other changes is the offer of a financial incentive for lone parents on income benefit to undertake training courses or work experience.

a) Explain why the two changes outlined above could be classified as supply-side policies.

b) Explain two reasons why someone might be reluctant to come off an incapacity-related benefit.

c) Discuss the effect on government spending in the short and long run of an increase in training financed by the government.

number of cases where there is a high risk of market failure.

Deregulation

Deregulation is the removal of rules and regulations that affect firms in the belief that it will give the firms greater freedom to make their own decisions and to increase competition by making it easier for new firms to enter an industry. For example, the UK government has removed some of the restrictions on firms competing with Royal Mail. In 2006, for instance, courier firms were allowed to apply for a licence to collect and distribute bulk loads of letters, handing them over to the Royal Mail for delivery on the last stage, to the letterbox.

In a number of countries including France and India, governments are considering reducing tight job protection laws that can make employers reluctant to take on new workers.

Policies to reduce unemployment

There is a range of policy measures a government may employ to reduce unemployment. The choice of measures will be influenced by the cause of the unemployment, the rate and duration of unemployment and the state of the other macroeconomic objectives.

DEMAND-SIDE POLICIES

If the economy is operating below its productive capacity, unemployment may be reduced by increases in AD. In such a case, expansionary fiscal and/or monetary policy can be used to create jobs. A government, using fiscal policy, could increase its spending and/or cut tax rates in order to raise AD. In practice, a rise in government spending has the potential to have more of an impact on AD and unemployment than cuts in taxes. An extra £10 billion of government spending, for example, would initially raise AD by the full £10 billion. In contrast, a cut in taxes of £10 billion may lead to an injection of only £6 billion of extra spending in the economy if, for example, £3 billion is saved and £1 billion is spent on imports.

Increases in the money supply or lower interest rates are also likely to raise AD. For instance, a fall in

interest rates and/or an increase in the money supply should stimulate consumption and investment. It may also raise net exports if it causes a fall in the exchange rate. Figure 6.5 shows the effect of expansionary monetary policy.

Expansionary fiscal and monetary policies may have undesirable side-effects. One consequence of a rise in AD may be a rise in the price level if the economy moves close to full employment. The higher level of spending may also increase any existing deficit on the current account of the balance of payments as UK residents buy more imported products.

In recent years, fiscal and monetary policies have not been used primarily to influence unemployment directly. Fiscal policy has been used mainly to promote economic stability, and monetary policy – in the form of interest rate changes – to achieve the government's inflation target. However, the Bank of England has been instructed by the government not only to maintain price stability but 'subject to that, to support the government's economic policies, including its objectives for growth and employment'.

Economic stability and low inflation will, of course, make low unemployment more likely, by encouraging investment and maintaining or increasing international competitiveness.

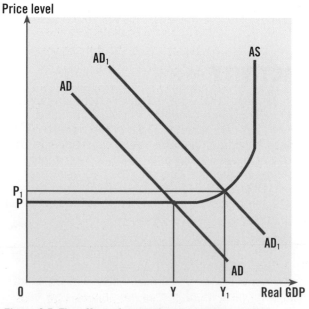

Figure 6.5 The effect of expansionary monetary policy

SUPPLY-SIDE POLICIES

Unemployment can exist even where there is not a shortage of AD if there are supply-side problems. Those people who are out of work when the level of AD is high, and there is no shortage of job vacancies, are likely to be in between jobs, lacking the appropriate skills, geographically or occupationally immobile, have family circumstances that restrict their ability to work or are lacking the incentives to move off benefits and find employment.

There are a number of factors that determine such unemployment. The time people spend finding a job after they have left another job is influenced by the quality of the information they have about job vacancies. Many of the long-term unemployed lack qualifications, have poor communication skills and are geographically immobile. Some may have lost the work habit, some may be having difficulty affording child care or overcoming prejudice in order to be permitted to work (for example, disabled people) and some may believe they are better off on benefits than in employment. In these circumstances, it is unlikely that raising AD will succeed in reducing unemployment. What is needed is an increase in the attractiveness of work to the unemployed and an increase in the attractiveness of the unemployed to employers.

Supply-side policies can be implemented to increase economic incentives and the quality of labour services offered by the unemployed. The quantity and quality of information available to the unemployed about job vacancies and to employers about those seeking jobs can be increased. Improved education and training and the provision of work experience may raise the skills of the unemployed. Greater provision of low-cost child-care may enable more lone parents to work. Legislation and the subsidising of special equipment and adaptation of buildings may facilitate the employment of more disabled workers.

The economic incentive to work may be increased by widening the gap between the income received from working and the income received in benefits. This might be achieved by, for instance, a reduction in income tax rates. Some economists also argue in favour of cutting the rules and regulations that firms have to follow in hiring, employing and firing workers.

Such rules and regulations, they claim, can make employers reluctant to take on new workers.

Of course, at any one time, unemployment may be the result of both a lack of aggregate demand and supply-side problems. In such a situation, a combination of expansionary demand-side and supply-side policies will be needed.

> ### ACTIVITY ⋯⋮⟩
>
> In September 2007, the French government announced its plans to overhaul the country's social security benefit system. It argued that the system was financially unsustainable and discouraged work. The planned reforms included the end of 'special pension schemes' for some public workers. These schemes were set up partly to compensate people for undertaking dangerous or demanding work. They allow a range of workers, including electricity, gas, railway and Paris Metro workers to retire early on full pensions. For example, train drivers can retire as early as 50.
>
> The government was also proposing to reform the country's rigid rules on employment contracts, to make it more difficult for people to claim state benefits and possibly to cut state benefit.
>
> a) Using an AD/AS diagram, analyse the likely effects on the French economy of the proposed change in the retirement regime for some public sector workers.
>
> b) Discuss whether a cut in unemployment benefit would reduce unemployment.

Policies to control inflation

If a country is experiencing inflation, the measures it implements will be influenced by what is thought to be causing the inflation. In the long run, it will use policy instruments in order to maintain price stability.

COST-PUSH INFLATION

There are a number of policy measures a government can take to control cost-push inflation in the short run. If a government believes that inflation is caused by excessive increases in wage rates, it may try to restrict wage rises. It can control wages in the public sector directly by restricting increases in government spending allocated to the pay of public sector workers. It can also restrict wage rises in both the public and private sectors by introducing an incomes policy. For instance, a government may place a limit on wage increases of 3 per cent or £2,000 a year. This measure seeks to reduce inflation without causing unemployment. It may, however, create inflexibility in labour markets. Firms wanting to expand will be limited in how much they can offer to attract new workers.

A government may try to lower firms' costs by reducing corporation tax. This will also have the advantage of stimulating investment. A government may also provide subsidies, so that firms can cover rising costs without having to put up their prices. This measure may reduce costs in the long run if some of the subsidies are spent on investment. There is a danger, however, that firms may become reliant on subsidies and do not strive to keep their costs down.

DEMAND-PULL INFLATION

To reduce demand-pull inflation, a government may use deflationary fiscal and/or monetary policy instruments. These are ones that seek to reduce inflation by decreasing aggregate demand, or at least the growth of aggregate demand. A government could, for instance, raise income tax. This would reduce people's disposable income and so their ability to spend.

The main short-run anti-inflationary policy instrument being employed in the UK and many other countries is changes in the interest rate. A higher interest rate is likely to reduce AD by reducing consumption, investment and net exports. Figure 6.6 illustrates a deflationary policy instrument reducing inflation.

INFLATION TARGETING

Inflation targeting can lower the chance of both demand-pull and cost-push inflation by reducing expectations of inflation. If people are convinced that a central bank has the determination, experience and ability to meet its target, they will act in a way that does not cause inflation.

Inflation targeting was first adopted by the Reserve Bank of New Zealand in 1990 and it is now widely used. It makes monetary policy more transparent and the central bank more accountable. If it is successful in keeping inflation low and stable, it means that the interest rate can also be low. This, in turn, is likely to encourage investment and economic growth.

Long run

In the long run, a government is likely to seek to reduce the possibility of inflationary pressure by increasing aggregate supply. If the productive capacity of the economy grows in line with AD, with rightward shifts in the AD curve being matched by

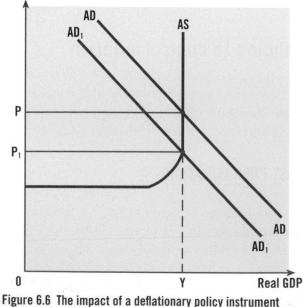

Figure 6.6 The impact of a deflationary policy instrument

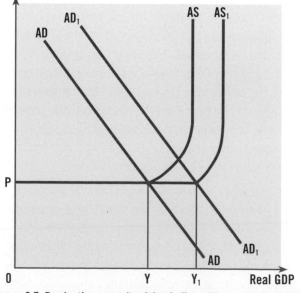

Figure 6.7 Productive capacity rising in line with aggregate demand

rightward shifts in the AS curve, the economy can grow without the price level rising. This combination of shifts is shown in Figure 6.7.

If AD and AS increase in line with each other, people will be able to enjoy more goods and services without the economy experiencing inflation and balance of payments problems.

To ensure that the quantity and quality of resources rise to supply more products, supply-side policies may be used. Using such policies is a long-run approach to controlling inflationary pressure. This is because most policy measures take time to have their full impact on productive capacity. They do, nonetheless, have the advantage that they do not usually run the risk of the adverse short-run side-effects on employment and output that deflationary fiscal and monetary policies may pose.

Policies to promote economic growth

A government may use different policies to achieve economic growth in the short and long run and to make economic growth more stable.

SHORT RUN

Increases in output in the short run can occur due to increases in AD if the economy is initially producing below full capacity. Such an increase may be stimulated by expansionary fiscal or monetary policy. Figure 6.8 shows the country's output increasing from Y to Y_1 as a result of AD increasing.

Some fiscal and monetary policy instruments have the advantage that they have the potential to increase both AD and AS. For instance, a lower rate of interest is likely to stimulate not only consumption but also investment. Higher investment will increase AS. Increases in some forms of government spending, for example, spending on education and research and development, will also shift the AS curve to the right.

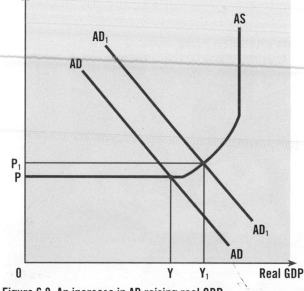

Price level

Figure 6.8 An increase in AD raising real GDP

LONG RUN

In the long run, increases in the country's output can continue to be achieved only if the productive capacity of the economy increases. This is why changes in AS are so important. So, for long-run economic growth to occur, the quality and/or quantity of resources has to increase. This is exactly what supply-side policies seek to achieve.

For instance, measures that raise investment will increase AS. The extent of the increase in AS will depend on the amount of extra investment, its type and how efficiently it is used.

To use capital efficiently, it is important to have educated and healthy workers. Investment in **human capital** should increase the productive capacity of the economy. However, again, the extent to which this occurs is influenced by the appropriateness and the quality of the investment. To be productive, workers need a range of skills including numeracy, literacy, ICT and interpersonal skills.

DEFINITION

Human capital: education, training and experience that a worker, or group of workers, possesses.

STABLE GROWTH

In seeking to promote economic growth, most governments aim for stable growth. This objective is

Education provides human capital

for actual growth to match trend growth and for that trend growth to rise over time.

Governments try to avoid AD increasing faster than the trend growth rate permits, since this can result in the economy overheating with inflation and balance of payments problems arising. They also try to prevent AD rising more slowly than the trend growth rate, since this would mean a negative output gap developing with unemployed resources. In other words, governments seek to avoid economic cycles.

ACTIVITY ····≻

Denmark's economy grew more rapidly than most of the EU's economies in 2005 and 2006. It also enjoyed the lowest unemployment rate in the EU at 3.3 per cent as measured by the LFS measure. In 2007, however, its economic growth rate slowed down and it was predicted that in 2008 it would decline even further. To counter this decline in economic growth, the Danish government was considering cutting the top rate of income tax and allowing more immigrant workers into the country.

a) How is economic growth measured?

b) Explain what happened to Denmark's national output in 2007.

c) Analyse how the policy measures proposed by the Danish government may increase economic growth.

Policies to improve the balance of payments

As with the other objectives, there are a range of policy instruments that a government can use to improve its balance of payments position. The short-run measures tend to concentrate on demand, while the long-run measures focus on improving the supply-side of the economy.

SHORT RUN

In the short run there are three main ways a government may try to raise export revenue and/or reduce import expenditure in order to correct a current account deficit. These ways are causing a fall in the exchange rate, reducing demand for all products whatever their source and specifically reducing demand for imports.

Exchange rate adjustment

A country may seek to reduce the exchange rate if it believes that its current level is too high and as a result is causing its products to be uncompetitive against rival countries' products. A central bank may seek to lower the exchange rate by selling its own currency and/or reducing its interest rate.

As noted at the end of the previous chapter, a lower exchange rate will cause export prices to fall and import prices to rise. But to succeed in increasing export revenue and reducing import expenditure, it is important that demand for exports and imports is price elastic, that other countries do not devalue and do not increase any import restrictions.

Lowering the exchange rate should increase AD and thereby raise aggregate output and employment in the short run, but it may increase inflationary pressure.

Deflationary demand management

To discourage expenditure on imports, a government may adopt deflationary fiscal and monetary policy instruments. Domestic spending may be reduced by higher taxation, lower government spending and/or higher interest rates. There is the risk, however, that the resulting reduction in spending may cause aggregate output to fall and unemployment to rise.

Import restrictions

A country may seek to reduce expenditure on imports by imposing import restrictions including **tariffs** and **quotas**. These measures, however, may have inflationary side-effects. For instance, imposing tariffs will increase the price of some products bought in the country, raise the cost of imported raw materials and reduce competitive pressure on domestic firms to keep costs and prices low.

Placing restrictions also runs the risk of provoking retaliation. If other countries respond by increasing their restrictions, the country may end up spending less on imports but also earning less from exports.

In addition, membership of an economic bloc, such as the EU, and a multinational organisation, such as the World Trade Organisation (WTO), limits the independent action that a country can take on import restrictions.

Long run

If a deficit arises from a lack of quality competitiveness, low labour productivity or high inflation, then reducing the value of the currency, deflationary demand-side policy instruments and import restrictions will not provide long-run solutions. In such a situation the most appropriate approach would be to implement supply-side policies.

As well as the supply-side policies already mentioned, a government may give subsidies to infant industries in the belief that they have the potential to grow and become internationally competitive. It may also increase funds for research and development at universities to encourage invention and innovation.

How successful supply-side policies are depends on the appropriateness of the policies. For example, training has to be in the right areas and firms and workers have to respond in a positive way to any incentives provided. Some supply-side policies can also take a relatively long time to have an effect and can be very expensive for the government.

> **learning tip**
> Policies to improve the balance of payments usually focus on instruments to influence the current account position.

CURRENT ACCOUNT SURPLUS

A balance of payments disequilibrium may also arise because of a current account surplus. A government may seek to reduce or eliminate a surplus in order

DEFINITIONS

Tariff: a tax on imports.

Quota: a limit on imports.

to avoid inflationary pressure and to raise the amount of imports it can enjoy. To reduce a surplus, a government may seek to raise the value of its currency, introduce reflationary fiscal and monetary instruments and/or reduce import restrictions.

ACTIVITY ····⫶

High spending by households in Latvia resulted in the country experiencing an inflation rate of 6.6 per cent and a current account deficit that reached 11 per cent of GDP in 2006.

To reduce inflation and to correct a current account deficit, the Latvian government moved from a budget deficit to a budget surplus in 2007. It also introduced a range of supply-side policies designed to improve export competitiveness by, for instance, increasing labour productivity.

a) Explain how the change in Latvia's budget position may have reduced the country's current account deficit.

b) What is the link between labour productivity and export competitiveness?

c) Analyse how one supply-side policy could increase labour productivity.

Effectiveness of fiscal policy

Fiscal policy has a number of advantages. As we have seen, a number of taxes and forms of government spending adjust automatically to offset fluctuations in real GDP. Changes in government spending directly affect the G (government spending) component of AD while changes in taxation affect C and I (consumer expenditure and investment) by altering the disposable income of households and the post tax income of firms.

Some forms of government spending and taxation, including cuts in corporation tax and training grants, have the potential to increase both AD and AS.

Fiscal policy, however, also has some potential drawbacks. Not only do changes in government spending and tax rates take time to have an effect on the economy; it can also take time to recognise the need for a change in policy and to gather the information on which to base the change. Then there is the time it takes to draw up and implement new tax codes and government spending plans.

There is also a time lag between introducing a fiscal policy instrument and that instrument having an

ECONOMICS IN CONTEXT

REPORT ON THE SPANISH ECONOMY – GOOD BUT COULD DO BETTER

Comunidad de Madrid
CONSTRUCCIÓN DE
140 VIVIENDAS Y GARAJES

Recent years have seen Spanish macroeconomic performance improve. Indeed, Spain has out-performed most other EU economies. The country's economic growth rate has been high, reaching 3.7 per cent in 2007. In that year, its unemployment, while still relatively high at 8 per cent, was continuing its downward trend. The country's price level has been relatively stable, averaging 2.8 per cent between

2000 and 2007. Over this period the country experienced a current account deficit on its balance of payments, but some of this was accounted for by interest paid back on loans undertaken by Spanish firms wishing to expand.

Some of the strengthening of the Spanish economy can be attributed to the policies pursued by the European Central Bank (ECB) and by the Spanish government. As a member of the single currency, Spain's interest rate is set by the ECB. In recent years, the rate has been relatively low and stable and this has helped to boost economic growth. The Spanish government has prevented AD rising too rapidly by allowing automatic stabilisers

to work. The budget position has moved from deficit to surplus as the economy has grown.

The Spanish government, though, is concerned that the economy is relying too much on the construction sector. The country has been enjoying a property boom and in 2007 construction accounted for 18 per cent of GDP. In an attempt to diversify the economy and raise productivity, the government has been using a range of supply-side policies. These include providing grants to encourage private sector investment in bio-technology, funding new research facilities and introducing a lower tax band for new, small firms.

impact on the economy. For example, households may take some time to adjust their spending when income tax is changed. If a government decides to build several new schools, the rise in spending will not occur immediately. It will take time to draw up designs for the schools, get planning permission and actually build the schools.

A number of forms of government spending are inflexible. It is, for instance, difficult to cut spending on health care and pensions. Also, once an investment project, such as new hospital or road, has been started, it may be politically and economically difficult to stop it.

For fiscal policy instruments to work effectively, they need to be based on accurate information. If, for instance, forecasts inaccurately predict a recession in the near future, a government may implement expansionary fiscal policy. If the economy is actually heading for an economic boom, such a move will add to inflationary pressure. It will reinforce the economic cycle rather than stabilise the economy.

Another reason why fiscal policy instruments may not work in the way the government expects is because households and firms may react in unexpected ways. For instance, a cut in income and corporation taxes may not lead to higher consumption and investment if households and firms lack confidence. Even if changes in taxation and government spending move the economy in the right direction, it may not alter economic activity to the extent the government wants. This may be because the size of the multiplier effect has been inaccurately estimated.

Changes in fiscal policy may also have an adverse effect on incentives and other macroeconomic objectives. A rise in income tax rates or an increase in state benefits may discourage some people from working. Higher corporation tax may discourage investment. A rise in taxation designed to reduce inflation may cut aggregate demand too far and cause a fall in real GDP and a rise in unemployment. Similarly, there is a risk that reflationary fiscal policy, while raising real GDP and lowering unemployment, may increase inflationary pressure and worsen a current account deficit.

Fiscal policy changes can also be offset by changes in economic activity in other countries. For example,

if the UK is pursuing an expansionary fiscal policy but its main trading partners are experiencing a recession, AD may not rise much in the UK.

> **learning tip**
>
> In assessing the effectiveness of any type of policy, consider both its advantages and its limitations. Also, remember that in an increasingly integrated global economy, the macroeconomic performance of a country is influenced not only by the policies of its own government but also by the policies of other governments.

ACTIVITY ····

US politicians in 2007 were considering cutting the country's corporate tax rate. In that year the overall rate was 39 per cent (adding state taxes to federal ones). This rate compared to 30 per cent in the UK, 25 per cent in China and 13 per cent in Ireland.

Those in favour of such a cut argued it would make US firms more internationally competitive and would make the country a more attractive place for firms to locate.

In practice, though, due to tax allowances, many US based firms were paying less than 30 per cent on average most were paying 23 per cent.

Tax rates are also not the only factor influencing where a multinational company decides to locate. Other factors include the availability of skilled labour and government subsidies.

A government considering cutting any tax rate also has to consider by how much it should cut the tax rate and what the implications for tax revenue will be.

a) Analyse how a cut in the US corporate tax rate could make US firms more internationally competitive.

b) Identify two reasons why firms might prefer to locate in the USA rather than the UK despite the US's higher corporate tax rate.

c) Discuss whether a cut in the corporate tax rate would reduce or increase tax revenue.

The effectiveness of monetary policy

As with fiscal policy, monetary policy depends on reliable information. There is a risk, however, that data, for instance, business confidence, may be misleading, and forecasts of trends in unemployment may be inaccurate.

Monetary policy instruments can be difficult to control. In the past, the UK and US governments tried to keep inflation in check by controlling the money supply. They did not find this easy. This was, in part, due to the strong profit motive that commercial banks have to increase bank lending.

A central bank can seek to influence the exchange rate by buying and selling currency and by changing the interest rate. Its attempts may, however, be offset by large movements of speculative funds.

The main policy instrument currently being used in the UK and a number of other countries to influence short-run economic activity is the rate of interest. The use of this policy instrument by the MPC is generally considered to have been very successful. The MPC, though, has received some criticism for overestimating the prospect of inflation and so keeping the interest rate too high and limiting economic growth.

It also takes time for an interest rate change to work through the economy. Interest rates offered to savers and charged to borrowers by commercial banks and other financial institutions do not always adjust quickly to reflect the change in base rate. A significant proportion of borrowing is now taken out on fixed rates. These take time to alter. Even when interest rates do change, it takes time for consumption, investment and net exports to adjust and for the alteration in AD to be reflected in the inflation rate. Indeed, it has been estimated that the process can take up to two years. As noted earlier (see page 144), this is why, if the MPC receives information indicating that on current trends inflation will rise outside its target range in two years time, it will raise the interest rate now.

There is also the question as to what extent AD will change in response to interest rate changes. A rise in the interest rate may not cause people to reduce their spending and firms to alter their investment if they are optimistic about the future. Indeed, expected changes in income may be more influential than changes in the interest rate.

A central bank's ability to change its interest rate may be limited by the need for it to remain in line with other countries' interest rates. This is because a noticeable differential may result in an inflow or outflow of hot money flows and these can disrupt financial markets. Those EU countries that are members of the single currency have limited independent control over monetary policy. In their case, the rate of interest is set by the European Central Bank and they do not, individually, have an exchange rate to influence.

Another limit with using interest rate changes is that when the interest rate falls to very low levels, a further cut is likely to be ineffective in stimulating economic activity. For instance, in June 2004, the US interest rate was at an historic low of 1 per cent and in September 2007, the Japanese interest rate was 0.6 per cent. Halving an interest rate from such low levels would be very unlikely to cause a rise in consumption, investment or net exports. For example, why would someone who was not prepared to borrow when the rate of interest was 1 per cent be prepared to do so when it is cut to 0.5 per cent?

Indeed, the effectiveness of interest rate changes to stimulate economic activity can be limited by their very success in tackling inflation. Low and stable inflation means that a central bank can keep the interest rate low. Such a situation, while having benefits, will leave the central bank with little room to cut the interest rate further.

The effects of monetary policy tend to be more concentrated on certain groups than do changes in income tax, for example. For instance, a rise in the interest rate will hit firms that export a high proportion of their output more than it will affect other firms. This is because they will be affected not only by higher costs but also by a likely fall in demand resulting from a rise in the exchange rate.

Any monetary policy instrument may also have undesirable side-effects. A rise in the exchange rate, designed to reduce inflationary pressures, may worsen the balance of payments position.

ACTIVITY ···

In 2007, Mexico's inflation rate reached 4 per cent. This was above its central bank's target of 3 per cent. The main cause was the rise in the price of basic food items. In particular, the higher world demand for ethanol had pushed up the price of maize and sugar. The higher inflation rate particularly harmed the 45 per cent of Mexicans who are classified as poor.

The country's central bank decided not to raise its interest rate because of concerns about the slow-down in economic growth.

a) How does Mexico's inflation target compare with the UK's?

b) Why may the poor be particularly harmed by inflation?

c) Explain why a rise in the interest rate may cause a 'slowdown in economic growth'.

d) Discuss one other policy instrument a government could use to reduce inflation.

The effectiveness of supply-side policies

Supply-side policies are selective, targeted at particular markets, and are designed to raise efficiency. Economists agree that if the supply-side performance of the economy can be improved, it may be easier for a government to achieve its objectives. Increasing AS enables AD to continue to rise over time without inflationary pressures building up. A higher quality of resources should also make domestic firms more price and quality competitive and so improve the country's current account position.

Increasing the productive potential of an economy on its own, however, will not be sufficient in raising economic performance if there is a lack of AD. In such a case, the extra capacity would not be used. Figure 6.9 (see over) shows AS increasing but output remaining unchanged.

Some supply-side policies, for example, spending on education, take a relatively long time to have an effect. They can be expensive to operate and there is no guarantee they will work. Indeed, as we have seen, there are also differences of opinion about the effectiveness of particular supply-side policies. For instance, economists disagree about whether firms operate more efficiently in the public or the private sector.

ECONOMICS IN CONTEXT

CHINESE MONETARY POLICY

The main monetary policy instrument used by the Bank of England, the US Federal Reserve and the European Central Bank is the rate of interest. The People's Bank of China (PBOC) also occasionally changes its interest rate to influence AD. The main policy instrument it uses, however, is changes in the money supply. The PBOC influences the money supply in a number of ways, including changing the amount of funds the country's banks have to hold at the PBOC and placing direct limits on the amounts the banks can lend.

The reason the PBOC favours changes in the money supply is that AD in the economy is relatively interest inelastic. A rise in the interest rate does not significantly reduce investment, as state-owned enterprises do not always consider very carefully the financial return on their purchase of capital goods. The balance between consumption and saving in China is probably being influenced more at the moment by other factors, including changes in health care and pension provision, and income levels.

The PBOC has recently been seeking to influence net exports by keeping the exchange rate low. It has been doing this, however, more by selling its currency, the yuan (sometimes also called the remnibi) than by changing the interest rate.

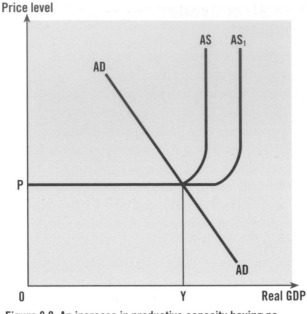

Price level

AS AS₁

AD

P

AD

0   Y   Real GDP

Figure 6.9 An increase in productive capacity having no impact on real GDP

Possible conflicts between policy objectives

The objectives of economic growth and low unemployment may benefit from expansionary demand-side policy measures. In contrast, such measures may make it more difficult for a government to achieve low inflation and a satisfactory balance of payments position.

The MPC may face a conflict when setting the interest rate. It may want to raise the interest rate to reduce inflationary pressure but be concerned about the effect such a move will have on the exchange rate and so on the balance of payments and employment.

Governments and central banks may seek to reduce the possibility of policy conflicts by using a variety of policy instruments. For instance, a government through its central bank may use the rate of interest to control inflation and labour market reforms to promote economic growth. Governments strive to ensure that increases in AD can be matched by increases in AS and that the economy works at full capacity.

Changes in the UK's pattern of international trade since 2000

International trade plays an important role in influencing output, employment and the price level in the UK. Firms in the country sell and purchase a wide range of products to and from countries throughout the world. They are internationally competitive in a number of goods, including telecommunications, aerospace engines and computer software. They are particularly strong in services, especially financial services. The City of London is the world's foremost financial centre, with a wide range of institutions dealing with banking, foreign exchange trading, share dealing, takeovers and mergers. Canary Wharf is often seen as a symbol of the success of the City.

ACTIVITY

The Federal Reserve (the Fed) is the central bank of the USA. Its Federal Open Market Committee (FOMC) is headed by the chairman of the Federal Reserve. It has four other members who are governors of the Fed appointed by the US president and five are drawn from the 12 presidents in charge of the associated banks based throughout the country.

The FOMC meets eight times a year and votes on whether to raise, lower or maintain its Federal Funds rate. This is the rate that the Fed charges when it lends to US financial institutions overnight. The FOMC is instructed by the US government to achieve both price stability and to promote economic growth.

On the 18 September 2007, the FOMC cut the Fed Funds rate from 5.25 to 4.75 per cent. It was the first cut in more than four years. The rate cut had been prompted by concerns over falling US employment and a slow-down in bank lending.

a) Identify two ways in which the FOMC differs from the MPC.

b) Analyse how a cut in the interest rate could raise employment.

c) Discuss whether the FOMC's cut in interest rate would achieve its objectives.

London's financial districts, such as Canary Wharf, are well situated for the international market

London has a range of advantages over the rest of the world's financial markets. The City is in the right place and the right time zone. It is located half way between the Asian and the US markets, so that traders can work almost 24 hours a day. People in the City speak the right language – English is the international language of business. The City also has a ready supply of skilled personnel and fewer rules and regulations than most financial centres.

The industries in which the UK is least competitive tend to be those dependent on heavy capital equipment or cheap labour.

A country's pattern of trade is concerned not only with the products it trades in but also with which countries it exports to and imports from. Table 6.1 shows the continued and increasing dominance of the EU as a destination of UK exports and source of UK imports. Table 6.2 (see over) shows the importance of individual countries in the EU with most of the countries in the UK's top ten trading partner countries being members of the EU.

It is interesting to note that, while China did not appear in the top ten sources of imports in 2000, it reached sixth position in 2006 and is expected to climb further in the future.

The three main categories of goods that the UK has been trading in are machinery and transport equipment, manufactures and chemicals. In most categories, the UK has had a trade deficit in recent years. An exception is chemicals, which includes pharmaceuticals. The UK has had a surplus over a long period of time. One category that has seen a significant change in recent years is fuels. In 2000, the UK had a surplus in this area. By 2005, this had turned into a deficit. Most of this reflects a change in the country's oil stocks. The UK used to be a net exporter of oil. With declines in its oil stocks, the UK became a net importer of oil in 2005.

The UK has continued to have a surplus on most service categories, doing particularly well in legal services, insurance, computer services, engineering consultancy and education.

Table 6.1 The areas of the world with which the UK trades

Area	Exports by area % share of total		Imports by area % share of total	
	2000	2006	2000	2006
EU	59.57	62.78	53.06	58.38
Other Western Europe	3.84	3.76	5.90	7.12
North America	17.94	15.06	15.15	9.58
Other OECD countries	4.27	3.55	7.11	4.17
Oil exporting countries	3.21	3.70	1.93	2.13
Rest of the world	11.17	11.15	16.85	18.61

Table 6.2 The UK's main trading partners

Top ten destinations of UK exports		Top ten sources of UK imports	
2000	**2006**	**2000**	**2006**
1 USA	USA	Germany	Germany
2 Germany	France	USA	France
3 France	Germany	France	USA
4 Netherlands	Irish Republic	Netherlands	Netherlands
5 Irish Republic	Netherlands	Belgium and Lux.	Belgium and Lux.
6 Belgium and Lux.	Belgium and Lux.	Irish Republic	China
7 Italy	Spain	Japan	Norway
8 Spain	Italy	Italy	Spain
9 Japan	Sweden	Spain	Italy
10 Canada	Switzerland	Norway	Irish Republic

Source: Annual Abstract of Statistics, 2007, ONS.

Crown Copyright material reproduced by permission of the Controller of HMSO and the Queen's Printer for Scotland

> **learning tip**
>
> Keep up to date with changes in the pattern of UK international trade by checking newspaper articles, the BBC news and the Office for National Statistics website. (You can go to www.heinemann.co.uk/hotlinks, insert the express code 2223P and click on 'Office for National Statistics'.)

Advantages that may be gained from international trade

International trade involves the exchange of goods and services across national borders. Being able to trade with other countries can bring a number of advantages. One is that it enables the country to specialise as the products it does not produce it can import.

Consumers can benefit from the lower prices and higher quality that results from the higher level of competition that arises from countries trading internationally. They can also enjoy a greater variety of products, including a few not made in the country.

Although firms will face greater competition in their domestic markets, they will also have access to larger markets in which to sell their products and from which to buy raw materials (enabling them to take greater advantage of economies of scale).

ACTIVITY ····❯

In January 2006, the UK exported £224,172m worth of goods to India and imported £257,548m worth of goods from India. A year later in January 2007, the UK exported £230,523m to India and imports from India had risen by 28.3 per cent.

The main products that the UK exports to India are metals, machinery, transport equipment, gold and diamonds. Its main imports from India are textiles, clothes and footwear.

a) i) What was the value of imports from India in January 2007?

   ii) What was the UK's trade in goods balance with India in January 2007?

b) Explain two possible reasons why the UK imports textiles from India.

c) Analyse two possible reasons why India may appear in the top ten destinations of UK exports in the future.

International trade poses challenges for countries. Competition from other countries and access to their markets results in some industries contracting and some expanding. This requires the shifting of resources, which can be unsettling and may be difficult to achieve due to, for example, **occupational immobility of labour**.

DEFINITION

Occupational immobility of labour: difficulty in moving from one type of job to another.

Despite the advantages of international trade, some countries restrict exports and most impose restrictions on imports. Restrictions may be placed on the export of certain products if they become in short supply. There are a number of reasons why a government may place restrictions on imports. The government may be concerned that, for example, certain undesirable products may be imported, that the continued existence of new and strategic industries may be threatened, and that other countries may not engage in fair competition.

Methods of protection

International free trade occurs when there are no restrictions imposed on the movement of goods and services into and out of countries. In contrast, **protectionism** results in the deliberate restriction of the free movement of goods and services between countries and economic blocs. A government engages in protectionism when it introduces measures to protect its own industries from competition from the industries of other countries.

DEFINITION

Protectionism: the protection of domestic industries from foreign competition.

TARIFFS

Tariffs are the best known method of protection. They can also be referred to as customs duties or import duties. They are taxes on imported products. They can be imposed with the intention of raising revenue and/or discouraging domestic consumers from buying imported products. For example, the EU's Common External Tariff, which is a tax on imports coming into the EU from countries outside, does raise revenue, but its main purpose is to encourage EU member countries to trade with each other rather than with countries outside the EU.

The effect of imposing a tariff is to raise prices for domestic consumers and, in the absence of any retaliation, shift demand from imports to domestically produced products.

QUOTAS

The second best known measure is probably a quota. This is a limit on the supply of a good or

---

ACTIVITY ···

Sales of Scotch whisky increased dramatically between 2000 and 2007 as a result of record rises in exports to China, India, Central, South and North America. Exports to China, for instance, increased from £1m in 2001 to £58m in 2006.

As a result of the significant increase in the volume of Scotch whisky being sold in foreign markets, new malt distilleries are being built in Scotland. Employment in the industry and related activities is rising. Demand for coppersmiths, who make and maintain whisky stills, and the coopers, who repair barrels, is increasing. Farmers are receiving much higher prices for malting barley.

a) Explain two possible reasons why the export of Scotch whisky increased.

b) Identify an area of the world that did not appear to experience a rise in sales of Scotch whisky.

c) Analyse the benefits that Scotland experiences from a rise in the sales of Scotch whisky.

d) Discuss whether an increase in the sales of Scotch whisky would necessarily have reduced the UK's current account deficit.

service. It can be imposed on exports. For example, a developing country may seek to limit the export of food during a period of food shortages. Quotas on imports, however, are more common. For example, a quota restriction may be placed on the import of cars. This may limit the import of cars to 40,000 a year or alternatively to, for example, £4m worth of cars.

The effect of a quota is to reduce supply. This is likely to push up price. Foreign firms would experience a reduction in the quantity they can sell but they may benefit from the higher price if demand for their products is inelastic and if the quotas are not operated via the selling of import licences.

VOLUNTARY EXPORT RESTRAINT

A **voluntary export restraint (VER)** is similar to a quota but this time the limit on imports arises from a voluntary agreement between the exporting and the importing country. A country may agree to restrict its exports in return for a similar limit being put on the exports of the other country or to avoid more damaging import restrictions being imposed on its products.

DEFINITION

Voluntary export restraint (VER): a limit placed on imports from a country with the agreement of that country's government.

FOREIGN EXCHANGE RESTRICTIONS

A government may seek to reduce imports by limiting the amount of foreign exchange made available to those wishing to buy imported goods and services or to invest or to travel abroad. This measure was used in European countries, including the UK, in the 1960s and 1970s and is still used in some developing countries.

EMBARGOES

An embargo is a ban on the export or import of a product and/or a ban on trade with a particular country. For example, a country may ban the export

ACTIVITY ┈┈▶

The Georgian economy has shown a remarkable turnaround in recent years. The former Soviet republic of 4.4 million people had been struggling at the start of the 21st century. But from 2004 to 2007, it experienced an average annual growth rate of 10 per cent.

A large part of the transformation of the economy has been attributed to the supply-side policies the Georgian government has introduced. These have included simplifying the tax system, introducing one low income tax rate of 25 per cent, deregulation and widespread privatisation, including of much of the country's health care system. The country's tax revenue has increased, although in 2007 there was a budget deficit equal to 2.3 per cent of GDP.

This improvement in economic performance is all the more remarkable as Russia, one of the country's main trading partners, imposed an embargo on goods from Georgia. In response to this, Georgia increased trade with its three other main trading partners, Turkey, Germany and Azerbaijan, and sought out new markets. The country had a trade in goods balance of −$2.82

billion but a current account surplus of $1.58bn.

The need to boost its exports did, however, mean that Georgia was reluctant to allow the country's currency, the lari, to appreciate. An appreciation might have reduced the country's inflation rate which in 2007 was 8 per cent.

a) What is meant by an 'annual growth rate of 10 per cent'?

b) What is the key aim of supply-side policies?

c) Using an AD/AS diagram, analyse the effects of a cut in income tax on an economy.

d) What does the information suggest about the relationship between tax revenue and government spending in Georgia in 2007?

e) i) Define an embargo.

   ii) Identify two other types of trade restrictions.

f) i) Explain how the appreciation of the currency may reduce a country's inflation rate.

   ii) Discuss the consequences of inflation.

of arms to a country with a poor human rights record, may prohibit the importation of hardcore pornography and is likely to break off trading relations with a country during a military conflict.

RED TAPE

Time-delaying customs procedures may be used to discourage imports. If it takes a long time to complete complex custom forms it will be more expensive to import products.

OTHER MEASURES

Two additional measures are quality standards and government purchasing policies. Quality standards may be set high and complex requirements may be put in place with the intention of raising the costs of foreign firms seeking to export to the country. A government may also try to reduce imports by favouring domestic firms when it places orders, even when the domestic firms are producing at a higher cost or lower quality.

ExamCafé
Relax, refresh, result!

Relax and prepare

Muttiah

I do a lot of revision with my friends from the class. We test each other on definitions and we work through some questions together. I really find it helps to work with my friends, as we can talk about the things we don't understand. Some friends of mine, though, prefer revising alone, as they can concentrate better on their own. But I find I get too easily distracted!

Karla

My teacher told me at the start of the course that I should 'engage in constant revision'. At first I didn't really understand what he meant, so I ignored him! But I didn't do as well as I'd hoped in my Unit 1 exam, so I asked him how to prepare for the Unit 2 exam. He said I should review my work after each lesson. Now, when I get home, I read over my notes. I sometimes look up points in my textbook and if I still do not understand, I ask my teacher at the start of the next lesson. It only takes me about 15 minutes to check over my work and I find it really helps.

Feodor

I like to revise by reworking my notes. I read through them and then put them in some other form. I try to draw up revision cards on each topic. I also use mind maps to help me get the links between points and I use tables to compare different problems and policies. This is a table I drew up on aggregate demand.

Components of aggregate demand

Component	Definition	Causes of an increase
Consumption	Household spending on goods and services	Reduction in income tax Rise in consumer confidence Lower interest rate Increase in population Increase in wealth
Investment	Firms spending on capital goods	Reduction in corporation tax Rise in business confidence Lower interest rate Advances in technology
Government spending	Government spending on e.g., defence, education, health	Desire to reflate the economy Approach of a general election
Net exports	Foreign expenditure on our exports minus our expenditure on imports	Higher incomes abroad Improved quality of exports Lower exchange rate Fall in domestic inflation rate

Refresh your memory

Quick-fire quiz

1. How does demand differ from aggregate demand?
2. What are the key causes of shifts in the AS curve?
3. How does demand-pull inflation differ from cost-push inflation?
4. Distinguish between fiscal policy and monetary policy.
5. What benefits do consumers and producers get from their country engaging in international trade?

Get the result!

Alex's answer

Comments on Alex's answer

Alex started well by defining fiscal policy and then recognising that expansionary fiscal policy is designed to reduce cyclical unemployment.

He then included two relevant and well labelled diagrams.

His comments then became rather confused and unfocused. The presence of cyclical unemployment would mean that the economy is operating below its potential capacity.

Alex sought to evaluate, but what he actually did was to assert rather strange points without explaining them. What forms of government spending are 'irrelevant' and why? How could government spending cause a fall in aggregate demand?

Alex could have made more of his comments in this paragraph. He could have moved towards evaluation by explaining that fiscal policy will not necessarily reduce frictional and cyclical unemployment.

Alex began well in this sentence but then failed to explain why lower prices might be experienced. Indeed, linking lower prices to an increase in disposable income was rather confusing.

The use of fiscal policy is designed to alter aggregate demand through changing either the amount of government spending and/or altering taxation. Primarily, fiscal policy is designed to increase aggregate demand, as this can reduce cyclical unemployment – unemployment caused by a lack of aggregate demand. Successfully increasing aggregate demand will not, however, always decrease unemployment, as shown below.

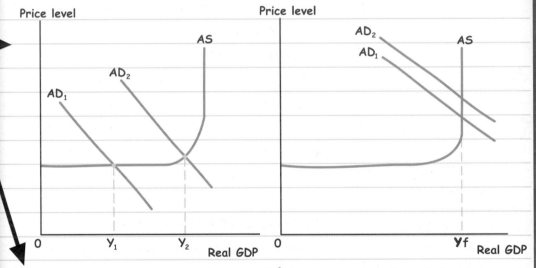

The cyclical unemployment can only be cured if the economy is producing below its productive capacity (Y_f).

An increase in government spending should stimulate economic activity. However, it depends on the nature of the government spending. Some things that are completely irrelevant will have no effect, or government failure could cause a drop in aggregate demand, which would increase unemployment.

There's only one type of unemployment caused by a lack of aggregate demand. The diagram shows a reduction in cyclical unemployment, and not frictional or structural. Increasing aggregate demand has negligible effects on these.

Decreasing taxes increases disposable income and leads to lower prices for consumers, which is the other tool of fiscal policy.

Tom's answer

Fiscal policy is a demand management policy that affects components of aggregate demand. Aggregate demand management can be used to reduce unemployment.

If there is a lack of demand, this causes an output gap and unemployment. Because there is little demand for goods, firms will not want to produce more goods and will not want to hire more staff. This can be solved by increasing aggregate demand through reflationary policy.

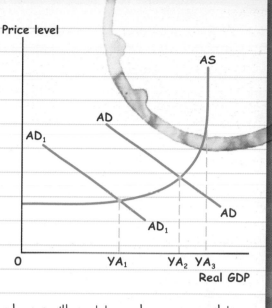

Comments on Tom's answer

Tom's answer started directly. He provided some clear analysis.

At the end of this paragraph he stated that 'spending on defence will not have a large effect on aggregate demand'. It is difficult to think why he thought this, especially as he did not explain this comment. He did, however, then go on to make a relevant evaluative point about structural unemployment.

In his comments on the effect on frictional unemployment he might have considered the impact of unemployment benefits on the incentive to work.

This last paragraph covered a relevant evaluative point and overall it was a reasonably strong answer.

By decreasing tax, households have more disposable income and a higher incentive to work.

Consumers will spend more and so producers will want to produce more, and to produce more, firms will hire more workers. Also, unemployed people will want to get a job more if taxes are lower, as the income they could earn increases. The government could also increase government spending. This would cause aggregate demand to shift to the right. However, this depends upon what the government spends the additional money on. Increased spending on defence will not have a large effect on aggregate demand. Also, it depends on the type of unemployment. Cyclical unemployment is easily affected by fiscal policy measures. However, structural unemployment is not as easily affected. A drop in tax rates does not enable people to take up jobs in sectors for which they are not trained.

Fiscal policy does not have a large effect on frictional unemployment either. Tax rates and spending on NHS/defence/roads does not enable people to find jobs faster. Government spending on unemployment benefits may make it easier for people to find jobs as they can afford to look for jobs.

The effectiveness of all fiscal policy measures on unemployment are affected by time lags. Fiscal policy measures take time to have an effect and time to be put in place. After the decision has been made on fiscal policy and by the time it is put into place, the problem may have changed or corrected itself. Then the fiscal policy may no longer have a large enough effect to significantly reduce unemployment.

Hot tips

As with Unit 1, the Unit 2 exam consists of data in the form of text and a diagram or table. There are usually between 12 and 14 questions set on this information.

The more straightforward questions tend to be at the start of the paper and the more demanding ones towards the end.

● On opening the paper, first read through the questions. You may want to highlight the command words and other key words. Then check the data, again highlighting any key words.

● Answer the questions in order. Forming your answers to the earlier questions should help you to answer the later questions. It should also mean that your answers do not overlap.

● Pay attention to the command words, how many marks are being awarded and the space provided in the answer booklet. For example, a question may ask you to *state* two components of aggregate demand. It may give two marks and the answer booklet may provide just one or two lines. In this case just write, for instance, consumption and investment. You should not waste time and effort stating more than two or describing or explaining two. In contrast, a question asking you to *explain* or *analyse* will require more depth. For example, in answering the question 'Explain the effect of a rise in the rate of interest on consumption', it would not be sufficient to just state that consumption would fall. You should analyse how the change in the rate of interest would affect the incentive to save, the cost of borrowing and discretionary income.

● Remember some of the questions on the paper will require you to *interpret* the data. This may, for instance, mean that you have to identify certain points from the text, explain what a table shows and *comment* on the trend shown in a graph.

● Ensure that you evaluate when you answer questions asking you to 'comment on' or '*discuss*'. These command words mean that you should go a stage further than analysis. In answering 'Discuss the effect of a rise in the rate of interest on consumption', you should explain why you would expect consumption to fall. Then you should discuss the factors that will influence the extent to which this may occur and why it may not reduce consumption. It is important that you do not just assert points. For instance, do not just state that a rise in the rate of interest may not decrease consumption – explain why not.

● Draw clear, well labelled and accurate diagrams where appropriate. On this paper the most important diagram is the AD/AS diagram. The other two main macro diagrams are a PPC diagram and an exchange rate diagram.

● Check over your responses when you have finished answering all the questions. You should have time to do this and it is important to do so, as it is easy to miss out a word, fail to fully label a diagram or make a careless mistake.

Exam practice paper

When you have revised, you may want to try answering this example of an exam question.

Will India's high economic growth continue?

In 2007, India became the twelfth country to produce a gross domestic product in excess of a trillion dollars. India is one of the fastest growing economies in the world, achieving a 9.2 per cent growth rate in 2006. Economists in 2007, however, expressed a number of concerns about the performance of the Indian economy. These concerns focused on India's growing trade deficit, high inflation and the rapid rise of the rupee.

The Reserve Bank of India raised the rate of interest in 2007, in a bid to reduce inflationary pressure. It also revised its annual inflation target to 5 from 5.5 per cent and stated it wanted to see 4–4.5 per cent in the medium term. Adopting a tighter monetary policy does run risks. It can push up the exchange rate even further, discourage investment, slow down economic growth and cause unemployment.

Figure 1 shows India's unemployment rate over the period 2002–07.

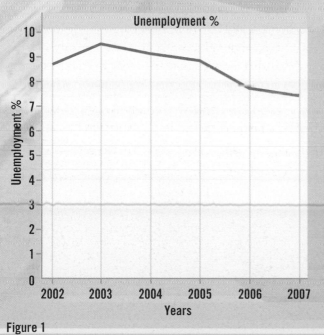

Figure 1

A report published by Goldman Sachs, the merchant bank, in 2007 argued that India's economic performance would be improved by encouraging more women in the country to enter the labour force. Increased participation in the labour force would increase India's productive capacity and potentially its economic growth.

a) Define:
   i) gross domestic product (line 2) (2 marks)
   ii) a trade deficit. (line 7) (2)

b) **i)** From the passage, identify one component of aggregate demand. (1)
   ii) Identify two other components of aggregate demand. (2)

c) Using Figure 1, explain what happened to India's unemployment over the period 2002–07. (4)

d) **i)** Explain two benefits of a fall in inflation. (4)
   ii) Analyse how a rise in the rate of interest may reduce inflation. (7)

e) **i)** Using an aggregate demand and aggregate supply diagram, analyse the effect of a rise in the exchange rate on an economy. (9)
   ii) Apart from a change in the exchange rate, explain one other cause of a trade deficit. (4)

f) Comment on one policy measure to reduce unemployment. (7)

g) Discuss whether an economy would benefit from an increase in its productive capacity. (18)

Further reading

Books

Bamford, C.G., and S. Munday, *Markets*, Oxford, Heinemann, 2002

Bamford, C.G., and S. Grant, *The UK Economy in a Global Context*, Oxford, Heinemann, 2000

The Economist Pocket World in Figures (latest edition)

Grant, S.J., *AS Economics*, London, Longman, 2006

Munday, S., *Markets and Market Failure*, Oxford, Heinemann, 2000

Smith, D., *UK Current Economic Policy*, Oxford, Heinemann, 2003

Wall, N., *The Complete A–Z Economics Handbook*, London, Hodder & Stoughton, 2005

Magazines

British Economy Survey

Economic Review

Economics Today

Glossary

aggregate demand (AD): the total demand for a country's goods and services at a given *price level* and in a given time period.

aggregate supply (AS): the total amount that producers in an economy are willing and able to supply at a given *price level* in a given time period.

allocative efficiency: where consumer satisfaction is maximised.

arithmetic mean: the sum of the items divided by the number of items.

asymmetric information: information not equally shared between two parties.

automatic stabilisers: forms of government spending and taxation that change automatically to offset fluctuations in economic activity.

average: see *arithmetic mean*; *weighted average*.

average propensity to consume (APC): the proportion of disposable income spent. It is consumer expenditure divided by disposable income.

average propensity to save (APS): the proportion of disposable income saved. It is saving divided by disposable income.

balance of payments: a record of money flows coming in and going out of a country.

bar chart: a diagram where the lengths of the bars show the different values of the items.

capacity utilisation: the extent to which firms are using their capital goods.

capital: man-made aids to production.

ceteris paribus (Latin: other things being equal): assuming other variables remain unchanged.

change in demand: this is where a change in a non-price factor leads to an increase or decrease in demand for a product.

choice: the selection of appropriate alternatives.

circular flow of income: the movement of spending and income throughout the economy.

claimant count: a measure of unemployment that includes those receiving unemployment-related benefits.

clearing price: same as *equilibrium price*.

command economy: an economic system in which resources are state owned and also allocated centrally.

complements: goods for which there is joint demand.

consumer confidence: how optimistic consumers are about future economic prospects.

consumer expenditure: spending by households on consumer products.

consumer prices index: a measure of changes in the price of a representative basket of consumer goods and services. Differs from the *retail price index* (RPI) in methodology and coverage.

corporation tax: a tax on firms' profits.

cost-push inflation: increases in the price level caused by increases in the costs of production.

cross elasticity of demand (XED): the responsiveness of demand for one product in relation to a change in the price of another product.

current account deficit: when more money is leaving the country than entering it, as a result of sales of its exports, income and current transfers from abroad being less than imports, income and current transfers going abroad.

cyclical unemployment: unemployment arising from a lack of aggregate demand.

deflation: a sustained fall in the general price level.

demand: the quantity of a product that consumers are able and willing to purchase at various prices over a period of time.

demand curve: this shows the relationship between the quantity demanded and the price of a product.

demand-pull inflation: increases in the price level caused by increases in *aggregate demand*.

demand schedule: the data that is used to draw the *demand curve* for a product.

demerit goods: their consumption is more harmful than is actually realised.

developed economy: an economy with a high level of income per head.

developing economy: an economy with a low level of income per head.

direct tax: one that taxes the income of people and firms and that cannot be avoided.

disposable income: income after taxes on income have been deducted and state benefits have been added.

dissave: spending more than disposable income.

distribution of income: how income is shared out between households in a country.

division of labour: the specialisation of labour where the production process is broken down into separate tasks.

economic cycle: the tendency for economic activity to fluctuate outside its *trend growth* rate, moving from a high level of economic activity (boom) to negative economic growth (recession).

economic efficiency: where both *allocative* and *productive efficiency* are achieved.

economic growth: in the short run, an increase in real GDP, and in the long run, an increase in productive capacity, that is, in the maximum output that the economy can produce.

economically inactive: people of working age who are neither employed nor unemployed.

economic problem: how to allocate scarce resources among alternative uses.

economics: the study of how to allocate scarce resources in the most effective way.

economic system: the way in which production is organised in a country or group of countries.

effective demand: the willingness and ability to buy a product.

efficiency: where the best use of resources is made for the benefit of consumers.

elastic: responsive to a change in market conditions.

elasticity: the extent to which buyers and sellers respond to a change in market conditions.

entrepreneur: someone who bears the risks of the business and who organises production.

entrepreneurship: the willingness of an entrepreneur to take risks and organise production.

equilibrium price: the price where demand and supply are equal.

equilibrium quantity: the quantity that is demanded and supplied at the equilibrium price.

exchange: the process by which goods and services are traded.

exchange rate: the price of one currency in terms of another currency or currencies.

exports: products sold abroad.

external benefits: the benefits that accrue as a consequence of *externalities* to third parties.

external costs: the costs that are the consequence of *externalities* to third parties.

externality: an effect whereby those not directly involved in taking a decision are affected by the actions of others.

deflationary: of policy measures designed to reduce *aggregate demand*.

discretionary fiscal policy: deliberate changes in government spending and taxation designed to influence *aggregate demand*.

disequilibrium: any position in the market where demand and supply are not equal.

factor endowment: the stock of *factors of production*.

factor of production: the resource inputs that are available in an economy for the production of goods and services.

factor services: the services provided by the *factors of production*.

fiscal drag: people's income being dragged into higher tax bands as a result of tax brackets not being adjusted in line with inflation.

fiscal policy: the taxation and spending decisions of a government.

free market mechanism: the system by which the market forces of demand and supply determine prices and the decisions made by consumers and firms.

free rider: someone who directly benefits from the consumption of a public good but who does not contribute towards its provision.

frictional unemployment: short-term unemployment occurring when workers are in-between jobs.

full employment: a situation where those wanting and able to work can find employment at the going wage rate.

goods: tangible products, i.e. products that can be seen and touched, such as cars, food and washing machines.

government bond: a financial asset issued by the central or local government.

government spending: spending by the central bank and local government on goods and services.

gross domestic product (GDP): the total output of goods and services produced in a country.

household: group of people whose spending decisions are connected.

human capital: education, training and experience that a worker, or group of workers, possesses.

hyperinflation: an inflation rate above 50 per cent.

hysteresis: unemployment causing unemployment.

imports: products bought from abroad.

income elastic: goods for which a change in income produces a greater proportionate change in demand.

income elasticity of demand: the responsiveness of demand to a change in income.

income inelastic: goods for which a change in income produces a less than proportionate change in demand.

index number: a number showing the variation in, for example, wages or prices, as compared with a chosen base period or date.

indirect tax: a tax levied on goods and services.

inefficiency: any situation where economic efficiency is not achieved.

inferior goods: goods for which an increase in income leads to a fall in demand.

inflation: a sustained rise in the price level; the percentage increase in the price level over a period of time.

inflationary noise: the distortion of price signals caused by inflation.

informal economy: economic activity that is not recorded or registered with the authorities in order to avoid paying tax or complying with regulations, or because the activity is illegal.

information failure: a lack of information resulting in consumers and producers making decisions that do not maximise welfare.

injections: additions of extra spending into the *circular flow of income*.

International Labour Organisation (ILO): a member organisation of the United Nations that collects statistics on labour market conditions and seeks to improve working conditions.

International Monetary Fund (IMF): an international organisation that helps co-ordinate the international monetary system.

investment: spending on capital goods.

labour: the quantity and quality of human resources.

labour force: the people who are employed and unemployed, that is, those who are economically active.

Labour Force Survey: a measure of unemployment based on a survey using the ILO definition of unemployment.

labour productivity: output of a good or service per worker in a given time period.

land: natural resources in an economy.

leakages: withdrawals of possible spending from the *circular flow of income*.

long-term unemployment: unemployment lasting for more than a year.

macroeconomic equilibrium: a situation where aggregate demand equals aggregate supply and real GDP is not changing.

macroeconomics: the study of issues that affect economies as a whole.

market: an arrangement that brings buyers into contact with sellers.

market economy: an economic system whereby resources are allocated through the free market mechanism.

market failure: where the free market mechanism fails to achieve economic efficiency.

menu costs: the costs of changing prices due to inflation.

merit goods: these have more *private benefits* than their consumers actually realise.

microeconomics: the study of how households and firms make decisions in markets.

mixed economy: an economic system in which resources are allocated through a mixture of the market and direct public sector involvement.

monetary policy: central bank and/or government decisions on the rate of interest, the money supply and the exchange rate.

Monetary Policy Committee (MPC): a committee of the Bank of England with responsibility for setting the interest rate in order to meet the government's inflation target.

movement along the demand curve: this is in response to a change in the price of a product.

multiplier effect: the process by which any change in a component of *aggregate demand* results in a greater final change in real GDP.

negative externality: this exists where the *social cost* of an activity is greater than the *private cost*.

net exports: the value of exports minus the value of imports.

net savers: people who save more than they borrow.

nominal GDP: output measured in current prices and so not adjusted for inflation.

non-excludability: situation existing where individual consumers cannot be excluded from consumption.

non-rivalry: situation existing where consumption by one person does not affect the consumption of all others.

normal goods: goods for which an increase in income leads to an increase in demand; goods with a positive income elasticity of demand.

notional demand: the desire for a product.

occupational immobility of labour: difficulty in moving from one type of job to another.

opportunity cost: the cost of the best alternative, which is foregone when a choice is made.

output gap: the difference between an economy's actual and potential real GDP.

overheating: the growth in *aggregate demand* outstripping the growth in *aggregate supply*, resulting in *inflation*.

polluter pays principle: any measure, such as a green tax, whereby the polluter pays explicitly for the pollution caused.

positive externality: this exists where the *social benefit* of an activity exceeds the *private benefit*.

price: the amount of money that is paid for a given amount of a particular good or service.

price elastic (or **price sensitive)**: where the percentage change in the quantity demanded is sensitive to a change in price.

price elasticity of demand (PED): the responsiveness of the quantity demanded to a change in the price of the product.

price elasticity of supply (PES): the responsiveness of the quantity supplied to a change in the price of the product.

price inelastic (or **price insensitive)**: where the percentage change in the quantity demanded is insensitive to a change in price.

price level: the average of the prices of all the products produced in an economy.

price system: a method of allocating resources by the free movement of prices.

private benefits: the benefits directly accruing to those taking a particular action.

private costs: the costs incurred by those taking a particular action.

privatisation: transfer of assets from the public to the private sector.

producer surplus: the difference between the price a firm is willing to supply and what it is actually paid.

production: the output of goods and services.

production possibility curve: this shows the maximum quantities of different combinations of output of two products, given current resources and the state of technology.

productive efficiency: where production takes place using the least amount of scarce resources.

productive potential: the maximum output that an economy is capable of producing.

productivity: output, or production, of a good or service per worker.

profit: the difference between the total revenue (sales revenue) of a producer and total cost.

progressive tax: a tax that takes a higher percentage from the income of the rich.

protectionism: the protection of domestic industries from foreign competition.

public goods: goods that are collectively consumed and have the characteristics of *non-excludability* and *non-rivalry*.

quasi-public goods: goods having some but not all of the characteristics of a *public good*.

quota: a limit on imports.

rate of interest: the charge for borrowing money and the amount paid for lending money.

real disposable income: income after taxes on income have been deducted and state benefits have been added and the result has been adjusted to take into account changes in the *price level*.

real GDP: the country's output measured in constant prices and so adjusted for inflation.

real interest rate: the nominal interest rate minus the inflation rate.

recession: a fall in real GDP over a period of six months or more.

reflationary: of policy measures designed to increase *aggregate demand*.

regressive tax: a tax that takes a greater percentage from the income of the poor.

retail prices index (RPI): measure of inflation that is used for adjusting pensions and other benefits to take account of changes in inflation and frequently used in wage negotiations. Differs from the *consumer prices index* (CPI) in methodology and coverage.

retained profits: profit kept by firms to finance investment.

saving: real disposable income minus spending.

savings ratio: savings as a proportion of disposable income.

scarcity: a situation where there are insufficient resources to meet all wants.

services: intangible products, i.e. products that cannot be seen or touched, such as banking, beauty therapy and insurance.

shoeleather costs: costs in terms of the extra time and effort involved in reducing money holdings.

shortage: an excess of demand over supply.

social benefits: the total benefits of a particular action.

social costs: the total costs of a particular action.

specialisation: the concentration by a worker or workers, firm, region or whole economy on a narrow range of goods and services.

structural unemployment: unemployment caused by the decline of certain industries and occupations due to changes in demand and supply.

sub-market: a recognised or distinguishable part of a market. Also known as a market segment.

subsidy: a payment, usually from government, to encourage production or consumption of a product.

substitute: a competing good.

supply: the quantity of a product that producers are willing and able to provide at different market prices over a period of time.

supply curve: this shows the relationship between the quantity supplied and the price of a product.

supply schedule: the data used to draw up the *supply curve* of a product.

supply-side policies: policies designed to increase *aggregate supply* by improving the efficiency of labour and product markets.

surplus: an excess of supply over demand.

sustainable economic growth: economic growth that can continue over time and does not endanger future generations' ability to expand productive capacity.

target savers: people who save with a target figure in mind.

tariff: a tax on imports.

third party: those not directly involved in making a decision.

time series: information shown at successive points or intervals of time.

tradable permit: a permit that allows the owner to emit a certain amount of pollution and that, if unused or only partially used, can be sold to another polluter.

trade-off: the calculation involved in deciding on whether to give up one good for another.

trade deficit: the value of imports exceeding the value of exports.

trade surplus: the value of exports exceeding the value of imports.

trend growth: the expected increase in potential output over time. It is a measure of how fast the economy can grow without generating *inflation*.

unemployment: a situation where people are out of work but are willing and able to work.

unemployment rate: the percentage of the labour force who are out of work.

unit cost: average cost per unit of output.

voluntary export restraint (VER): a limit placed on imports from a country with the agreement of that country's government.

want: anything you would like, irrespective of whether you have the resources to purchase it.

wealth: a stock of assets e.g. property, shares and money held in a savings account.

weighted average: an average that takes into account the relative importance of the different items.

World Trade Organisation (WTO): an international organisation that promotes free international trade and rules on international trade disputes.

Index

Note: Page numbers in **bold** indicate defined terms.